June 8, 1992
Royalty Monthly

Sept. 1969
The Tatler

Lord Rhodes, Mr. D. J. Green, Princess Alexandra and Mr. T. R. Grieve at the opening by Princess Alexandra of Shell-Mex and B.P.'s new oil terminal at Haydock, Lancashire, bringing into operation a new type of internal traffic control system for the loading of road tankers.

Mollie Lee Pryor

Mollie Lee Pryor

PRINCESS ALEXANDRA

Margaret: A Woman of Conflict
Diana: One of the Family?
Anne: The Working Princess
At Her Majesty's Service
At Home with the Royal Family
The Royal Almanac
The Secret Journals of Queen Elizabeth II
The Secret Royal Love Letters
Prince Philip's 101 Great Games
Excuses, Excuses...
It's a Weird World

PRINCESS ALEXANDRA

Paul James

Weidenfeld and Nicolson
London

First published in Great Britain in 1992 by
George Weidenfeld & Nicolson Limited,
91 Clapham High Street, London SW4 7TA

British Library Cataloguing-in-Publication Data
(available on request)

Printed and bound in Great Britain by
Butler & Tanner Ltd, Frome and London

Dedicated to
Denise and Peter Wood
Samuel, Hyru and Joseph

HOME FROM NORTHERN IRELAND: PRINCESS
ALEXANDRA OF KENT RETURNS FROM HER
HOLIDAY WITH THE DUKE AND DUCHESS OF
ABERCORN. SHE WAS MET AT LONDON AIRPORT
BY HER MOTHER, PRINCESS MARINA, IN THE
EVENING OF OCTOBER 2.

October 14 1951
The Illustrated
London News

Contents

Illustrations

Acknowledgments

For some thirty years I have been watching the Royal Family from very close quarters. Born on the borders of the Sandringham estate, in one of my earliest childhood photographs I am looking, not at the camera, but at my own reflection in the glossy paintwork of the Queen Mother's Daimler. For the last decade my career has involved broadcasting, writing and commenting about every possible aspect of royal life. Along the way I have gathered such a wealth of information that when I was asked to write biographies of the Princess Royal, the Princess of Wales and, more recently, Princess Margaret, my job involved bringing together all the pieces of the jigsaw into an easily assimilated form, discarding those that did not quite fit. Often it was as difficult knowing what to leave out as to what should be put in. Princess Alexandra, however, presented a much greater challenge. Described by journalists as, 'tantalisingly mysterious', she has consistently refused to grant interviews throughout her life and has managed to steer clear of almost any trace of scandal in over thirty-five years of public duty. A senior member of the Royal Family, fulfilling more than her fair share of engagements, invariably polled as one of our most popular royal figures, yet much of her life has passed unrecorded.

In *The Irish Times*, the novelist Maeve Binchy wrote jokingly that 'royal biographies are a kind of game in which everyone has the same pieces of a picture; they throw them up in the air to see how they will come down this time, and then publish another book as a result.' A truism, for a subject's life history *cannot* change. Only the biographer's perspective differs, each writer hopefully providing fresh insights. With Princess Alexandra, however, the picture is hazy, the pieces difficult to find let alone toss up into the air. I hope that the results of my looking at Princess Alexandra's life more closely than anyone has perhaps attempted to do in the past will result in a clear portrait of one of the most respected members of the Royal Family, who has managed to stay in the forefront of the public arena but out of the full glare of the spotlight.

In my task I have been helped and guided by a large number of people over the years. Many have requested anonymity, which I respect. I would particularly like to thank Miss Mona Mitchell CVO, Private Secretary to Princess Alexandra from 1968 to 1991; Sir John Garnier, Private Secretary to Princess Alexandra; the staff of the Press Office at Buckingham Palace; Barbara Bentley JP, Director of the Cystic Fibrosis Research Trust, and Mrs Bobbie Burton who first introduced me to the work of the Trust in 1976; Gillian Greenwood, National Director of Alexandra Rose Day; Cecil Mountford for memories of Queen Mary and Princess Marina; Peter Russell, who worked for both Princess Marina and the present Duke and Duchess of Kent and has in the last decade offered perhaps the greatest insight into life at Coppins and Kensington Palace, being part also of Princess Alexandra's twenty-first birthday celebrations and a guest at her wedding; to L. Foulkes; the Central Office of Information; *Bygone News* to David Horne for acting as guru; to J.M., E.M. and the girls for our sharing of royal stories over candlelit suppers. Special thanks go to Julian Clegg and the staff of BBC Radio Sussex, particularly in this instance for providing an opportunity to watch Princess Alexandra at work. Since May 1987 I have regularly broadcast my 'Royal Diary' and 'Royal Watch' and many of the guests on the programme have each offered their own invaluable insights into the Royal Family, both on and off the air, especially Theo Aronson, Jeannette Charles, Tom Corby, Nicholas Courtney, Jayne Fincher, Neil Mackwood, Josephine Ross, Ivor Spencer, Judy Wade and Alison Weir, the latter's *Complete Genealogy of Britain's Royal Families* being an incomparable source of reference. Last, but certainly by no means least, my gratitude goes to David Roberts; my ever enthusiastic agent, Andrew Lownie, and my editor, Amanda Harting.

In any book of this nature there are invariably anecdotes and stories which are apocryphal and open to conjecture. This is unavoidable when the only person who knows the truth is Princess Alexandra. I have tried, therefore, to include facts that I have been able to verify and in several cases I hope that I have been able to set the record straight. Any opinions expressed are my own, as are any unwitting errors or omissions.

In the course of my work as an author and broadcaster, I have come into contact with many hundreds of people who tell me that Princess Alexandra is their favourite member of the Royal Family. They cannot explain why, indeed they know very little about her. Some of the younger generation scarcely know who she is. I hope that this book will help redress the balance by shedding a little light on this popular Princess, who is at times too modest and has remained in the shadows for far too long.

PAUL JAMES
Brighton, 1991

Prologue

Her Royal Highness Princess Alexandra, the Hon. Lady Ogilvy, shares with her brothers, the Duke of Kent and Prince Michael, the unique distinction of being at one and the same time a cousin of the Queen through her father *and* the Duke of Edinburgh through her mother. Not only is she a perennial favourite with the general public, but is reputed to be the most popular member of the family within the Royal Family itself. Nicknamed 'Pud' by the Queen, Alexandra is godmother to Prince Andrew and Prince William, and it is said that Prince Charles always takes a silver-framed photograph of her in his suitcase whenever he travels. Indeed, when the Prince and Princess of Wales embarked on a 'second honeymoon' cruise off the coast of Italy in August 1991 to celebrate their tenth wedding anniversary, Princess Alexandra went with them.

Dubbed the Princess who never puts a foot wrong, Princess Alexandra's success stems from an inherent inner dignity combined with outward approachability. Yet, in her youth she was very much the ugly duckling just waiting to turn into a swan and even today she is not above making an unintentional *faux pas*. Visiting St Michael's Hospice in Herefordshire she innocently asked a question about the establishment's finances. 'Are you well endowed?' she enquired of consultant Dr Jeff Kramer. Noting his blushes, the Princess's lady-in-waiting steered her towards the retiring room where they both collapsed with laughter.

It is Princess Alexandra's naturalness that endears her to the public and the Royal Family alike. Visiting the Chelsea Flower Show in May 1990, the Princess was busy shopping at the National Trust stall when someone tapped her on the shoulder. It was the Queen. Taken by surprise, Alexandra quickly gave her cousin the customary kiss on each cheek. Suddenly she blushed, realizing that she had forgotten to curtsey and immediately did so as royal etiquette dictates. 'I do take you rather by surprise sometimes,' grinned the Queen at her cousin's gaucherie.

Born sixth in line to the throne, Princess Alexandra's upbringing was geared towards a life of royal duty, dictated by protocol. She was pushed into public engagements the moment she reached maturity and there are occasions when her apparent friendly approachability can be deceptive. Within a short space of time I encountered Princess Alexandra in what appeared to be two conflicting lights. In 1976 I approached the Princess with a request to write the foreword to a book I was compiling, the royalties of which raised money for the Cystic Fibrosis Research Trust, of which she is Patron. I received a long letter in return which went to great lengths to explain why it was with 'particular regret' that the Princess felt unable to comply. Having refused other writers in the past she felt that an exception to the rule in my case would 'create an awkward precedent for the future' and hoped that I would 'understand her predicament'. When the book was eventually published I arranged for Princess Alexandra to receive a copy and once again I was sent a lengthy reply saying how 'extremely touched' she was by the presentation and that the Princess 'well remembered the previous correspondence'. As a young writer I too was extremely touched by her obvious sincerity and interest in my project.

A few months later I came across Princess Alexandra in person, shopping privately with her daughter Marina in Harvey Nichols, the Knightsbridge department store. As so frequently happens when royalty shop, the Princess was not permitted to deal with any sales assistant direct but a senior floor manager stepped in to act as intermediary. If the Princess or her daughter wished to look at any item they asked the senior floor manager, who in turn gave orders to the humble sales assistant. At one point, Princess Alexandra requested a particular garment.

'Will you fetch this in Princess Marina's size,' the floor manager gave her command to the anxious young sales assistant. Immediately Alexandra's expression clouded over as if the wraith of her stern grandmother, Queen Mary, had momentarily taken her place. Quietly, but very firmly, an unanticipated admonishment came. 'She is *not* Princess Marina, she is *Miss* Marina Ogilvy.' Both daughter and floor manager were put swiftly in their place.

I was momentarily shocked by this unexpected and, what on the surface seemed, unnecessary sharpness. Yet I realized then that Princess Alexandra is first and foremost a member of the Royal Family, and despite her friendly and sympathetic approach there is an innate sense that she must always do the right thing. An inbred conditioning that sets those born royal apart from those who marry into this extraordinary family. A propensity that would not let Princess Alexandra forget to curtsey to her cousin, albeit slightly mistimed; that did not allow her to make an exception to an unwritten rule and write a foreword to a book; that could not ignore the misuse of a title. It is a characteristic that the Queen, Princess Margaret and the Princess Royal constantly display. When a photographer in Australia shouted to Princess Anne, 'Look this way, love,' she retorted, 'I am not your *love*, I am your Royal Highness.' When photographers wanted the Queen to pick up a starving baby while in Senegal, she refused. Only too aware of the stark contrast of one of the world's richest women holding one of the poorest people in the world. How different in every instance would have been the reactions of Diana, the Princess of Wales, and Sarah, the Duchess of York, who have experienced a life other than as members of the Royal Family and are quite prepared to allow lapses in protocol to pass unnoticed.

Surprisingly, those who know Princess Alexandra well say that she is ambivalent. On the one hand wanting to uphold tradition and maintain the mystique of her position, comfortable with court etiquette and commanding respect, yet on the other revelling in the unexpected and enjoying opportunities to eschew formality herself. As a schoolgirl she was asked what it was like to be a Princess and she replied, 'The bother is that I sometimes forget that I am one.' On one of her early public engagements when a young boy greeted her with 'Wotcher!' she immediately retorted 'Wotcher!' back in response. When she accidentally sat on the Governor of Queensland's top hat on a visit to Australia, squashing it completely flat, she simply roared with laughter and held it up for the delighted crowds to see. Indeed it was she who initiated the 'royal walkabout' back in 1959, long before other members of the Royal Family adopted the impromptu opportunity to meet the crowds. Actions that may seem trivial in the 1990's but in the context of the time, Alexandra was a revelation. When she embarked on the round of royal duties there was a distinct shortage of Princesses and the Royal Family were still remote. Many people had only recently acquired their first television sets in Coronation year and the media still maintained a discreet distance. The Queen's Christmas Day broadcast was not to be televised until 1958 and the British Royal Family never gave interviews, indeed unless you actually came into physical contact with them there was no way of even knowing how they spoke. Interviewing the future King Hussein of Jordan, the respected broadcaster Richard Dimbleby asked falteringly, 'May I ask you a *very* personal question?' Those fortunate enough to have a television set listened in wide-eyed anticipation as to what this perhaps impertinent question was going to be. 'Are you ever worried about your own safety?' came the searching enquiry.

It was in this deeply respectful climate that Princess Alexandra matured. Her early childhood had been dominated by the Second World War, which not only took her father's life but kept her separated for long periods from her own mother during formative years, which were spent instead with the austere Queen Mary. As a teenager she was overshadowed by her elegant mother, Princess Marina the then Duchess of Kent, and later by her higher profile cousins the Princesses Elizabeth and Margaret. With her roots bound by royal tradition she was as much a 'second-born syndrome' rebel as her cousin Princess Margaret. At heart Alexandra may have preferred to have been born a generation later when she would have appreciated the informality that has been introduced into her family, in an age when she would have been more likely to succeed at the nursing career for which she once trained.

In many ways Princess Alexandra was a pioneer of the modern Royal Family as we accept it today. She was the first Princess to be educated at boarding school rather than under private tutorage, thus paving the way for Prince Charles and later Princess Anne to follow suit. Despite the opportunity of accepting the hand of any number of European Princes, she chose to marry commoner Angus Ogilvy for love, and became the first Princess to include the suffix 'Mrs' in her title. A style which Princess Anne later adopted. Taking Alexandra's lead, Princess Anne also refused to allow her husband to accept a title purely for the sake of it. It was not until 1989 that Angus Ogilvy was finally knighted.

It is this duality in Princess Alexandra's character that makes her so fascinating. She somehow bridges the gap between a time when royalty were revered from a respectful distance and the late twentieth century belief that the Royal Family can be treated as soap opera stars. She has the dignity and elegance that is so much admired, but like the favourite auntie of the family is also prepared to let her hair down and send herself up. Journalists love her, the public admire her. When she visited the Côte d'Azur on the 150th anniversary of the founding of this resort, journalist Colin Mackenzie asked Angus Ogilvy if he and the Princess would walk down the Croisette for his photographer so that he could picture them in a typical Cannes setting. It was not the kind of question you could have asked of the Queen, but Princess Alexandra's 'approachability' made it acceptable. Not only did the Ogilvys pose as requested, but asked if they should do it again to make sure that the picture was what the photographer wanted.

From the general public there has always been sympathy. Sufficiently set apart from the pressures that some royals encounter, Princess Alexandra has been able to take a more relaxed approach to her work. Although she has conscientiously attempted to stay out of any controversy, there have been times when she has been dragged unwillingly into the mêlée, such as in 1976 when Angus Ogilvy became embroiled in the Lonrho affair and chose to resign from his sixteen business directorships, and more recently in 1990 when their own daughter, Marina, chose to sell her story to a tabloid newspaper. Throughout any such 'scandals' Princess Alexandra has managed to emerge with her own reputation intact, her public standing enhanced. She has never attracted the bad press of her cousin, Princess Margaret, or her sister-in-law, Princess Michael of Kent, because she is co-operative within the bounds of dignity. On a visit to Bangkok she was anxious that the Press contingent that followed her should not insult her hosts by spelling their complicated Thai names incorrectly in the newspapers and so discreetly handed them a personal note. 'I've written down the names for your captions,' it said. 'Don't get them wrong!'

Within the main cast of the Royal Family today, Princess Alexandra may no longer be a juvenile lead but still takes on more than a supporting role. As the Kents are officially excluded from the Civil List that covers the expenses for public duties, and now that there is a larger collection of younger royals to fulfil obligations, few would object if

Princess Alexandra opted for a quieter life in her mid-fifties. Yet, each year her engagement diary appears fuller: she attends well over 100 functions annually, deputizing for the Queen on occasions, and frequently it is she who is sent to the airport to meet visiting Heads of State and escort them to Windsor Castle or Buckingham Palace, and less widely known is the fact that she acts as an ambassadress for Britain when overseas. Since she enjoys foreign travel, her diary frequently includes more visits to far-flung corners of the globe than any other member of the Royal Family. She may not be photographed in the poorer regions of Bangladesh or the Upper Volta like Princess Anne, which makes news, but quietly carries out her duties where most appreciated. In Hong Kong, which she last visited at the end of 1990, Princess Alexandra is known as *Ngar Lai Sun Kwun Tzu* – the Princess Elegant and Beautiful Coral; in Australia 'The Dinkum Princess' and in Japan 'The Pearl Princess'. Each country has an image as to how a Princess of the royal blood should look and behave. Princess Alexandra never lets them down. Soignée, her once plump features now settled into the classic wistful beauty of Princess Marina, and still retaining an aura of mystery, it is easy to see why her popularity is universal.

When Princess Alexandra left Heathfield School in the winter of 1952 her final report said: '. . . all the lovable qualities of quick sympathy, affection and generosity, laughter and total honesty are still there in abundance.' Some forty years on, no one could deny that the assessment of her character then is just as valid today.

1

The Christmas Child

Princess Alexandra symbolized hope. For the Royal Family it had been a subdued Christmas Day, at the close of a traumatic year. King George VI felt too emotionally drained to make a customary broadcast to the nation, but as he and Queen Elizabeth left the small Church of St Mary Magdalene with the little Princesses Elizabeth and Margaret Rose, they found that some 6,000 well-wishers were waiting outside to cheer them and prove that support and affection for the monarchy had not diminished. A new era was dawning and it was with gladdened hearts that the Royal Family returned to Sandringham House on this mild December morning to be greeted with the news that Princess Marina, the Duchess of Kent, had given birth to a $6\frac{1}{2}$-pound baby daughter. The weary features of Queen Mary, who had not been feeling well that day, broke into a smile of relief. 'The only nice thing to have happened this year,' she said.

The timing of Princess Alexandra's birth on 25 December, 1936, had somewhat ironically been heralded by three Kings. In January of that year her grandfather George V's life had passed peacefully to a close; on 11 December her uncle, Edward VIII, abdicated after finding it 'impossible to carry the heavy burden of responsibility ... without the help and support of the woman I love', and so her father's second brother, the ill-prepared George VI, took on the mantle of Kingship and came to the throne just two weeks before she was born. Although the stable and manger were missing, gynaecologist William Gilliatt noted with a wry smile on entering Princess Marina's stylish black and silver bathroom after the delivery that on the wall hung a painting of shepherds by Joseph Sert.

From the second-floor bedroom of 3 Belgrave Square, once the home of Queen Victoria's mother, where the newborn baby lay, could clearly be heard the sound of distant church bells. Outside in the Square a lone musician played carols to entertain photographers and reporters who had forsaken their own family celebrations to await the news of this auspicious birth. No snow fell to add the finishing touch to an otherwise idealized scene, but Princess Alexandra's arrival at 11.20 am was cheered by waiting newsmen who now had their story and could still be home in time for Christmas dinner, already fortified by a festive drink from the expectant father. In thousands of homes news of the birth on the radio made up for not having the King's Speech.

When Independent Labour Party MP, James Maxton, that year tabled a motion in the House of Commons to replace the monarchy with 'government of a republican kind' it was defeated by 403 votes to 5, showing overwhelming support for the Crown. With a new family installed at Buckingham Palace stability had been restored and the birth of Princess Alexandra provided a sign of continuity – a focus of fond attention after all the perplexity that had surrounded the Abdication. So great was the attention that when you look back over the newspapers of the day, progress reports were made on an almost frivolous level well into 1937, long after there had been anything newsworthy left to say about an infant of only a few weeks old. Ultimately *The Times* was reduced to the revelation that baby Alexandra was gaining weight.

Sixth in line to the throne at the time of her birth, as a daughter of the then Duke and Duchess of Kent,★ Princess Alexandra Helen Elizabeth Olga Christabel was christened on 9 February, 1937, in the old chapel at Buckingham Palace. She was the last baby to be baptized there as the chapel was completely destroyed during the Battle of Britain when a bomb scored a direct hit. The Queen's Gallery was later built on the site. In line with the Royal Family's desire for continuity, Princess Alexandra wore the traditional Honiton lace christening gown made for Queen Victoria's first child in 1840. It was later to be worn by Alexandra's own children and was still being put into service 150

★ Preceding Princess Alexandra in the line of succession were: Princess Elizabeth, Princess Margaret, Duke of Gloucester, Duke of Kent, Prince Edward of Kent.

years after it was made when Princess Eugenie of York was christened at Sandringham in December 1990. Another link with the past at Princess Alexandra's own christening was one of the godmothers, eighty-year-old Princess Beatrice, the youngest daughter of Queen Victoria, and an even greater stir was caused by the presence in the chapel of Princess Louise, Duchess of Argyll, Queen Victoria's fourth daughter. Just a month short of her eighty-ninth birthday, she had been christened, in 1848, wearing the same gown, at the same chapel.

Princess Alexandra's other godparents were her maternal grandmother, Princess Nicholas of Greece; her mother's sister, Princess Olga of Yugoslavia; her mother's brother-in-law, the Count of Toerring-Jettenbach – known as Uncle Toto; her own great-aunt, Queen Maud of Norway, a daughter of Edward VII; Queen Mary's brother, Alexander the Earl of Athlone; and her father's brother and sister-in-law, King George VI and Queen Elizabeth. With Queen Mary and the future Queen Elizabeth II also present, it was an illustrious gathering to witness Princess Alexandra's public début.

Princess Marina and Prince George chose Christian names for their daughter that had many family associations on both sides. Queen Alexandra, the wife of Edward VII, was both Prince George's grandmother and Princess Marina's great-aunt. Prince George had the middle name Alexander himself and Princess Marina in her complicated ancestry from the Greek and Danish Royal Family, and the Russian Imperial Family, had almost too many relatives to count that bore the name in some form, from her father's sister, Alexandra of Greece, to her great-uncle Alexander II, Tsar of Russia. Even her sister had christened her son Alexander. The name Helen was that of Princess Marina's mother, *and Olga that of her sister and grandmother. Elizabeth was not only *[born a grandduchess of Russia, Olga married George I of Greece] the name of Marina's second sister, but also a perennial favourite with the British Royal Family. Finally, the name Christabel was added in honour of her Christmas birthday.

'She's highly strung and somewhat emotional. It's all that foreign blood in her,' commented Queen Mary as her granddaughter grew up, and for someone who today is the epitome of Englishness, Princess Alexandra does have a remarkably rich variety of blood in her veins. As her father, the Duke of Kent, and King George VI were brothers, Princess Alexandra has the same paternal ancestry as the Queen, that can be traced directly back to William the Conqueror and beyond. A varied mixture of Hanoverian, Saxe-Coburg-Gotha and Windsor genes were inevitably passed on. On her mother's side, Princess Alexandra is a direct descendant of Catherine the Great. Although Princess Marina was Greek by birth, her father was originally from the Danish royal House of Glücksburg, her mother part of the Romanov dynasty of Russia, she was the progeny of kings and kaisers, emperors and grand-duchesses. This colourful and cosmopolitan background was to have a profound influence on the development of Princess Alexandra's character.

At the time of their marriage in 1934, Princess Marina and Prince George received exactly the same public attention that today surrounds Charles and Diana. Marina's hairstyle, clothes and hats were copied by women throughout Britain and once the engagement was announced the flat where she was temporarily staying was besieged by press photographers, many climbed up lampposts, attempted to hide in the lift, followed her to the hairdressers or dressmakers, pushed microphones at her in the hope of getting a few words. Scenes reminiscent of 1981 when the young Lady Diana Spencer received exactly the same treatment. Prince George, the fourth son of George V and Queen Mary, was publicly regarded as the most stylish man in the Royal Family. Apparently sensitive and shy in public, he was known as 'rakish' to his own circle. His good looks had led to many liaisons with often unsuitable women, he had experimented with drugs, and was believed to be bisexual, supposedly having had an affair with Noël Coward. Much of this naturally remained concealed from the general public and suppressed amongst his intimates, so that his reputation has remained intact. One ex-member of the Royal Household to whom I spoke remembered seeing the Prince going out to nightclubs 'in full make-up', which would have been scandalous in the Thirties had it been common knowledge. It was to the King's relief that Prince George announced that he would like to marry Princess Marina, whom he considered, 'the most beautiful princess in Europe – and the poorest!', in the certainty that she would have a stabilizing effect on him. One was quite irrefutably needed. In 1925 the author Ursula Bloom had what was then a typical experience of the Prince's boisterousness. At Cowes week that year she was on board the *Royal Oak* which was acting as guardship for the royal yacht, *Victoria and Albert*. When a party was held on the *Royal Oak* one night the noise was kept to a minimum so as not to disturb Queen Mary on the royal yacht, an extremely light sleeper. Suddenly the peace of the calm waters was shattered by the sound of a small boat heading straight towards the *Victoria and Albert* in which sat a drunken Prince George, with a lavatory seat around his neck, attempting to play the concertina. There are many such reminiscences surrounding Prince George's bachelor days and it was not until marriage and fatherhood that he appeared to mature.

Prince George married Princess Marina on 29 November 1934 in Westminster Abbey and that same month received the titles Duke of Kent, Earl of St Andrews and Baron Downpatrick in a private ceremony at Buckingham Palace. The new Duke and Duchess of Kent began married life at 3 Belgrave Square in London, leased from Lady Juliet Duff, and it was here on 9 October, 1935, that their first child Prince Edward was born, followed by Princess Alexandra some fourteen months later. Although they retained the Belgrave Square home until the outbreak of war, in 1936 the Kents inherited a country house called Coppins at Iver, Buckinghamshire, from Princess Victoria the second daughter of Edward VII. Coppins became the family home and the focus of Princess Alexandra's childhood and by 1937 it was redecorated and fully furnished. At Belgrave Square the Duke and Duchess of Kent could enact their glamorous role as leading lights in the Royal Family and at the hub of British society, but at Coppins they were an hour's drive from London and sufficiently in the country to enjoy the much-needed privacy that enabled Prince George to work in the garden and Princess Marina to take walks unnoticed through the streets of Iver. Even in the late Fifties there was no police protection at Coppins and, when returning from an engagement, Princess Marina would often get out of her chauffeur-driven car on the outskirts of the town and walk home across the fields. Coppins lacked the rigid formality that pervaded other royal homes at this time.

It was, nevertheless, a home of contrasts for the young Princess Alexandra. Although devoted to each other, Princess Marina and Prince George were like chalk and cheese. He was the one who made all the decisions regarding the furnishings, decorations and reorganization of the garden. She even revealed at one dinner party early in their marriage that she often did not know what they were going to eat until it arrived on the table and throughout the rest of her life she often only met her chef at Christmas and kitchen staff could frequently change without her knowledge. Whilst George was passionate about fast cars and loved flying, Marina hated both and never learned to drive and flew only if it was necessary to shorten a journey. He drank gin-based cocktails, she seldom drank alcohol. For one noted for her stylish wardrobe, even before her marriage, there were raised eyebrows at one dinner party when the Duke revealed that he always told Marina which clothes and jewels to wear. 'She was totally under his control,' one of their circle revealed. While he settled comfortably into married life, Marina constantly felt homesick for Greece and ran up enormous telephone bills talking to her relatives throughout Europe on a daily basis. Yet the couple shared a love of biographies, paintings, collecting small art treasures, the theatre, cinema and music, and most importantly of all, their children. They once described a weekend at Coppins alone with the children as their idea of paradise.

However 'ordinary' the Kents attempted to make life at Coppins it was very much an illusion of normality. While the Duke referred to the house as their 'country cottage', the building had over twenty rooms and was much more of a Victorian mansion with two sitting rooms, a music room, dining room, a nursery and playroom, six bedrooms, bathrooms, kitchen and staff quarters which included a complete cottage for the butler on the estate. Whilst George and Marina spoke of their enjoyment at being alone with the children, they were never in reality alone, with a minimum staff of twelve, which included a butler, footman, valet, lady's maid, housekeeper, chef, daily maid, cleaners, two chauffeurs, two gardeners, and an 'odd-man' whose varied job involved the 'dirty' work from bringing in the coal to cleaning the silver. When the Kents took up residence at Coppins they removed the heavy Victorian furniture and covered the brown paintwork, creating a bright home with pale walls and chintz upholstery. Each room always had an abundance of flowers, guests were restricted to family and friends, never official visitors, and yet it was impossible to ignore the fact that this was a *royal* residence. Prince George was a stickler for punctuality and dinner was served formally in the dining room. The entrance hall was dominated by a marble bust of Edward VII, and even the housekeeper's room was adorned with a portrait of Queen Victoria. On the Steinway piano in the drawing room were the inevitable framed photographs of royal relations that seem, even today, to be a feature of any royal sitting room. Formal, posed pictures with the subject in evening dress or full uniform that would not look out of place in any embassy. On the walls hung portraits of Prince George and Princess Marina by the Russian artist Sorine and Philip de Laszlo, leaving no doubt that this was the home of the Duke and Duchess of Kent.

Without the furore that in later years was created when Princess Margaret, the Princess of Wales and, more recently the Duchess of York, went abroad leaving their babies in the care of a nanny for a few weeks, the Duke and Duchess of Kent in 1937 were able to take a six-week holiday shortly after Princess Alexandra's christening – without criticism. During this time Alexandra and her brother Edward were left not only in the capable hands of their Nanny, Ethel Smith, but from time to time in the care of the woman who had been Princess Marina's own Nanny, Miss Kate Fox. Known as 'Foxy', she had gone from England to Greece in 1906 to look after Prince Nicholas's children and even when Princess Marina was an adult, still referred to her former charge as 'my baby'. When she finally retired from service she would still meet with Princess Marina once a week, right up to the day before her death in November 1949, and did not cease treating Marina as a child. 'Why are you wearing that, it's not warm enough,' Foxy would say, or 'powder your nose, it's all shiny', never forgetting her Norland training. For Princess Marina, Foxy was a much needed link with her Greek past and she knew that her children would be safe under this experienced eye.

As Princess Alexandra's birth occurred during the year in which Queen Mary lost not only her husband of forty-two years but saw her son give up the throne and forced into exile, she sought consolation in her new granddaughter and was a frequent visitor to 3 Belgrave Square. Occasionally Princess Alexandra would be driven to Buckingham Palace where the dowager Queen would push the baby in her pram around the parklike gardens whenever she was visiting from nearby Marlborough House. Today's experts who claim that the first few weeks of a baby's life are crucial in building the bonds between mother and child will understand the close relationship that Princess Alexandra was to enjoy with her grandmother. Whilst the world saw Queen Mary as the austere face of royalty, never comfortable with her newly inherited title 'Queen Mother', to Princess Alexandra she was a matronly bosom on which to climb that offered ropes of pearls on which to pull, and was first and foremost a doting grandparent. From Queen Mary, Alexandra learned how to maintain the stiff upper lip in public, retaining dignity regardless of the situation. When Princess Marina, for example, became a widow her late husband's name could not be mentioned in her presence in case she broke down, yet Queen Mary outlived her husband and three of her sons but not once did she shed a tear outside the privacy of her own home.

Whilst the Duke and Duchess of Kent were very much to the fore during the Coronation of George VI in May 1937, Prince George riding on horseback immediately behind the Coronation Coach as a Personal Aide-de-Camp to the King and Princess Marina sharing a box with Queen Mary in Westminster Abbey itself, Alexandra was naturally too young to attend the proceedings. Just a few weeks later, however, the seven-month-old Princess made the newspaper headlines herself following an incident that might easily have bought her life to a premature end.

Born close to the blue waters of the Mediterranean, Princess Marina always loved the sea and many of her childhood photographs show her on the beaches of Europe. On a visit to England in 1911 she and her sisters, accompanied by Foxy, spent the first of many holidays on the sands of Bognor Regis – a town with many royal associations. Following the upheaval of the Coronation, Princess Marina decided to take her young children to the coast for what was most certainly Princess Alexandra's first experience of the sea. On a sunny summer's day they set out on a journey towards a quiet stretch of Kent coast, Bloody House Point, once a battlefield overlooking the now peaceful Sandwich Bay. Princess Alexandra lay asleep in a basket carrycot between the Duchess and Nanny Smith, when suddenly the car crashed into another and as the windows shattered, razor sharp slivers of glass showered down on to the baby. No serious injuries were sustained, but Princess Marina lost her sapphire engagement ring in the accident and was still searching anxiously for it when the police and a relief car arrived for them to continue the journey. What began as a quiet visit to the sea soon became a public concern and as the children later played on the beach, Press photographers were already training their lenses on them. Too young to comprehend the situation, it was nevertheless an indication that Alexandra had been born into no ordinary family.

The Kents tried hard to spare their children from the burden of royal birth. Like the Queen's son Prince Edward today, Prince George was the son of a monarch yet sufficiently down the line of succession now to ensure that he would not inherit the throne. But there is an inescapable destiny that sets all royal children apart and Alexandra was to be no exception. Seldom could they travel even the shortest distance as a family without the inevitable detective in tow; when these children complained about the lack of sand on the beach at Sandwich a special sandpit was built for them, purely because of their royal birth, and from an early age whenever Alexandra met her Uncle Bertie (George VI) or her grandmother (Queen Mary) she was encouraged to curtsey.

Marina and George were constantly in demand to fulfil more and more public engagements in the late Thirties. There were only so many that the King and Queen could do, the then Princess Royal (George's only sister, Mary) although fulfilling her fair share disliked appearing in public, and the Duke and Duchess of Gloucester never quite managed to attain the glamorous image of the Kents. This meant constant separation from the children, especially when foreign tours, which usually entailed lengthy sea voyages in those days, were involved. During the week this often meant that the Duke and Duchess saw Alexandra and Eddie for a short time after their nursery breakfast and again in the evening for an hour's family play before bedtime. Whilst the Kents avoided the situation of becoming almost strangers to their own children, as occurred in many an aristocratic household during this period, inevitably there were times when Princess Alexandra saw more of Nanny Smith than she did of her own mother.

In 1938 the Duke and Duchess of Kent were not only at the height of their popularity in Britain, where Marina set a fashion for wearing cotton dresses and revived Lancashire's flagging cotton industry, but also became overseas ambassadors. Their marriage had naturally brought greater ties to Greece; in Poland there was a suggestion that the Duke should become their King, and so great was affection for the couple in Australia that in the autumn of 1938 it was agreed that George should become Governor-General. After the initial consternation Marina agreed and a date was set for November 1939 when the Kent family would emigrate permanently to the antipodes. Government House in Canberra was to become their official residence and throughout 1939 the building was redecorated, new furniture was installed and personal items, including their own horses, were shipped over. This was the first time a member of the Royal Family had been given such a position, and whilst George was enthusiastic about the prospect, revealing that he felt his children would have 'the time of their lives', Marina was less so. In January of 1938 her father, Prince Nicholas of Greece, had died. For one so close to her family this left a gaping hole in her life, and Marina did not relish the thought of being so far away from her mother and sisters. The journey from Britain to Europe was bad enough, but the distance from Australia seemed unbearable. However, it was the Duke who made the decisions and George had decided that a new start was needed. The Australian climate suited his temperament and in Canberra he would be in total control of his family's lives and not under the influence of British protocol.

Although popular with the Duke of Kent, the decision to emigrate to Australia was not accepted by the British press who had no desire to lose such a newsworthy and photogenic family. Even less enamoured were Marina's dress designers who felt that her departure would have 'an adverse effect on the whole fashion industry. The Duchess has made fashion history. She has given London the leadership that belonged to Paris and fashion houses fear that ... in her absence London will lose that lead again.'*

Whilst the preparations went ahead and personal items at Coppins were packed up, the young Prince Edward and Princess Alexandra were taken to the seclusion of Sandringham under the watchful eye of Queen Mary. The first of many such separations that were to draw the children closer to their grandmother. Alexandra took her favourite toys, which not surprisingly were dolls dressed in European national costumes, soon to be discarded in favour of one rubber doll dressed as a nurse. Only in retrospect, in the knowledge that Alexandra studied nursing, does this choice have any significance. Called 'Christabel',

* Lead story on the front page of the *Sunday Express*, 1938.

because like Alexandra herself she arrived on Christmas Day, the doll remained a popular toy, but never as popular as her brother's mechanical toys for the Princess's 'tomboy' nature was quick to assert itself. Just as many years were to pass before any relevance could be placed in Alexandra's bias towards the nurse doll, equally in the scheme of things it was then insignificant that Alexandra was sent to Sandringham while her cousins Elizabeth and Margaret Rose were staying at Balmoral enabling them to attend a birthday party. Celebrating his birthday was the grandson of Lady Airlie, Queen Mary's lady-in-waiting, Angus Ogilvy.

As the time approached for the Kents to move from Coppins to 'Yarralumla', the Government House in Australia, an event hailed by Winston Churchill as 'a master stroke of Imperial policy', so too came the threat of war. The announcement of the Duke of Kent's appointment as Governor-General in the autumn of 1938 coincided even then with the rumblings of hostility. In March Hitler's troops had invaded Austria in an attempt to claim what he called Germany's 'lost territories'. Next on his list was Sudetenland, part of Czechoslovakia. In September Chamberlain, the British Prime Minister, met with the French premier Daladier, Hitler and Mussolini at Munich and an agreement was made granting the German-speaking fortified frontier to Hitler, while the rest of Czechoslovakia would remain under the protection of the other powers. Chamberlain thought he had averted war, but he had only delayed it. In August 1939 the Duke and Duchess of Kent made a visit to Europe to say farewell to Marina's relations. During their stay the possibility of war became greater and the Duke returned alone to England to take stock of the situation and within days telegrammed his wife to return to England immediately. It was alone in the Music Room at Coppins, the Duke in London, Alexandra and Edward still at Sandringham, that Princess Marina heard Neville Chamberlain's broadcast announcing that Britain was at war with Germany. Like so many families in 1939, the six years that followed were to alter the course of their lives irrevocably.

For the Kents, a new life in Canberra was no longer a possibility, and the Duke's appointment as Governor-General was postponed indefinitely, never to be taken up. Not yet three years old, Princess Alexandra had a prestigious background and a promising start but faced a blighted future. Instead of the freedom she would have experienced growing up in Australia, her destiny was to spend her childhood within the grisly shadow of the Second World War and the inevitable restrictions that this imposed. The life that had begun as a fairytale was about to turn into a tragedy. The symbol of hope into an object of pity.

2

A Wartime Tragedy

In 1964 Princess Marina visited Australia for the first time, making a poignant journey to Government House in Canberra that might once have been her home. There, surrounded by furniture that the Duke of Kent had himself chosen in 1939, Marina said: 'Well, I'm here at last. It's taken me twenty-five years to get here. War and tragedy prevented it. That's what war does to a person.'

The declaration of war had naturally caused consternation within the Royal Family. Princess Alexandra was not to see the nursery of 3 Belgrave Square again as the Duke of Kent decided not to renew the lease. Gone too was the calm chintzy world of Coppins, now temporarily closed up for fear that it should become a target for enemy attack being so close to Windsor Castle. Instead the Kents rented a house at Tetbury, Gloucestershire, the same small market town where the present Prince of Wales was by coincidence to purchase a house some forty years later. Princess Alexandra's first real taste of war came less than twenty-four hours after it had begun. At 2.45 am on Monday 4 September the air raid sirens sounded at Sandringham. A hideous sound for an adult, let alone a young child, in the dead of night. The Princess and her brother Eddie were carried in the darkness to the basement of Sandringham House, where the reassuring figure of their grandmother arrived some time later. Queen Mary, somewhat typically, having chosen to dress immaculately first.

The following morning Queen Mary decided to take the children to the relative safety of her niece's house at Badminton. After breakfast they set out with an entourage of more than sixty servants and a fleet of twenty cars and vans. One can only imagine the Duchess of Beaufort's expression, having anticipated receiving a seventy-two-year-old lady and two small children with perhaps the minimum of staff, when this regal procession eventually arrived at Badminton House. For the next six months Princess Alexandra was to see her own mother just once a week, her father even less.

Although the separation was distressing for Princess Marina, it was nothing new for Alexandra and unlike many evacuated children she was not in a house of complete strangers and certainly not noticeably deprived of luxury. One of England's stateliest homes, Badminton House has rooms designed by James Wyatt, wood carvings by Grinling Gibbons, magnificent Canalettos and Van Dycks, and most famous of all the entrance hall which is the size and shape of a badminton court for it was here that the game originated. On the second floor a set of rooms was turned into a nursery suite, once used by earlier generations of Beaufort children, with impressive views across the 50,000 acres of parkland. An air raid shelter was created for them on the ground floor which offered greater degrees of comfort than the Sandringham cellars. From the moment they arrived Queen Mary took charge, not only of the children but also of the house. 'Pandemonium was the least it could be called,' the Duchess of Beaufort wrote to her friend, Osbert Sitwell, when the royal party arrived. 'The servants revolted and scorned our humble home. They refused to use the excellent rooms assigned to them ... The Queen [Mary] quite unconscious of the stir, has settled in well, and is busy cutting down trees and tearing down ivy.'

Queen Mary's hatred of ivy is now legendary and the young Princess Alexandra was quickly conscripted into helping tear it down from buildings and trees. As she grew older she helped also with her grand-mother's salvage expeditions to collect scrap metal. On one occasion a battle royal erupted when Queen Mary wanted to chop down a cedar tree that grew outside her bedroom window, positive that it was infested with bugs that were pervading her room. At first the Duchess pointed out to her aunt that the 5th Duke of Beaufort had planted the tree 150 years earlier, but for one who had lived a life surrounded by treasures of great antiquity this small point meant nothing to Queen Mary. She demanded that the tree be removed. The Duchess was adamant that it should stay. The battle went on for days, until ultimately the matter was resolved by making Queen Mary's bedroom bug-proof and the tree remained. For a time it was like a scene from Thomas Hardy's *The Woodlanders* in which Marty South's father is convinced that the tree outside his bedroom window will be the death of him.

In Queen Mary, Princess Alexandra had the toughest character within the whole Royal Family as a mentor and subconsciously she was being trained for her future role. The Queen had a knack of tempering play with learning. An early gift from her to the young Princess Elizabeth was a set of toy building blocks and she was quick to point out that each brick came from a different part of the Empire. Equally a childish game at an early age with her grandmother taught Princess Alexandra how to curtsey. It was noted that the young Princess Alexandra possessed a certain dignity and even if out picking fruit with her grandmother or collecting eggs, she was always smartly dressed and even wore the obligatory hat. It may have been many years before she was to undertake official duties, yet she accompanied Queen Mary on local visits to the Army and handed out presents to the soldiers at Christmas. Without her realizing it, her training had begun.

Although Princess Alexandra was safely cocooned at Badminton, sheltered from the harsh realities of the war, for her parents it was a different story. Princess Marina was no longer able to make her daily telephone calls to her mother and sisters, which left her feeling isolated from her family. Even worse, her sister Elizabeth had married the German Count Charles of Toerring-Jettenbach (one of Alexandra's godparents) and was technically considered to be an enemy. Three of Prince Philip's sisters were in the same position. King George VI was determined that his family should do their part for the war effort and Marina was made Chief Commandant of the Women's Royal Naval Service in 1940. This involved travelling all over Britain visiting each unit, boosting morale, touring bomb sites, talking to the bereaved and injured and taking an active involvement in every aspect of the WRNS work. Besides travelling some 500 miles a week in this capacity, she still continued to fulfil her former duties as a member of the Royal Family whenever necessary.

As Prince George was first a Rear-Admiral in the Navy stationed at Rosyth in Scotland and later a Welfare Officer attached to the Inspector-

General of the Royal Air Force, the opportunities for the family to be together were infrequent. Once the war had been in progress for a year and their lives had begun to settle into a pattern, they decided to open up Coppins again as a family home. In 1941 they agreed to risk having the children to stay for a while and Princess Alexandra and Prince Edward were allowed to return. Inevitably there were tensions. All had been apart, both George and Marina had risked their lives in air raids, and in many ways they were almost strangers. Princess Alexandra was becoming exuberant and boisterous, perhaps allowed too much of her own way as compensation for the separation. Occasionally she was moody and disobedient, once kicking over a tea trolley when angry and she went through a period of pretending to be a horse and refusing to speak other than in neighing sounds. At the root of her behaviour was confusion. She did not fully understand the war, she no longer had one secure base and lacked a proper family life. On occasions she would spend time at Windsor Castle with her cousins and sometimes she would be taken to York Cottage on the Sandringham estate but for eighteen months of her short life much of her time had been spent incarcerated at Badminton with her grandmother. For the same reasons her brother, Eddie, became very withdrawn, often too serious and pensive for one so young. Taken to a sweet shop by Queen Mary, Prince Edward spent a long time pondering over how to spend his pocket money. When asked what the problem was, he replied anxiously, 'Rising prices.' Both children had what one member of the family described as 'pent-up restless energy'. Occasionally, with Alexandra, it exploded.

However much the Duke and Duchess of Kent wanted to spend time with their children, they possessed the inherent royal quality of placing public duty before private desire. Besides being Commandant of the WRNS, sometimes attracting new recruits simply because she looked elegant in the uniform, Princess Marina worked as a nurse at the local cottage hospital in Iver, and later became a VAD (Voluntary Aid Detachment) at University College Hospital in London. Known as 'Nurse K', she managed to keep her identity a secret for a long time, even when patients remarked on how much she resembled the Duchess of Kent. One potentially embarrassing moment came when the Duke of Kent paid an official visit while she was on duty, but she simply curtseyed along with the other nurses and kept a discreet distance. On another occasion, when some soldiers beyond medical help were brought in, the Matron told Marina that the best service she could do them was to remove her nurse's uniform, put on her hat and coat and go to the men's beds as the Duchess of Kent, pretending that she was visiting officially. In this capacity she was able to offer greater comfort. Eventually her cover was blown when a dressmaker, who naturally followed the Duchess of Kent's fashions closely, recognized 'Nurse K' and soon the whole hospital, and the Press, knew her real identity. Once public knowledge, it greatly enhanced the Kents' reputation. Princess Marina 'retired' from her nursing career with a secret of her own. She was expecting another baby.

Princess Alexandra's second brother, Prince Michael of Kent, was born on 4 July, 1942, at Coppins. He was given the names Michael George Charles Franklin, the latter in honour of his birth on American Independence Day. The then President, Franklin D. Roosevelt, agreed to be one of the godparents. Although Princess Alexandra and Prince Edward were at Badminton with Queen Mary at the time, they were quickly brought to Coppins so as not to feel excluded. Had it not been wartime the situation would have been idyllic. The Kent family could have no inkling of the tragedy that lay in store.

In many ways the war suited the Duke of Kent's restless nature and he enjoyed the element of danger that existed. On several occasions he narrowly escaped injury during air raids in London and appreciated the opportunities it afforded to escape the routine round of royal engagements. Like his niece, Princess Margaret, he hated boredom and revelled in the unexpected. As the war progressed he lamented the fact that he was 'too protected' as a member of the Royal Family and deliberately kept out of any real danger. His wife had been able to undertake valuable war work, not without personal risk for the hospital where she had worked was in the shape of a cross and looked from the air like a prime target for enemy bombers. When bombs did rain down, Princess Marina was always too busy to get to the hospital shelter. Prince George, however, felt that his war work lacked purpose. 'It's not very exciting to spend an awful lot of time looking at ablutions,' he said after numerous visits to factories and bomb sites. In the spring of 1942 he had lunch in London with the film star Douglas Fairbanks

Jr., then an officer in the American Navy on leave in England. The Duke told him that he wished to see more action and that some involvement with the American Air Force might be the solution. Fairbanks arranged for him to see an American General, but he never knew the outcome of their subsequent conversation.

One month after his birth, on 4 August, Prince Michael's christening was combined at Windsor Castle with the forty-second birthday celebrations of Queen Elizabeth. It was a more subdued affair than Princess Alexandra's. Although all royal christenings are private, because of the war no foreign members of the family were able to travel and it was decided to keep the occasion simple. The Duke stood proxy for the United States President, and staff from Coppins mixed on a social level with royalty. Exactly three weeks later on 24 August, the Duke of Kent set out on a tour of inspection in Iceland. That day he said his goodbyes to Princess Alexandra and her brothers. As he drove away down the drive of Coppins, Princess Marina felt compelled to watch the car until it was completely out of sight. At the last moment the Duke turned to look back at her and smiled. Before he left he had made a special point of stroking his favourite Chow dog. 'What will you do with him when I'm gone?' he asked.

This was intended to be his last such tour of inspection, and the Prince told Marina to expect him home within seven to ten days. That morning he drove to Invergordon from where he was to fly the next day from the RAF base on the Cromarty Firth. On Tuesday 25 August, as planned, the Sunderland 'flying-boat' took off at 1.10 pm with a crew of ten for the 900-mile flight to Iceland. On board were five passengers, including the Duke. As it was wartime, depth-charge bombs were also carried should enemy submarines be spotted *en route*, much of the seven-hour flight being over the sea. It was a calm but overcast day and as the aircraft flew north-eastwards over the Dornoch Firth the cloud began to thicken. The events that happened in the twenty minutes after take-off have never been adequately explained. It is known that the flying-boat cleared a hill, near Berriedale on the coast, called Eagle's Rock. At 900 feet this was one of the lower peaks in the Scottish Highlands that the aircraft would have encountered. Two crofters walking through the hills suddenly saw a brilliant flash of orange light and heard two explosions which they later described as 'like the worst kind of thunder'. The plane had crashed into the hillside on the other side of Eagle's Rock. The younger of the two crofters, Hugh Morrison, ran to his motorcycle and raced into Berriedale to alert the police and rescue services. Although a search party set out, the mist became too thick and it was not until the search could be resumed on the following day that the wreckage of the aircraft was found. Fourteen of the fifteen men were dead. The local doctor identified the Duke of Kent's body by his watch, a birthday present from Marina. It was stopped at 1.32 pm, the time of the crash.

One man miraculously survived. Flight-Sergeant Andrew Jacks, who had been travelling in the rear turret and had only joined the crew after the toss of a coin with a rear-gunner, had been able to pull seven bodies from the plane at great personal risk to himself before the flames became too great. He had then crawled six miles to get help, too late to save the flight engineer who had been breathing but bleeding profusely after the crash. Andrew Jacks was the one man who could later explain what had gone wrong but scarcely was he settled in the hospital at Grangemouth than RAF intelligence officers made him sign an Oath of Secrecy. Jacks died in 1978, never having publicly explained the crash, although he had met with Princess Marina privately on several occasions and presumably told her his story. The only consolation was that the Duke of Kent had died instantly. He was thirty-nine.

The Secretary of State for Air, Sir Archibald Sinclair, said in a statement to the House of Commons that the findings were: 'First, the accident occurred because the aircraft was flown on a track other than that indicated in the flight plan given to the pilot, and at too low an altitude to clear the rising ground on the track. Secondly, that the responsibility for this serious mistake in airmanship lies with the captain of the aircraft. Thirdly, that the weather encountered should have presented no difficulties to an experienced pilot. Fourthly, that the examination of the propellors showed that the engines were under power when the aircraft struck the ground.'

This was the official version that is now generally accepted, the blame lying fairly and squarely with the Captain, Flight-Lieutenant Frank Goyen, a twenty-five-year-old highly experienced pilot. It was automatically assumed that it was he who was flying the plane. In the fifty years that have followed since the Duke of Kent's death, there have been many theories as to why the plane crashed, from 'magnetic rocks' affecting the craft's controls to the depth-charge bombs prematurely exploding. The weather should not have been a problem to such a craft or pilot, and the wreckage of the craft was cleared with such extraordinary speed that no independent check was allowed to be made on the remains. Perhaps the most likely clue comes from the Royal Family themselves. The author and historian Michael Bloch was given access to the Duke of Windsor's papers in 1982 and subsequently wrote that the Duke heard that his brother had actually been piloting the plane himself.★ From whom would the Duke of Windsor have heard of the Duke of Kent's death? He received a telephone call from King George VI. The King had himself had a long private conversation with survivor Flight-Sergeant Andrew Jacks. There was no reason for Jacks to lie and it was he, after all, who had pulled George's body from the wreckage. It is unlikely too that the Duke of Windsor would have been ill-informed. He would most certainly have known whether George was passenger or pilot.

Was this then the reason for the fatal plane crash, that the less experienced Duke of Kent was flying the craft himself and misjudged the high ground? Was this also the reason for the subsequent secrecy surrounding the events and the eventual blame on the dead Frank Goyen who could not defend himself? The *one* survivor was made to sign an Oath forbidding him to tell his side of the story, yet his was surely a tale of heroism that would otherwise have been harmless. Certainly it is in character with the Duke of Kent's craving for adventure that he would ask to take over the controls and how could a young, albeit experienced, pilot refuse what on the surface appeared to be a harmless request from a royal Duke, the King's own brother? It also ties in with the Duke's earlier conversation with Douglas Fairbanks Jr. that he wanted to see more action and this should have been his last such tour of inspection.

By coincidence, Douglas Fairbanks Jr. was to have spent the following weekend at Coppins with George and Marina, but at the last minute George had written to postpone the visit because he had to fly north on an assignment. Fairbanks received the letter at the same time as his newspaper. On the envelope was the Duke's familiar handwriting.

★ See *The Duke of Windsor's War* by Michael Bloch, Weidenfeld & Nicolson 1982.

The large headline announced that the Duke of Kent was dead.

At Coppins, Princess Marina was already in bed when the news came. It was Sir Archibald Sinclair, the Secretary of State for Air, who telephoned and it was Princess Marina's devoted Foxy who took the call. With Prince Michael still only seven weeks old, and the Duke away from home, Kate Fox had come to take care of her former charge. She who had been with Princess Marina through a troubled childhood, had shared the joys of her entry into the British Royal Family and marriage to the Duke, the birth of three children, and was her closest confidante, now had to break the most tragic news of all. Hardly knowing what to say, the elderly nurse walked slowly up the stairs towards Princess Marina's room. Hearing the telephone and Foxy's footsteps, Princess Marina knew what had happened even before Foxy had opened the door. At Sandringham, Princess Alexandra slept, unaware of the tragedy that had unfolded itself. The news was kept from her until she could be taken to Coppins to hear it from her own mother, but as an astute child she must have known that something was wrong by the people around her long before she heard the news.

Princess Marina was devastated. George had been the centre of her world. It was he who had made every decision, often even down to how she should style her hair or which dress she would wear. For the first day she cried inconsolably or sat staring blankly into space, attempting to take in the full horror of the situation. George was dead. Prince Michael would never know his father. Prince Edward would now be Duke of Kent. How would she cope with bringing up the children alone? Who knows what, if any, practicalities went through Princess Marina's mind. Just before his death Prince George had planned to sell Coppins and buy a larger house called 'Dropmore', an eighteenth-century Buckinghamshire mansion. This could not now go ahead. The Duke of Kent's £25,000 Civil List allowance came to an end that day. Marina had no source of income. As she wept through that night and the following day there can have been no light at the end of a very dark tunnel.

At Badminton, Queen Mary 'felt so stunned by the shock I could not believe it', but told her lady-in-waiting, Lady Cynthia Colville, to begin packing her clothes in preparation for a trip to Coppins. 'I must go to Marina tomorrow,' she said. For the Duchess the arrival of her mother-in-law at Coppins was the first faint glimmer of hope. Queen Mary shared a mutual loss and could offer the necessary words of comfort, herself also a widow. Typically the Queen's words were not syrupy platitudes, instead she pointed out that Marina had a *duty* to her country, her family and her children and must not allow herself the luxury of self-pity. The message struck home and although Princess Marina never seemed to fully recover from her loss, she did not withdraw from public life as anticipated. 'I am just one among thousands of war widows,' she said and ten weeks after the Duke's death she began undertaking engagements again, taking on many of her late husband's duties and the patronages of some thirty organizations with which he was associated. Any portrait of the Duke had to be taken down before her arrival, however, and no mention was allowed of his name for it upset her too greatly. The funeral at St George's Chapel, Windsor, where only weeks earlier their son had been christened, was Marina's greatest ordeal. Throughout she was supported by the heavily veiled Queen Mary and Queen Elizabeth. On two occasions she seemed on the verge of collapse. 'I have attended very many family funerals in the Chapel, but none which have moved me in the same way,' wrote King George VI in his diary. 'Everybody there I knew well, but I did not dare to look at any of them for the fear of breaking down.'

In the early days there were fears as to how Princess Marina would cope. The elderly Foxy could not bear the sole responsibility for her, and eventually it was decided that Marina's sister, Princess Olga should be brought to England. Married to Prince Paul of Yugoslavia, Princess Olga had been exiled to Kenya during the war after Yugoslavia's pact with the Germans. This presented political problems in getting Olga out of Kenya, but after a lengthy journey, part of which was on board a battleship, the sisters were re-united for the first time since the war began. She alone could help her sister piece her life back together again.

Once again Princess Alexandra was parted from her mother and joined Queen Mary at Badminton House where they were to remain for the rest of the war. As if influenced by the events around her, the Princess seemed confused, at times rebellious. She would kick and scream if things did not go right for her and Queen Mary called her 'an impossible child'. Yet there was much for the young girl to come to terms with. The war itself meant by its very nature that it was impossible to live a normal childhood. Coupled with this, Alexandra had in a short space of time suddenly stopped being the 'baby' of the family and had been superseded in this role by Prince Michael, who not only seemed to receive all the attention when they were together as a family but was also the one who now remained behind at Coppins with their mother. Princesses Elizabeth and Margaret had been older when the war came and were used to Windsor Castle, and saw their parents frequently; their cousin Alexandra, however, had not been to Badminton until she was evacuated there and she was too young to fully understand exactly why she kept being taken away from her parents. To a childish mind it seemed like banishment. In the midst of this she had to face the trauma of a tearful mother telling her that she would never see her father again. Although devoted to Queen Mary, she could never take the place of two contented parents in peacetime. Difficult days lay ahead for them all.

Now with two brothers, it was not surprising that Princess Alexandra turned into a tomboy. She and Prince Edward played at being Commandos, once blacking both their faces with watercolour paints to everyone's absolute horror. To provide them with a sense of responsibility they were given animals to look after, firstly rabbits, then two calves at a nearby farm to feed and take care of. So determined was the Princess that hers would be in better condition than her brother's that she groomed the unsuspecting creature two or three times a day, once using an entire bottle of 'Brilliantine' to ensure that hers had the shiniest coat. Like her cousin Elizabeth, Princess Alexandra was passionate about horses. Indeed, many members of the Royal Family have looked upon riding as a form of escapism enabling them to release tension. Not only an exciting sport in itself, there is the added attraction of being alone with a creature that has no conception of the word 'royal'. Wanting desperately to be 'like other girls', many years were to pass before Alexandra stopped feeling self-conscious about being a Princess. When she won a rosette at a local show with her white pony 'Tony' at the age of eight, she announced proudly that she had one ambition in life. To be a bareback rider in a circus. Queen Mary carried on doing her crossword puzzle without comment.

When the Second World War finally came to an end in 1945 Princess Alexandra finally returned to Coppins. Less worldly than she might have been as an evacuee from any other family, Alexandra faced an uncertain future in a house that had suffered a dramatic change. The man who had loved it and ruled over it was gone and although Princess Marina was far from destitute, economies had to be made. While the lifestyle of her cousins, Elizabeth and Margaret, appeared to improve dramatically once the war was over, life became less easy for nine-year-old Alexandra. To her great embarrassment she no longer seemed to receive new clothes but instead came gifts of her cousins' cast-offs. To the outside world her home life appeared enviably secure, but she now lacked a father to bring her under control and no longer had the firmness of Queen Mary to guide her. Princess Marina would need all her strength to prevent her daughter from turning into a rebel.

The contradictions which seem to dominate Princess Alexandra's life began almost as soon as she returned to Coppins. Marina decided that her children would benefit from a period of study in a local establishment rather than having lessons in the traditional royal manner with a private tutor or governess. For too long the war had incarcerated them in the countryside and she felt that they should begin mixing with other children. A select school was chosen, run by a Mrs Parnell, who already taught the local doctor's twin sons and a few aristocratic children. Marina wanted Alexandra and Edward to learn how to socialize with their own peer group and experience life as 'ordinary' children, yet no sooner was Alexandra beginning to experience non-royal life for the first time, than she was suddenly on the balcony of Buckingham Palace with the rest of the Royal Family for the VE Day celebrations, being told that she must behave like a Princess.

This was Princess Alexandra's first experience of royal adulation, an unbelievable sight for a child to see thousands of people thronging in the Mall to cheer her family. The following week she went with Princess Marina and Prince Edward to St Paul's Cathedral for a Service of Thanksgiving to mark the end of the war, again witnessing the cheering, waving crowds of well-wishers. Back home in Iver she was later admonished for waving over-enthusiastically out of the car window on an ordinary private journey, believing that this was now expected of her. By the time summer came and the Kents were at Balmoral for the traditional royal holiday, the Princess had developed a complex about being seen in public. 'It's no good saying they're not looking at me,' Alexandra said to her brother, 'I know they *are*, and it's too awful.'

There were two facets to Princess Alexandra's life and it was now up to her to reconcile them.

3

Paving the Way

Slightly too plump, tall for her age and preferring to condense her name to 'Sandra', Alexandra was far from the fairytale vision of a Princess. 'I don't know what to do with her. She's the very limit,' complained Princess Marina. Clumsy, untidy and quite often downright disobedient – hiding in the garden when it was time for bed – there were frequent battles between mother and daughter. Once again Alexandra's life seemed unable to establish itself towards a comfortable pattern, and now her brother Prince Edward, who had been a constant companion since the day she was born, was to be taken away from her. Sent to a school in Wokingham, scarcely twenty miles away from Coppins, Eddie was to return home only for school holidays and one Sunday afternoon a month. After prep school he was to go on to Eton, finishing his education in Switzerland before embarking on an Army career at Sandhurst. His childhood at home was effectively at an end. Coppins was not to become a permanent home for him again until he was married.

As if seeking compensation, the Princess immersed herself in the world of horses, entering innumerable gymkhanas with sufficient success to encourage her to continue. By this time her career ambition had changed from wanting to enter the circus to dreaming of being a prima ballerina. Like the Princess of Wales, who nursed a similar ambition, her height was against her. In an era when Princesses did not embark on full-time careers, it is intriguing that Alexandra had such aspirations, and right up to the time when she began undertaking royal duties she still harboured desires to work in other spheres. As she grew up many felt that she had sufficient talent to become a concert pianist. She was fluent in French and, had she wished, it might have been possible for her to teach the language. She could also have chosen a full-time nursing career, following her mother's lead. It is intriguing that her childhood choices were in the world of entertainment and many have likened royal duty to 'an acting job'.

In October 1946 the first opportunity for Princess Alexandra to 'perform' in public presented itself. She was chosen to be a bridesmaid at the wedding of Lord Mountbatten's daughter, Patricia, to Lord Brabourne. For Alexandra the greatest excitement was not so much the role of bridesmaid as the fact that she was actually to have a new dress for the occasion. The greatest coup was that it turned out to be identical to those worn by her cousins, Elizabeth and Margaret Rose, and for once she did not feel like the poor relation. Unbeknown to Alexandra the wedding at Romsey Abbey was to mark yet another turning point. Relieved when the ceremony passed without incident and without embarrassment to herself, her behaviour at the reception afterwards was regarded as over-vigorous by the family. Perhaps Princess Marina had allowed her daughter too free a hand, some felt; her boisterous nature was obviously far from under control. 'If Marina had only kept with tradition and employed a governess,' said the King, 'Alexandra would learn discipline.' Since the death of his brother, King George felt a certain responsibility towards his niece. Princess Elizabeth had experienced no education other than from her governess, Marion Crawford, and eventually special private lessons in the history of the British constitution with Sir Henry Marten, the Vice-Provost of Eton. Measured against 'Cousin Lilibet', Alexandra certainly lacked decorum. A family conference ensued and it fell to Princess Alice, the Duchess of Gloucester, to gently persuade Marina that Princess Alexandra would benefit from a more formal training. Alexandra quite obviously had the intelligence, but her energy needed to be channelled more effectively.

Having myself studied in depth the lives of Princess Margaret and Princess Anne, both second-born children, there are striking parallels with Princess Alexandra. Notably, all three experience difficulty in coming to terms with their royal status, all had periods of rebellion and were much more outgoing in personality than the first-born brother or sister. Prince Edward of Kent, Princess Elizabeth and Prince Charles are outwardly more serious and deeper thinkers than their younger counterparts. It is as if Alexandra, Margaret and Anne felt that they had to use their personalities in an effort to prove second-born did not mean second-best. Princess Alexandra, however, lacked the volatile nature of Princess Margaret and Princess Anne, and instead of kicking back at tradition and rebelling against her royal status, her greatest worry was that she would not come up to expectations. As she grew older, she was happy to do her duty but lacked confidence in her own abilities. Always able to see humour in everything, while being initiated into the royal way of life Princess Alexandra looked upon it all in a characteristically down-to-earth and bemused manner. After the house party at Windsor Castle for Ascot week in 1947, her first experience of the event, her sentiment was, 'Eton boys stand around and we stand around, and you never see anyone for more than five minutes. First they're changing, then you curtsey, then you're off to the races. About the only thing to do is eat strawberries and cream.'

On returning to Coppins, Princess Marina pondered as to whether it had been a wise decision to send Alexandra to the local school. Much has been made today of the 'normal' lives and schooling that modern royals try to give their children, but even in the Nineties total freedom is impossible. When the Prince and Princess of Wales decided in 1991 that they wanted to put their eldest son's name down for Eton, they were advised against it on security grounds. Too close to a public road, it would prove impossible to protect Prince William. Security and not the quality of the school was to be the key factor in the future King's education. The fact that Princess Alexandra went to a local school with other children, was able to walk about the Iver shops with her friends, seems trivial now but it was a breakthrough for the Royal Family in the Forties. The confusion for Alexandra stemmed from the fact that she wanted to be treated like other girls with whom she now mixed, which was encouraged to an extent so that she did not think herself superior, yet at one and the same time her mother insisted, 'You are not a girl, you are a Princess.' Alexandra must have felt in limbo.

The first step on the road to royal maturity came with the employment of a Scottish governess who came, it is believed, at the Duchess of Gloucester's recommendation. Little is now known about the governess, but a popular fallacy is that she was Miss Catherine Peebles who taught the Queen's four children, Princess Margaret's two and for a time Princess Alexandra's own children in the Sixties. Even the most authoritative books will state that 'Mispy', as Catherine Peebles was known, entered the Queen's employment after a period as Princess Alexandra's governess, but the Princess has told her staff that it is simply not true. The anonymous governess, whom Alexandra apparently nicknamed 'Bambi' because of her big brown eyes, was said to be in her twenties and had an approach that was 'firm but fair' and if her pupils worked diligently there were always rewards such as trips to the zoo or a visit to an exhibition. Always instructional but a refreshing change from the schoolroom for her charges. The day would begin with a Bible reading followed by traditional tuition in the 'three R's'. There was room also to develop creative talents, royal children were always encouraged to paint, but it was in music that Alexandra particularly excelled and once nurtured it was to become a lifelong passion for her. Princess Marina adored opera and went to Glyndebourne and Covent Garden as often as possible, Verdi and Puccini being her favourites, and it is today followed with equal fortitude by her son Eddie and the present Duchess of Kent. Princess Alexandra's tastes are more varied, ranging from jazz, like her father, to Beethoven.

Under the private tutor Princess Alexandra matured noticeably. Perhaps it was because she was growing older anyway, more probable was the fact that with Eddie away at school she no longer felt the need to compete for attention or make her presence felt. She had a lively talent to amuse and Princess Marina now included her in small cocktail parties at Coppins where guests could include the likes of Noël Coward and Malcolm Sargent. Often Alexandra would be handing round nuts or canapés, but as her confidence increased she would occasionally entertain on the piano. Whether it was 'Bambi's' success, Alexandra's maturity or a compromise between Princess Marina and King George VI, is unrecorded but eventually it was agreed that Alexandra should attend a school so as not to become too insular in her outlook. The compromise being that, like royal sons, she would be sent away to boarding school so that she would be completely immersed in an academic environment. This way she would learn how to communicate on a social level with other girls, would be able to study a wider range of subjects than a governess could ever offer, and at the same time would benefit from the discipline that would be necessary in such an establishment.

Many girls' schools were considered, but eventually Heathfield was chosen for a variety of reasons. One of Alexandra's friends, Lady Diana Herbert, was also a pupil which meant that Alexandra would have someone there that she knew, and, more importantly from Marina's point of view, the school was situated at Ascot only a short drive from Coppins.

'I don't know what I'm going to do without Alexandra,' Marina confessed privately.

Founded by Miss Beatrice Wyatt in 1899, with the object of 'giving girls a sound education within a religious framework', Heathfield School stands in thirty-four acres of ground adjacent to Swinley Forest. The environment is peaceful with no external distractions, the school building itself originally a late Georgian house to which many wings have since been added. Even today the school insists that, despite the wider curriculum offered than in Princess Alexandra's time, as in 1947 'the domestic and social graces are not ignored'. Although new pupils have to take a common entrance exam, this was not the case when the Princess joined the school and Marina expressed doubts at her daughter's ability to pass one.

The motto at Heathfield School is 'The Merit of One is the Honour of All', a maxim that the Royal Family could easily adopt as an institution. For Princess Alexandra the school rather surprisingly provided a reassuring haven of security in a life that had previously been unpredictable. She seemed to appreciate having a routine, and wearing the regulation off-the-peg navy blue uniform, with a red cape in winter, made her equal to the other girls. It also meant she no longer had to wear ill-fitting second-hand dresses. 'I am expected to wear my cousin Margaret's clothes,' Alexandra confessed, and even at the age of eleven she was taller than her 5' 2" cousin of sixteen.

Today there are some 200 boarders at Heathfield whose parents pay in the region of £9,000 a year in fees for their daughters' education (£9,150 p.a. in 1991); although there were on average only seventy-five girls in Princess Alexandra's time, the fees were presumably of a comparative rate. Princess Marina was quick in pointing out to the headmistress that she was not wealthy and could only afford the basics for her daughter. Alexandra was to receive no special privileges for being royal and had come to expect none. It was to surprise many with whom she came into contact that she was genuinely grateful for anything that was given to her, however small the gift or deed.

Much as it must have been daunting for Alexandra at first to enter such an alien environment, the other girls were unimpressed by titles and she was quickly accepted once it became apparent that she had no airs and graces. Indeed, the school was peppered with daughters of the very rich, who came from grander homes with a larger staff than the Kents – Princess Alexandra seemed quite ordinary in comparison. Many stories abounded of girls who arrived at the school without the vaguest notion of how to dress themselves or style their own hair without a maid. In some areas Princess Alexandra had far less to learn. Alexandra was given the option of a single room or sharing a dormitory with five other girls and she chose the latter, enjoying the experience of new friends. Whilst others in her position might have felt intimidated by the whole concept, to her it was an adventure and she seemed to revel in the freedom. It was a genuine opportunity to be a girl and not a Princess. In then typical fashion, this new found liberty manifested itself as boisterous energy.

On one occasion a pillow fight after 'lights out in the dorm' became so frenetic that a chandelier almost came down on the headmistress at work in her study below. When called into the study the next morning to explain the fracas, Princess Alexandra gushed, 'Oh gosh,' in her best Joyce Grenfell voice. Sometime later she was gated for throwing a bucket of water over matron, and frequently she was asked to modulate her voice which rang out around the school when excited. 'She was like one of the worst from St Trinian's,' said a contemporary.

One advantage of a royal upbringing was that Princess Alexandra was never apprehensive or lost for words when meeting strangers, nor was she intimidated by people in authority. Many girls are in awe of their headmistress, but the principal of Heathfield, a Miss Kathleen Dodds, seemed scarcely older than her cousin Lilibet and the Princess identified easily with her. A drawback of being royal, which Princess Anne was to discover at Benenden in the Sixties, was that whilst other girls would return from school holidays and enthuse about their family and various activities, Princess Alexandra had to remain quiet. She could not give out details of what had gone on while staying with the King and Queen at Balmoral or Christmas at Sandringham. It was an early lesson in discretion. How desperately she must have longed to talk when in the winter term of her first year at Heathfield she was chosen to be a bridesmaid at the wedding of Princess Elizabeth to Prince Philip in Westminster Abbey. With the date of the wedding not even announced by Buckingham Palace, there was no way Alexandra could pass on such privileged information. At the same time she harboured a fear that this duty as 'Princess' was going to encroach on her life as 'schoolgirl' and she would be singled out as being different from the others. Even when it did become common knowledge she did not speak with any great enthusiasm about it and had been forbidden to reveal any secrets.

Marina did not allow Alexandra to have time off school for dress fittings and Norman Hartnell, who designed the bridesmaids' clothes along with Princess Elizabeth's wedding gown, had to give Alexandra the first fitting during Heathfield's half-term holiday. Final adjustments could only be done by sneaking the dress into the school itself, where an embarrassed Princess had to be given a private room, for her own dress would have given any onlookers a clue as to how the bride would look. Surprisingly, once the ceremony was over on 20 November 1947, and Alexandra had joined the other members of the Royal Family for an appearance on the balcony of Buckingham Palace, followed by the wedding breakfast, she was quickly driven back to school. Any other girl at Heathfield would have been allowed the entire day off, even for a much less auspicious wedding than that of the future Queen Elizabeth II, but Marina was firm.

In the wedding photographs taken after the ceremony, Alexandra stands immediately behind her brother, Prince Michael, who was a page at the ceremony, and next to her cousin, Princess Margaret. Alexandra looked extremely mature and it is difficult to believe that she was still a month away from her eleventh birthday. In a later family group photograph she is at least as tall as Queen Elizabeth, who was no doubt wearing her favoured three-inch heels. When it was announced that the entire school at Heathfield was to be taken to see a film of the wedding, Alexandra was panic-stricken and asked to be excused from this 'special treat'. Many reported that the Princess was too shy to see herself on the screen, but shyness was never part of her nature. Instead it seems that she was probably embarrassed at being made to feel different. She was intrigued at seeing herself on film, and would no doubt have done so had it been in private, but to possibly be made an object of ridicule in front of all the other girls filled her with horror. Even today she does not like having her photograph taken and as a child she would often kick and scream in the presence of a camera. Unphotogenic, it was she who was eventually to blossom and the camera never to flatter. Her great fear in the film of Princess Elizabeth's wedding was that she would look awkward and ungainly as she walked down the aisle. Such doubts about her abilities and appearance were to dog her for years to come.

Suffering from an acute lack of confidence in herself, Princess Alexandra tended to over react, occasionally going out of her way to prove that she was just one of the girls. She would volunteer to sweep the classroom floor, served behind stalls at the school bazaars, and joined the teams to play rounders, tennis and lacrosse. When she was made head of her small dormitory she was placated by being told that it had nothing to do with being a Princess, but was a position usually given to the rebellious girls. This was based on the supposition that a little responsibility would make a girl mature more quickly.

Princess Alexandra's five years at Heathfield were academically unremarkable. She excelled at music, enjoyed theatre and literature, and it became apparent that, like her cousin Princess Margaret, she had deep-seated religious beliefs. Before going to school her nanny had taught the Kent children to say their prayers aloud each night before going to bed, and it was a habit Alexandra found difficult to drop. Of above average intelligence, the Princess learned to speak French fluently, and it was a good all-round education that she required far more than gaining any qualifications which would prove to be of little practical use in the years ahead. It was Princess Marina who had at first insisted that Alexandra master the French language and it is a skill that the Princess has been able to put to good use in her royal career. Perhaps their wide number of European relatives had some bearing on their aptitude to learn languages, or maybe it is mere coincidence, but all the Kent children appeared to experience few difficulties. Prince Michael is the only member of the Royal Family who can converse fluently in Russian.

The Heathfield years stand out for Princess Alexandra not because of her scholastic endeavours but because she continued to be dogged by misfortune. Events happened beyond her control and her sunny disposition belied the disappointments she suffered. Frequently she would look forward with mounting excitement to school holidays, and time and again her plans would go awry. Although she enjoyed staying at Birkhall on the Balmoral estate in the summer, the prospect of a holiday in Jersey in the summer of 1949, her first overseas trip albeit only to the Channel Islands, was something she had looked forward to for weeks. No sooner had Alexandra Kent, as she called herself on private visits, arrived on Jersey than an outbreak of polio forced her to promptly fly straight home. She had to return to Heathfield and reveal that she had spent the time at Clymping, Sussex, instead.

When she did eventually make it to Jersey the following summer, the enjoyment was harried by frustration at being away from London where her cousin, Elizabeth, now Duchess of Edinburgh, was giving birth to her second child, Princess Anne. Two months later she was excluded from a visit to Rome with her mother and Prince Michael simply because Marina chose to go *after* Alexandra's half-term holiday from Heathfield. Alexandra was forbidden to have time off school. Even when she had her adenoids removed, the operation had to be performed during the Easter holidays of 1951 so as not to interrupt her education. Ever conscious of money, perhaps Princess Marina wanted value out of Heathfield, not wishing to pay for her daughter's absences.

Illness seemed to disrupt Alexandra's plans also. Although her adenoid operation put an end to her constant snoring, which the other girls complained about, it meant that her break from school was spent recuperating. Only a few months earlier her Christmas vacation had been ruined when her elder brother, the present Duke of Kent, contracted measles and they had to be kept apart. In 1951 when Alexandra was due to be confirmed in Heathfield Chapel in the presence of her grandmother, Queen Mary, not only did the latter take to her bed with a heavy cold forcing her to cancel, but Alexandra woke up to what at first appeared to be cold symptoms yet with the onset of a rash turned out to be German measles. Alexandra was confined to bed, her confirmation cancelled. Instead of taking place before her whole school, which on this occasion she did not object to, she was later confirmed privately at Windsor in front of family and only four Heathfield friends. 'Why does *everything* seem to happen to me?' Alexandra asked Miss Dodds.

That summer was to be the last carefree holiday at Balmoral Castle with the King and Queen. Princess Marina had decided to take Edward away from Eton College to complete his education at Le Rosay in Switzerland, not only for academic reasons but because the young Duke suffered constantly from allergies and hay fever and it was believed that the Swiss air would have a beneficial effect. This meant that Alexandra would now see even less of her brother than she did already. Eddie seemed to be growing up and she feared that they might grow apart. They stayed as usual at Birkhall, they fished in the River Dee and uncharacteristically, one would think, Marina would herself cook bacon and eggs on the river bank. It used to surprise her staff when, late in life, Princess Marina whenever alone at Kensington Palace would often request a supper of bacon and eggs with two boiled potatoes as a special treat. Not only did Alexandra feel subdued that summer because of Eddie's imminent departure, but it was also clear that the King was not in the best of health. While the Kents were still at Balmoral the King returned to London to see a leading chest surgeon, Clement Price Thomas. Although the King was never told, tests revealed that George VI had cancer.

The first public indication that all was not well had been on Thursday 3 May, 1951, when he opened the Festival of Britain on the south bank of the River Thames. He looked pale and drawn, later he began wearing make-up at evening functions to restore a healthy pallor but an X-ray that same month had already revealed to his doctor a patch on the lung. Although the King probably suspected his condition, the true nature of the disease was kept from him and he was told simply that there was a blockage in the left lung which would necessitate its removal. The operation was carried out on 23 September at Buckingham Palace and although the news bulletin said that 'His Majesty's post-operative condition is satisfactory,' it did not reveal that some of the nerves of the larynx had also to be removed, which meant that the man who had suffered a severe stammer for most of his life might only ever speak in a faint whisper. The King had smoked heavily throughout his adult life, the cause of his condition became obvious. Princess Marina cut her Greek cigarettes in half and began smoking each piece as a whole in a deliberate effort to cut down.

Although the King's recovery was slow, the operation appeared to be a success. On 21 December, Princess Marina and her family travelled to Sandringham for the traditional family Christmas. It was a particularly affectionate Christmas for the Royal Family, each trying to shut from their minds the seriousness of the King's condition. Princess Alexandra was told nothing more than that her 'Uncle Bertie' was very ill. In January the Princess returned to Heathfield, Princess Marina flew to Munich to visit her sister Elizabeth, the Duke of Kent went back to Switzerland, while Prince Michael remained at Sandringham until the end of the month. On the morning of Wednesday 6 February, Princess Alexandra was taken to one side by her headmistress to be told that just a few hours earlier King George VI had died in his sleep. Her cousin Lilibet was now Queen.

Princess Alexandra had been too young to attend her own father's funeral, but when taken to Westminster Hall where the late King's coffin lay in state, she became aware that Princess Marina's grief of a decade earlier had been rekindled. In silence they paid their respects, the Imperial State Crown glittering in the candlelight beside the golden orb and symbols of Sovereignty resting on the catafalque. In one poignant scene were two images that Princess Alexandra had been fighting to come to terms with. The glittering crown as the public emblem, yet underneath the contrasting mortal remains as proof that royalty are only human. At the funeral in St George's Chapel, Windsor, she became conscious of the words, 'We brought nothing into this world, and it is certain we can carry nothing out.' She had been hounded by the words, 'You are not a girl, you are a Princess.' In the face of death, titles seemed irrelevant. But being *royal* for Alexandra was a fact of life. From now onwards she would never again be able to meet her cousin Lilibet without curtseying first. Only ten years older than Alexandra, the heavy burden of Sovereignty had fallen on to Elizabeth's shoulders.

With the death of King George VI, Alexandra's brother, as Duke of Kent, like her found a greater awareness of royal status. He was officially head of the Kent family and as such had to walk behind the gun carriage bearing the King's coffin. Within a short time both Edward and Alexandra were to face new responsibilities. Edward, it was agreed, would accompany Princess Marina on an official tour of the Far East as an initiation into royal service. In the summer of 1952 Princess Alexandra was given her first official position and at the instigation of Lady Airlie (Angus Ogilvy's grandmother) became Patron of the Junior Red Cross.

Whether noting Alexandra's increased maturity, or moved by the death of her brother-in-law, Princess Marina took her eldest two children to Eagle's Rock to the spot where their father had died. Although Marina had been there alone, four years after the Duke's death, having taken a long time to summon enough courage, it was Princess Alexandra's first visit. The long black scar in the hillside that had been clearly visible to Princess Marina on that first traumatic pilgrimage had faded on this tenth anniversary of the Duke's death. A simple granite cross erected by his widow was the only tangible evidence of the tragedy. The Kent family walked silently on the two-mile walk through the heather to the spot, each lost in their own thoughts. Princess Alexandra seemed to return to Balmoral that evening more grown-up than when she set out. It seemed to mark the passing of her childhood and a new era was dawning. Already that summer the house party at Balmoral had changed; the castle was now twenty-six-year-old Lilibet's home and an abyss seemed to have opened up between the dignified Queen and the very inexperienced Princess. Alexandra returned to Heathfield that autumn for the final time.

4

In the Shadow of Marina

[i]

Princess Alexandra was in tears. Any excitement she had felt about the planned visit to France had abated on learning that she was to be present at a formal dinner party with the Comte de Paris. 'I'll knock something over. I dread meeting new people,' she howled. 'My hands go clammy and I can't think what to say. They'll put me next to some elderly prince who can't be interested in me and he'll think I'm stupid. If mother wasn't going to be there it wouldn't be so bad...'.

If *mother* wasn't going to be there. That was the crux of Princess Alexandra's problems in adolescence. Princess Marina had high standards. She was noted for her elegance and style. Princess Alexandra had no interest in clothes and felt intimidated by her mellifluous parent. Marina appeared graceful, even lighting her strong Greek cigarettes, and smoking them in a holder gave her a Hollywood glamour. There was too much for Alexandra to live up to. She felt large and ungainly in comparison, and as she blossomed into womanhood it was inevitable that onlookers would compare mother and daughter.

Their relationship, however, was not one of rivalry. At least not on Alexandra's part. She looked up to her mother, even as a young child she would sit and stare at her, reputedly once saying to her brother Edward, 'Aren't we lucky to have such a beautiful mother?' Yet, when one studies photographs of mother and daughter throughout Alexandra's teenage years, the latter looks positively dowdy, her dresses matronly, her hairstyle ageing, her shoes flat and unfashionable. The assumption would be that the elegant Marina would have instilled a sense of style in her not unattractive daughter. Did Marina perhaps fear the competition? Having influenced fashion for so long herself did she hold Alexandra back for as long as possible to prevent her position being usurped? Even if Alexandra had no real interest in clothes, surely when she was of an age to wear what her mother *told her to wear* she would have worn something less restrained. Perhaps, with limited resources, the money went instead on Marina's wardrobe until Alexandra was of an age to enter the public eye. Or was it that she wanted to bring her daughter up understanding humility and with a proper sense of values? When Princess Alexandra was first initiated in royal duty and began accompanying Marina on engagements one would have expected all eyes to be on the blossoming daughter, yet it was the former who at first attracted most of the attention. It was not until the Princess had reached full maturity that she was able to upstage her mother. When a friend of mine worked at Coppins while Princess Alexandra was a teenager, Marina often seemed to put her daughter down, telling her in front of both staff and guests that she looked 'unbecoming in that dress'. As Marina had bought Alexandra the outfit in the first place it can have done little to boost the Princess's confidence. It says something, perhaps, about Alexandra that she accepted such treatment with such good grace. It would be hard to imagine Princess Margaret, or even Princess Anne, accepting humiliation without comment.

Her Heathfield education was now behind her and plans for the Coronation in 1953 seemed to dominate Princess Alexandra's life. Although she was not to take an active part in the ceremony itself, her brother Eddie was, and the Kent family were prominent in the Abbey as principal members of the Royal Family. As with Princess Elizabeth's wedding, Norman Hartnell was chosen to design both the Queen's Coronation dress and the gowns to be worn by Alexandra and Marina. When Alexandra saw the design for hers, described by Hartnell as 'a diaphanous garment of white lace tulle lightly threaded with gold', with its low neck, narrow-belted waist and full skirt embroidered with sequined flowers, she panicked. 'I can't ever look like that,' she squealed. The stylized sketch of a slim, elegant model bore no resemblance to herself. Princess Marina had the final say in the designs, and whilst Alexandra's outfit had a lacy effect, not unlike the dress she had worn for Princess Elizabeth's wedding, Marina's had a satin base that shone in the lights like a shimmering ballgown. Marina wore a tiara, Eddie had a coronet, but Alexandra was to go bare-headed, her hair styled like her mother's.

Shortly before the Coronation, Princess Alexandra had to face one of the most distressing losses of her life. Queen Mary, her grandmother and mentor, died on 24 March 1953, at Marlborough House. On her deathbed she had insisted that under no circumstance was the Coronation to be cancelled and the crowning went ahead ten weeks later as planned. One of Queen Mary's last wishes was to see her granddaughter, Elizabeth, crowned and St Edward's Crown was taken in secret to Marlborough House so that the young Queen could pay homage to the old. For Elizabeth the burden of duty superseded grief, but Alexandra felt the loss more than most. She had been too young to be greatly affected by her own father's death, but throughout the war years Queen Mary had become a second mother. Whilst many were intimidated by the austere matriarch, there was a rapport between Queen Mary and Princess Alexandra that united the two. The Queen always listened and seemed to understand Alexandra's problems, offering sage words of advice. They shared the same sense of humour and of all her grandchildren, Alexandra seemed the closest in spirit. It was Queen Mary who had taken Alexandra to the cinema for the first time to see Charlie Chaplin's *The Gold Rush* when she was five; once she took her unexpectedly to see *Peter Pan* at the theatre, and on another occasion to Madame Tussaud's where she gave the Princess pennies to play on the slot machines.

Queen Mary felt sympathetic towards Alexandra, realizing perhaps that she felt inferior to Elizabeth and Margaret, lacking their glamorous public image and the private security that they had known. Although ten years younger than the Queen and less outwardly sophisticated, Alexandra was in many ways more worldly. Elizabeth would never have to wear second-hand clothes, scarcely knew what it was like to go out shopping alone, had never been to school and experienced the camaraderie of sharing a dormitory for five years. Although Elizabeth was thrifty and knew how to economize with her money, she would never need to sell *objets d'art* like the Kent family to raise capital. Queen Mary knew astutely that Princess Alexandra lacked the privileges and comfort that her Windsor cousins would know.

When Queen Mary died, Alexandra lost not only a grandmother but a friend and confidante. There was a gap that would be impossible to fill and one that Princess Marina could not bridge. It was one more blow to Alexandra's security, one more push towards adulthood. The State Banquets and receptions held before the Coronation threw Alexandra in at the deep end, she was not yet conversant with small talk, appearing only to relax when her mother was out of earshot. True to form, the most enjoyable moment of Coronation Day came at the end of the celebrations when she put on a headscarf and raincoat, sneaked out of Buckingham Palace and stood in the rain-soaked Mall with the crowds, completely unrecognized, to cheer the newly-crowned Queen. This was where Alexandra felt she belonged, among the people.

After the Coronation the Queen faced a dilemma. There was a distinct shortage of royals to undertake duties. The bereaved Queen Mother was still grieving and was undertaking few engagements; as the Queen and Prince Philip were about to embark on a six-month tour of the Commonwealth, this left Princess Margaret, Mary the Princess Royal, the Duke and Duchess of Gloucester and Princess Marina. From the press point of view only Margaret and Marina had the charisma to be newsworthy.

In July 1953 Princess Marina decided that Alexandra should begin official duties. It was not as if Alexandra had not seen her family at work, indeed she had accompanied Queen Mary on sporadic engagements, at the age of eleven, for example, joining her on a tour of the British Industries Fair at Olympia. Although Princess Marina and the Duke and Duchess of Gloucester ('Uncle Henry and Aunt Alice') were amongst the royal party, it was Alexandra who had dominated the newspapers on the following day much to Queen Mary's embarrassment. At a toy stall the Princess was offered a small toy as a souvenir. It was the 'girl' and not the 'Princess' side of her that chose the largest item on display, a stuffed cat bigger than she was. Calmly Marina told her daughter to choose something smaller and it was a subdued Alexandra who came away with a tiny wooden dog. It was another royal lesson learnt. It was an example of practical experience and Marina now felt that in order for Alexandra to fully appreciate her future role she must undertake a solo visit.

The first solo visit for any member of the Royal Family is always a daunting experience and so Marina agreed that Alexandra should present prizes at the open day of the local comprehensive school. Only the local Press would be present and if the Princess was an unmitigated disaster it would soon be forgotten. Not even seventeen herself it must have been particularly horrifying for Alexandra to be performing as a member of the Royal Family in front of local children, many of whom were her own age. She arrived in her mother's official car, toured the school, practised her smalltalk, and presented the prizes. Just when she had relaxed into the part and all seemed to be going well, her clumsiness came to the fore. A tea cup she was holding fell from her grasp and smashed to pieces on the floor of the domestic science room. Instinctively she sank to the ground and began gathering the pieces. Although it endeared her to those present, Marina would have raised her hands in horror.

That same month Princess Alexandra attended one of the annual garden parties at Buckingham Palace given by the Queen to thank people from all walks of life who have been of service to the community. In the early part of her reign the Queen held two garden parties a year at Buckingham Palace, increasing the number in 1958 to accommodate more guests. In 1953 strawberries and cream were still on the menu for the 8,000 partygoers and it was this that appealed to Alexandra more than the two hours of polite conversation. The following day fashion editors noted in the newspapers that whilst Princess Marina looked half her age, Alexandra appeared double hers. Her beige shoes, they wrote, looked as if they had 'once belonged to the late Queen Mary'. Her blue and white dress was 'in a beltless almost shapeless style and too long for a teenager'. Whilst the Press criticized Alexandra's appearance they did not lay the blame at her door. Instead they, quite rightly, held Princess Marina responsible. The problem, fashion experts realized, was that whilst Marina knew how to appear stylish herself as a forty-eight-year-old she had assumed that her sixteen-year-old daughter would look equally stylish if dressed the same. The theory did not work in practice. 'Rid Alexandra of the old-maid hairstyle of stiff waves,' one newspaper boldly advised Marina. Whether she read the articles or not, Marina knew that Alexandra lacked the necessary sophistication and that something would have to be done.

That summer, Alexandra accompanied her mother on an official visit to Lancashire. The two-day tour, beginning on 13 October 1953 in Accrington, was to include visits to numerous cotton mills and printworks – an industry that had Marina to thank for a revival in the Thirties when fashionable women had copied her choice of cotton-print summer dresses. Again Alexandra appeared dowdy in a dull brown beaver-trimmed coat that added twenty years to her age. The whole tour did nothing to boost Alexandra's confidence and she returned to Coppins no nearer being a leader of fashion than when she had set out. The tour, organized by the Cotton Board, had unrelentingly tried to pack too many visits into too little time. Their official car sometimes had to travel at eighty miles an hour to maintain any semblance of schedule and the two Princesses arrived late for every engagement. Well-wishers who frequently lined the route in the pouring rain caught sight of little more than a car flashing by at great speed with Princess Alexandra holding on tightly to her seat. Parts of the tour had to be cancelled altogether; it drizzled continuously and Princess Alexandra began to wonder if this was what royal duty was all about. At the first factory they faced a reception committee made up of eighty people, all management and local dignitaries, nobody that actually worked on the factory floor. Walking round the cotton mills, Alexandra tried to rectify the matter by shaking hands with as many of the girls as possible. In two days it was calculated that she had shaken some 600 hands. Through Accrington, Padiham, Nelson, and Broad Oak, they visited five cotton mills, three town halls packed with dignitaries, colleges, exhibitions, they put on overalls at a calico printing works to print the armorial bearings of Accrington on to handkerchiefs, and by the time they reached a Didsbury Research Institute, Princess Alexandra was visibly flagging. At a reception later that day Alexandra turned to Princess Marina and said, 'Are *all* engagements like this?' Just as her voice had rung out around Heathfield School, so her question reverberated throughout the Mayor's parlour. Alexandra grinned gauchely. Marina smiled resolutely.

It had been a bad start to public life. The Princess disliked the fact that they had been confronted continually with fawning officials and seldom the real workers, she hated the relentless pace that they had needed to work which prevented them from looking at anything in

49

great detail. It seemed as if the tour had achieved nothing. Possibly she made no conscious decisions then, but her solo engagements since have allowed the Princess to work at a much slower pace and are organized so that she can meet and talk with those who work the hardest. In a similar style the Prince of Wales today will often break away from the official reception committee lined up to meet him and will ask to see the man who sweeps the floor. Whilst the Lancashire people had noted Princess Alexandra's ever cheerful smile whatever the situation, Princess Marina knew she alone was incapable of instilling the necessary polish that her daughter lacked. No one doubted Alexandra's kindness, her generous nature and concern for others. From a character point of view she had faultless qualities which in anyone else would have been sufficient. In a Princess they were not enough.

In the Twenties Princess Marina had herself lived in Paris at the same age as Alexandra was now. Although her family were in exile and as such Marina has been saddled with the 'tragic Princess' image, she did live in the luxurious Hotel Continental which overlooked the Tuileries Gardens. It was an elegant world of potted palms and *haute couture* and she learned the meaning of *chic*. In 1923 Princess Marina spent twelve months at a finishing school run by a Princess Meterchesky, where she studied languages, literature and art. In her spare time she went with her mother and sister to Paris fashion shows and it is said that when she returned home she would imitate the models she had just seen. In the afternoons the girls would be taken to Versailles, Fontainebleau, art galleries, the Louvre and places of historical interest. In the evenings they went to concerts or the theatre. The family eventually purchased a flat near the Avenue Henri Martin, where not only exiled European members of the family would gather, but poets, writers and artists. In 1924 Marina travelled to England, where her sister Olga was staying at White Lodge in Richmond Park (close to where Princess Alexandra lives today) and again visited galleries and museums in London to broaden her knowledge. In Paris, Princess Marina blossomed from being a plump schoolgirl into a woman noted for her beauty. A beauty that led Prince George, Duke of Kent, to fall in love with her.

Princess Marina knew that the transformation she had experienced herself in Paris could happen again to Princess Alexandra. Within two weeks of returning from the ill-fated Lancashire tour, Princess

Alexandra was on her way to the French capital to undergo a meta-morphosis. She was not convinced that it would be a success.

Princess Alexandra was enrolled at Madame Anita's finishing school at number ten, Rue de l'Amiral d'Estaing, which in the Fifties was considered to be the smartest school of all. 'Mademoiselle' Anita, as she was called, was an elderly woman by this time, with ramrod straight deportment, her hair tied tightly into a bun, and was described by one of her ex-pupils as having the ability to govern the girls with 'inflexible authority'. Mademoiselle Anita's actual background always remained a mystery and few even knew her surname. Whatever her past, her talent for turning unruly adolescents into sophisticated ladies was unquestionable and her period of training in Paris was to be the making of Princess Alexandra. When she made a brief visit to England for Christmas in 1953, the change in her was already dramatic.

Whereas many girls spent long periods at finishing school, and even Princess Marina herself lived in Paris for several years, whether for economic reasons or the necessity for her to begin royal duties as soon as possible, Princess Alexandra was allowed just six months to turn herself into a lady. Again Princess Marina called on her many relatives to help out. For the days that she studied at Mademoiselle Anita's, Princess Alexandra would lodge with Marina's sister, Olga, and Alexandra's cousin, Princess Elizabeth of Yugoslavia. The rest of the time was spent with a more distant relation, Henri d'Orleans, the Comte de Paris, the man Alexandra had once been so terrified of meeting. His sister, Françoise, had married one of Marina's uncles. Henri was a direct descendant of Louis XIV and as he was classed as a pretender to the French throne, Princess Alexandra's association with him raised a few eyebrows within the British Royal Family. Marina ignored any gossip. Not only did Alexandra benefit from Mademoiselle Anita's instruction, but almost as much from her host and his family. They lived in a château near Versailles called *Manoir de Coeur Volant*, the Manor of the Flying Heart, and to Alexandra's delight they had eleven children! Isabelle, François, Anne, Diane, Jacques, Michel, Claude, Chantal, and Thibault, many of whom did not speak English which encouraged the Princess to bring her Heathfield French into everyday usage. Princess Isabelle had herself been a pupil at Mademoiselle Anita's, so could offer Alexandra advice, and fifteen-year-old Princess Anne started at the school on the same day, so Alexandra instantly had a friend and ally. More excitingly for the Princess, she did not stay in the main château but in a small whitewashed cottage nearby called *Blanche Neige* with some of the children. It was like being back in the dorm at Heathfield.

Mademoiselle Anita's maxim was to give her girls lessons 'in all the arts, but chiefly in the art of living', so instead of studying only academic subjects such as French literature and grammar, Russian literature (in French), the girls learned about fashion, housekeeping, cookery, even typing and shorthand. Princess Alexandra benefited most from lessons in deportment, she was taught general etiquette, how to walk, move, sit, stand, get out of a car gracefully, how to dress elegantly, do her make-up, how to wear jewellery. Her former teachers at Heathfield would have laughed at Alexandra's lessons in voice modulation, Mademoiselle Anita insisting that ladies 'never speak loudly'. When Princess Alexandra returned to Coppins briefly for Christmas 1953 after only two months' training her family were already aware of an improvement. Princess Alexandra wore simple but well-cut clothes, her hair had been elegantly styled, and she had a new dignity and inner serenity that Princess Marina had seldom noticed before.

Although Princess Alexandra undoubtedly benefited from her six months at finishing school which polished off her rough edges, she also blossomed because she was away from Marina and the influence of the Royal Family. In Paris she had freedom and independence that she had not experienced before. At Heathfield she had been under the strict guidance of teachers and had to conform. It gave her social skills and a good general education, but did not give her room to develop. In the shadow of Marina at home Alexandra felt inferior and trapped by her royal status. Yet in Paris she lived with eleven Princes and Princesses, there were even five Princesses studying at Mademoiselle Anita's, so the title became irrelevant. She could travel on the metro alone and unnoticed in Paris, shop for clothes of her own choice using the guidelines she had been taught at finishing school and so develop her own personal style. She became wrapped up in the culture and elegance of Paris and the French people, which inevitably rubbed off on her, and she found a new sense of maturity and responsibility. She was no longer Marina's child, but was treated for the first time as an adult in her own right. Her once stifled character was allowed to emerge. Instead of being a clone of Princess Marina, which is how she seemed to the British public from her dress and hairstyle, she discovered the real Princess Alexandra. For the first time she liked what she saw, and when she returned to England finally at Easter 1954 it was with self-confidence.

The tragedies that periodically seem to dominate Princess Alexandra's life continued. She arrived back at the airport to find Princess Marina dressed in black. On the previous day Martha, the wife of Crown Prince Olav (later King Olav of Norway), a cousin of the Duke of Kent,★ had died and the royal court was in mourning. It was a less than joyous homecoming. Five days later Princess Alexandra's own cousin, Prince Nicholas of Yugoslavia, the son of Marina's sister Olga, was killed in a car crash just a few miles from Windsor Castle. He was twenty-five. Again Marina was in bed when footsteps approached her room to tell her the news just as she had been in 1942 when her husband died. At first she feared the news was of her son, Eddie, who had a motorbike and had only recently passed his driving test. Ironically, just eight weeks later Marina heard that Eddie had been knocked uncon-scious in a car crash, but had suffered no permanent damage.

Although preoccupied with her cousin's untimely death, Alexandra had by now mastered the royal art of publicly hiding emotions and was determined to embark on full-time royal duties as had already been arranged by Philip Hay, Marina's Private Secretary. On returning to England Alexandra, now in her eighteenth year, had been given a lady-in-waiting of her own. Six years older than the Princess, Lady Moyra Hamilton, the dark-haired daughter of the Marquess of Hamilton (later to inherit the title Duke of Abercorn), had been one of the six Maids of Honour at Queen Elizabeth II's Coronation a year earlier and was well-suited to the role. The Princess and Lady Moyra had been friends and in the early Sixties there was even speculation that Alexandra might marry her younger brother, James, the present Duke of Abercorn. The Princess shared the same sense of humour as her lady-in-waiting and they had many interests in common, including music and horses, but for Alexandra Lady Moyra had one special quality. She was tall. Always conscious of her own height, it is no coincidence that not one of

★ Olav's mother was Queen Maud, a daughter of Edward VII.

Alexandra's ladies-in-waiting throughout her royal career has been noticeably shorter than herself.

On 5 May 1954, Princess Alexandra officially became a fully-fledged working member of the Royal Family, exactly one month after leaving Mademoiselle Anita's. A visit to the British Red Cross Society was on the agenda and newspapers entered the details in the Court Circular. The Princess wore the distinctive Red Cross uniform and was guest of honour at a reception where she received the gold Patron's badge with the emblem marked out in diamonds and rubies. She read a prepared speech with confidence and felt that Marina would have been proud of her, although one journalist subsequently complained that Alexandra's speaking voice was 'too soft'. A strange comment, considering 150 people present seemed to hear the Princess say loudly 'Was I awful?' after her speech. Neither Mademoiselle Anita or Princess Marina would have approved.

Alexandra knew that she could only learn by practical experience and with each engagement she improved. In quick succession followed a visit to the British Industries Fair at Olympia, which brought back memories of her childhood visit when she had requested the large toy cat; she attended a Junior Red Cross rally, the Chelsea Flower Show, the Rose Ball at Grosvenor House, went to Northern Ireland for the Ulster Show, opened a college extension in Belfast and planted a tree at an old people's home. She accepted the Presidency of the Guide Dogs for the Blind Association, became Vice-Patron of the YWCA, Patron of the Royal Alexandra Hospital for Sick Children and the National Association of Girls' Training Corps. From touring the Alexandra Rose Day depot to a Civic Luncheon in her honour at Belfast City Hall, Princess Alexandra was quite literally thrown in at the deep end and packed more engagements into those first two months than any other member of the Royal Family had previously done on their initiation.

Inevitably there was the odd Press criticism, one news report saying after an engagement that Alexandra had 'mislaid her handbag, twice dropped her gloves, spluttered pink-cheeked through her speech and then escaped with obvious relief to the sandwiches and eclairs', but she was never to receive the vicious and sometimes malicious attacks that have been made on other members of the Royal Family. It was perhaps fortunate for Princess Alexandra that her début coincided with the legendary period when Princess Margaret wanted to marry Group Captain Peter Townsend and speculation regarding their relationship filled the gossip columns. While Princess Margaret's love life both before and during her stormy marriage made her fair game for public sniping in the Fifties and Sixties, superseded by Princess Anne in the Seventies, Princess Michael of Kent in the Eighties and the hapless Duchess of York, the much maligned 'Fergie', in the Nineties, Princess Alexandra has consistently managed to remain out of the firing line.

What the Press *did* pick up on, however, was Alexandra's change in appearance. Gone was the puppy fat and whilst she lamented her height, fashion experts translated it as 'tall and elegant'. Under Mademoiselle Anita's direction, Alexandra knew how to dress to her advantage, shunning frills, flounces, bows, and opting for strikingly pale colours in plain materials that gave her a look of sophistication. For the first time she sparked off dozens of magazine and newspaper articles, with headlines such as 'Princess Alexandra Grows Up' and 'The Blossoming Alexandra Rose'. She was both embarrassed and flattered at one and the same time.

When Princess Alexandra next appeared in public with her mother, for the first time cameramen allowed their lenses to stray from the Duchess of Kent and on to her daughter. Now Alexandra was newsworthy. Her voice had a rich deep quality that the Queen's piping tone lacked, commentators wrote; Alexandra's features now pushed her into the 'classic beauty' category. One phrase was repeated time and time again and it was something that twelve months earlier Princess Alexandra would not have believed possible. She was now considered to be the very image of the young Princess Marina. Unwittingly Alexandra had stolen the limelight.

5

A Spreading of Wings

The Duchess of Kent stepped forward to lay a wreath at the war memorial. It was always of poignant significance to her to commemorate those who gave their lives during the Second World War. As she waited to be handed the floral tribute, red-faced officials realized that the wreath had been forgotten. There was nothing for Princess Marina to lay. The solemn moment of remembrance was in danger of turning into a farce. Instinctively Princess Alexandra handed over her bouquet and her mother laid it gently at the memorial without batting an eyelid. Alexandra had saved her from an otherwise embarrassing situation.

'Am I supposed to carry this about?' Princess Alexandra had asked six months earlier when handed her first official bouquet. Now on a royal visit to Montreal she behaved like a seasoned performer. A joint tour of Canada with Princess Marina was to be the highlight of 1954, and was the point when Alexandra became known internationally. The initial reason for the visit had been an invitation for the Duchess of Kent to inaugurate a new power-generating station at the Niagara Falls, and like the earlier joint tour of Lancashire it was to be an introduction before embarking on solo overseas tours. Alexandra was to have two rehearsals with Marina, in Canada and America, then a later tour of Mexico, Chile and Brazil. From then onwards she was to be on her own.

For the first time Princess Alexandra was excited rather than apprehensive on an official visit. The few brief overseas visits she had made already to Greece, Italy and France had sharpened her appetite for foreign travel and that excitement for going abroad has never diminished. In many ways Princess Alexandra seems a great deal more relaxed on engagements in other countries – it is as if she is filled with the holiday spirit. Her thirst for knowledge is that of any tourist and she enjoys asking questions out of a genuine desire for more information. The trip to Canada was her longest actual flight at that time and it was not long before she was taken to the cockpit with the pilot, although reports that she had taken over the controls were later denied.

Like her cousin, Princess Margaret, Alexandra enjoyed the sense of adventure that travel offered and was always ebulliently enthusiastic. Marina, who disliked flying intensely even when the Duke of Kent was alive, would only travel in planes out of necessity. Once when woken up on a flight to be told that they had encountered a storm and the flight might be bumpy, she grumbled, 'I wouldn't have known anything about it if you hadn't told me.' Lady Moyra Hamilton accompanied the Princess on the trip and when not actively involved in official duties they were like two girlfriends on vacation. Flying to Quebec, once the formal introductions were over the two escaped to explore unrecognized, wide awake because of a five-hour time difference. As Lady Moyra had friends in Toronto and Alexandra knew people in New York, there were plenty of non-official visits to make on the tour. Even Princess Marina took the opportunity to visit her mother's cousin, Grand Duchess Olga Alexandrovna, the sister of Tsar Nicholas II of Russia. Ten miles outside Toronto, the Grand Duchess was living in squalor with chickens wandering freely into the house. Marina was shocked by what she saw.

The Canadians were enthusiastic about Alexandra and her photograph was featured on the cover of national magazines even before their arrival, a novel experience for the Princess so used to seeing the more glamorous Princess Margaret in the British magazines. For some reason, however, the Duchess of Kent's office (still at Marlborough House at this time) had issued instructions that no close-up photographs were to be taken of them on the tour and that Press photographers were to remain at least fifteen feet away. The official reason given was that Princess Marina wanted to 'protect' Alexandra, but the edict caused ill-feeling and many suspected that it might well have been Princess

Marina's vanity that wanted photographers kept at bay. Next to the flawless complexion of her daughter, in close-up Marina would have looked her age. Needless to say the instruction was hard to enforce and when cameramen moved in ten feet nearer than they had been told to nobody tried to prevent them. Conscious of the animosity this unnecessary ruling had begun to cause on the tour, at Niagara Princess Alexandra relieved the tension by grabbing one of the cameras and taking photographs of the pressmen amid much laughter. One of the pictures she had taken was actually published by a Detroit newspaper under the headline 'The Princess packs a bigger punch than Niagara!' It was something Alexandra was proud of, and gently flouting the rules in favour of the Press has almost become a trademark. After writing a biography of Princess Margaret, of the many letters I subsequently received, one comment was common, as in this extract from a reader in South Africa: 'I certainly agree with you when you suggest that a great deal of misconception could have been avoided had the Princess, or her staff, been able to meet the Press half-way.'*

In great contrast to Princess Margaret, Alexandra has frequently gone out of her way to co-operate with the Press. On a later tour journalists were informed that they were not under any circumstances to ask the Princess questions. By now she was used to fielding the occasional question thrown at her with an innocuous, wry comment and again sensing the animosity she turned the tables and began asking the journalists questions. That way they got their story without going against their instructions. Instead of the love/hate relationship that many of the Royal Family now have with the media, Alexandra won them over from the outset. Some criticized her for the apparent lack of formality, but she was astute enough to realize the advantage of having the Press on her side.

Compared to their working schedule in Britain, the Canadian tour was relaxing, and the Princesses left Halifax, Nova Scotia, on their way to New York, leaving behind a craze for the 'Princess Sandra' hairstyle among teenage Canadian girls. It was the first time Alexandra had started a trend. While in New York Alexandra, Marina and entourage stayed privately with Mr and Mrs John Barry Ryan, whose daughter

* Denis Slaney, Natal, South Africa.

Virginia had married David Ogilvy two years earlier. David is Angus Ogilvy's elder brother, now the 13th Earl of Airlie, and Virginia has been a Lady of the Bedchamber to the Queen since 1973. As Princess Alexandra slept in Virginia's old room in New York, even she could not have predicted that they would one day be sisters-in-law. From the family wedding photographs grouped on display, Angus Ogilvy's smiling face looked down on the Ryans' royal guests. To add the final seal to this adventure, Alexandra and Marina sailed home across the Atlantic on board the luxurious liner *Queen Mary*. It had been a personal triumph for Alexandra, and had succeeded in its original aim of promoting goodwill with Canada and increasing export orders to Britain.

Just before their departure for Canada in the summer of 1954, the Queen had decided that as Princess Alexandra was now undertaking engagements in her own right, she and Princess Marina should have a central base in London, rather than continuing to travel to and from Coppins in Buckinghamshire. As the Duke of Kent's Civil List allowance had died with him, and Marina had declined the Royal Air Force widow's pension, finances were continually tight. The Queen, therefore, offered the Kent family a grace and favour apartment at Kensington Palace. It was the ideal location, barely a mile from Buckingham Palace itself, and had been empty for fifteen years. Formerly the home of Princess Louise, Duchess of Argyll, who had lived there until her death in December 1939. By that time all the Royal Family had homes of their own and as it was wartime nobody wanted to move to central London where the risk of bombing was greater. Indeed Kensington Palace was itself bombed with incendiary devices in 1940, which left their mark. By the time the war ended in 1945 this part of the Palace had been uninhabited for nearly six years, was damp, had death-watch beetle, dry rot, and was even less appealing than before. Much of Princess Louise's heavy Victorian furniture remained, as did the oppressive brown paintwork.

By giving it to the Kents, the Queen felt that it would put the former royal palace to good use and would not only be a private residence, but would provide office space and a further building for official entertaining. Princess Alexandra was excited by the idea, Princess Marina less so. On looking round for the first time the cold building not only seemed forbidding, but Princess Marina was horrified by the fact that it had some forty-two rooms. Even with Alexandra, Edward and Michael each having their own bedroom and sitting-room it was still much too large, the renovation costly. Eventually it was decided to divide the wing in half, making a smaller compact three-storey unit. Today it is the London home of the Duke and Duchess of Gloucester. The other half that Marina did not want was eventually turned into a home for the Snowdons and Princess Margaret has now lived there for thirty years.

The problem that faced the Royal Family was the cost of the repairs to make the building habitable. The first estimate was £80,000, to be paid for by the Government as it was an official royal residence and in theory belonged to the nation. The actual cost came closer to £130,000 once the much-neglected building had been given a new roof, had heating installed, wet rot and dry rot treated, windows repaired, completely re-wired and plumbing updated, original ceilings and plaster mouldings restored, then eventually every room redecorated. This led to inevitable criticism in Parliament with regard to the justification of the project. With no less than eight new fireplaces being required, such a furore was caused at the cost of just one original Adam fireplace that Marina purchased the rest out of her own funds. Eventually the building was habitable and the Kents took up residence in 1955, the work having taken a year to complete.

Coppins still remained as the family home for weekends and holidays, but Princess Alexandra lived at Kensington Palace for much of the week. Keen to economize, Princess Marina could not afford to fully staff each residence and so her small retinue, including Bysouth the butler and Mrs Keeble the cook, travelled between the two – usually going in advance of Marina to ensure that all was in order. Occasionally when the staff had to remain at Coppins while the Kents briefly visited London, Alexandra and Marina would 'picnic at the Palace'.

Princess Alexandra enjoyed living at Kensington Palace. It had the atmosphere of a small village and was sufficiently far from the Bayswater Road and Kensington High Street to be free of traffic noise. They had their own private garden, and there was the vast expanse of Kensington Gardens and Hyde Park for the Princess to escape into for long walks where she would be unnoticed. This was to be her home for eight years.

Unlike Coppins, Kensington Palace was more formal in appearance as an official residence. Guests entered by the main front door down a long corridor hung with tapestries, into a main hall dominated by a large mahogany table in the centre on which a collection of the late Duke's snuff boxes would be displayed for visitors. Looking down on to the hall was an almost lifesize portrait of Princess Alexandra's maternal grandmother, Princess Nicholas of Greece. Each evening the painting was emphasized by a special picture light from above, so that her figure dressed in black became haunting and inescapable. So proud was Princess Marina of this portrait that staff only forgot to switch on the light at their peril. When Princess Nicholas eventually died in 1957, Marina ordered that the light be switched off, never to be lit again.

Princess Marina's sitting-room was at the end of a short corridor leading off the hall and it was here that the family would gather. Green-carpeted, decorated in white and gold with crystal glass chandeliers and gilt-framed mirrors, family portraits, and eight long windows looking out on to the garden, it was also a scene for formal entertaining. Just off this room was Marina's private boudoir where she used to work on her official papers. On the ground floor was also the formal dining-room, with a mahogany dining-table that could seat up to twenty-four people, an office for the Private Secretary dealing with Alexandra and Marina's engagements, and a small sitting-room-cum-study for Alexandra's brother, the Duke of Kent.

On the second floor were six bedrooms, one for each member of the family and two guest bedrooms, bathrooms, the bedroom of Princess Marina's dresser, Edith Arter, and two workrooms where clothes could be made, hats re-feathered or shoes polished and blouses pressed. On the top floor were three staff bedrooms, a laundry room and a boxroom for storage. There was also an attic room for storing everything from old toys to Marina's hat boxes. The kitchen was on the ground floor and the basement housed numerous extra rooms, more staff bedrooms, storage rooms for food, china and a staff sitting-room.

This was Princess Alexandra's home and it had been a novel experience for her helping her mother to choose the decorations and furnishings. Both 3 Belgrave Square and Coppins had been styled to the Duke of Kent's taste in the Thirties, but Kensington Palace had an obvious feminine touch. With Alexandra's brothers Edward at

Sandhurst and Michael at Eton, the house was essentially the Princesses' house. Alexandra's own room was predominantly pink, with a chintz print and wallpaper with small pink carnations. She had her own small sitting-room with a piano – on which she would practise for an hour-and-a-half each day – a private bathroom and a dressing-room. For her eighteenth birthday, on Christmas Day 1954, her present had been her own lady's maid, Marjory Dawson. Once again Alexandra had not been allowed to forget her royal status; this private 'gift' to help her with official duties. Reminiscent of her cousin Lilibet, who at eighteen had received a lady-in-waiting and her own coat-of-arms.

These were Princess Alexandra's securest years: ever gaining confidence in her public role, she was no longer faced with the pressures of maintaining Marina's standards. Once Alexandra had matured it was as if Marina compromised and became less critical, their relationship ever developing into that of sisters rather than mother and daughter. They became noticeably closer after the premature death of Princess Marina's sister, Elizabeth, at the age of fifty in the New Year of 1955. Whenever Edward and Michael were at home, Alexandra seemed at her happiest. They called each other 'Ed', 'Mow' and 'Puddy' respectively, and Princess Marina was occasionally known as 'Min', in keeping with the Royal Family's love of nicknames. When visiting her Windsor cousins as a child, Alexandra found that 'Lilibet' had a name for everyone. Her nurse, Clara Knight, was 'Alah', her dresser Margaret Macdonald became 'Bobo', their governess was 'Crawfie', and even Queen Mary was 'Gan Gan' to them all.

Staff who worked for the Kents remember Princess Alexandra as being almost permanently cheerful, always greeting them with a bright 'Good Morning!' if they encountered her on the deep blue carpeted stairs or in the corridor, whereas her brother Edward, perhaps weighed down with his title 'Duke of Kent' and position as theoretical head of the household, would shout at staff if he saw standards slipping or his clothes were not laid out for him. Prince Michael was perpetually untidy and unpunctual, but had sufficient schoolboy charm to win anyone over and seemed the least concerned about his royal status. Princess Alexandra was always the favourite of the household and staff found her more approachable if they had a problem than facing Princess Marina, who remained aloof and unyielding where her staff were concerned. Although Bysouth the butler remained with the Kents for some twenty-five years he had many tussles with his employer, Marina, who nearly always succeeded in getting her own way.

The influence Princess Marina had over Alexandra at this time became more subtle. She would use the unsuspecting Marjory Dawson as an intermediary, graciously 'allowing' her to watch her own dresser, Miss Arter, at work. Telling her how a hat should be worn stylishly, or a scarf tied elegantly, hoping that these 'tips' would eventually filter back to Princess Alexandra. Ultimately Princess Alexandra's head was so full of advice from Mademoiselle Anita and Princess Marina that her dress designer, John Cavanagh, had difficulty persuading her to have as much as a single covered button on a dress as adornment. A frill or bow would not even be considered. Whether for reasons of economy, or simply a desire to keep one foot in a non-royal world she frequently shopped for ready-made, mass-produced clothes. Whilst we accept it of Princesses in the Nineties, it was practically unheard of in the Fifties.

Princess Marina had her own method of economy. She would borrow clothes from a couturier, such as Norman Hartnell, wear them for one event and then return them. Because she had been born with a twisted left foot, which necessitated wearing different sized shoes throughout her life, and had a weak leg on that side, Miss Arter used to alter the hems of dresses to make them hang straight. When the borrowed dresses were eventually returned they were out of shape for another client.

The Kents' financial position obviously had a great bearing on Princess Alexandra's life and much has been written about the 'poor' relations. This is not strictly accurate and is based on the assumption that because Princess Marina received no Civil List allowance she had no money. The Civil List is, however, never an income for any member of the Royal Family but merely a reimbursement of expenses for fulfilling public duties. It is not theirs to spend as they wish and all require a private source of income. Whilst Princess Marina was certainly thrifty and did not fritter money on needless extravagances, it would have been impossible for her to run and furnish two homes the size of Coppins and the Kensington Palace apartment without money.

Although the contents of royal wills remain secret, Princess Alexandra's father was certainly left no less than £300,000 in King George

V's will; some estimates put the amount as high as £750,000, although this was probably an exaggeration. It was, nevertheless, a sizeable amount which the Duke of Kent invested wisely in stocks and shares, he left money in trust for Alexandra and his two sons, and spent a great deal on paintings, silver, antiques and *objets d'art*. He owned paintings by Van Dyck, Veronese, and Reynolds. He always had an eye for an investment. In 1940, for example, he paid 3,700 guineas for three paintings by Claude Lorrain. Princess Marina sold them in 1947 for £50,000, a considerable sum at that time. Princess Marina had her first sale to raise funds in 1943, twelve months after the Duke's death, selling furniture which had been left to them in Princess Louise's will. This raised nearly £20,000. In 1947 she had the first sale of art treasures at Christie's in London. Over three days in March a variety of items were sold at auction: porcelain, period furniture, paintings, drawings, jade figures, a Limoges dinner service, candelabra and chandeliers, all of which raised £92,341. 'Not much of a sum for the public humiliation,' scoffed Marina, but she continued to periodically send paintings and silver to auction, and occasionally clocks, the Duke having collected far too many clocks for two homes, some rooms at Kensington Palace having no less than three timepieces.

In 1960 a further well-publicized auction at Sotheby's relieved Marina of many Fabergé items, more silver, some of the Duke's snuff boxes and cigarette cases, even shoe buckles and buttons. The Fabergé alone raised in excess of £15,000. The sheer quantities of items available to sell proved that Princess Marina had more than she would ever need. Possibly her apparent poverty was only when measured against the treasures owned by her niece, Queen Elizabeth II. When Marina died boxes containing priceless antique silver, Fabergé eggs, china and glassware that the family did not want were simply packed away in boxes in an attic at Hampton Court Palace. When discovered one day by Princess Michael of Kent in the Eighties they went back on display in the Duchess's old home. Ironically, before Princess Michael had time to thoroughly search the boxes that had not seen the light of day for over fifteen years, a fire on 31 March 1986 destroyed part of Hampton Court and Princess Marina's remaining treasures.

Whilst Princess Marina was excluded from the Civil List, in 1952 a fund was set up for members of the Royal Family who undertook public duties but were not included from which she was awarded £5,000 a year for her official expenses. As she kept staff wages deliberately low, made unexpected economies such as changing the card on floral gifts given to her and sending them on to someone else, her financial position was certainly not as bad as she led people to believe. When Princess Alexandra and the Duke of Kent began to undertake official duties they too received an allowance out of the Queen's own Civil List payment, a practice which still happens today.

Although Princess Alexandra was now enjoying her public life and by 1956 had mastered the inevitable round of tree planting, ship launching and plaque unveiling; had spent time blindfolded with a guide dog for a greater understanding of their work and had gone up in a hot air balloon with paratroopers to appreciate theirs, there was still a part of her that felt unfulfilled. Possibly it was because her brother Prince Edward was by this time in the Army, eventually becoming a Lieutenant-Colonel in the Royal Scots Greys; Prince Michael planned to follow his brother and was actually to spend nineteen years with the 11th Hussars, and Princess Alexandra, although resigned to a life of royal duty, was keen to experience life in the 'real world' first. There was no tangible reason why she could not provide some kind of service like her brothers, but she had no idea what.

A popular misconception is that Princess Alexandra had a lifelong vocation, a desire to be a nurse. This is not true, and is an example of how tiny clues can be misinterpreted. Possibly it stems from her family for the general public knew of Princess Marina's experiences as a nurse during the war and the Duke of Kent once told the matron of University College Hospital, 'If I could have chosen my job I would have liked to have gone in for medicine more than anything.' His own sister, Alexandra's 'Aunt Mary', the Princess Royal, had also chosen to be a nurse during the Second World War. Even when Princess Alexandra was at Mademoiselle Anita's in Paris, the Comte d'Paris's daughter, Princess Isabelle, had been training to become a State Registered Nurse at the Croix Rouge Peupliers and often Alexandra would visit her at the hospital. So when it was suddenly announced that Princess Alexandra had enrolled for a course at Great Ormond Street Hospital for Sick Children in London, all these factors were put together by 'experts' – those really in the know remember that Alexandra even had a doll in a nurse's uniform as a child – and it was assumed that Princess Alexandra had always wanted a career in nursing.

The truth of the matter seems to be that, although Alexandra was certainly not opposed to the course, it was Princess Marina who pushed her towards nursing, perhaps wanting her daughter to follow in her own footsteps. In March 1956 Princess Alexandra joined the Queen on a private Mediterranean cruise in the royal yacht, *Britannia*. The ship was on an exercise for the Royal Navy with the Duke of Edinburgh as part of the crew and without any publicity the two cousins took advantage of *Britannia* to have a rare holiday together. There is no doubt that the two discussed Alexandra's future. The Queen is very astute and saw that although nursing might not be Alexandra's first choice, the Princess expressing a private fear that she was too clumsy for the work, it could prove to be a useful and worthwhile experience. When Princess Alexandra returned home she agreed to enrol for the course at Great Ormond Street Hospital. The choice was not without consideration. Not only did the hospital have an excellent reputation, but as the Princess would be working with babies and young children there was a greater chance that she would be spared the recognition by patients which had hounded Marina's nursing career. To her young charges she would be just another nurse. At the end of September 1956 Princess Alexandra began her training. She was to be known simply as 'Nurse Kent' and be treated in exactly the same way as her fellow students, just as the edict had been given to Heathfield School ten years earlier. Dressed in her regulation pink and white uniform with starched apron and cap, it did not please Alexandra to be greeted by hordes of photographers, cheering crowds and a bouquet from the matron on her first day. This mock official visit was precisely what she had wanted to avoid. She worked hard to break down the royal barrier that surrounded her, but her status always set her apart. The more menial the tasks she undertook to show she was just one of the girls, the more impressed people seemed to be. It would have seemed trivial to even comment that a nurse had changed a baby's nappy or bandaged a child's foot, so why, she wondered, was it ever worthy of comment when she performed tasks that millions of anonymous nurses did each day as a matter of course? In her head she must almost have heard Princess Marina's voice. 'You are not a nurse, you are a Princess.'

The knowledge gained through the Patronage of the Junior Red Cross had provided a good foundation for Princess Alexandra's study of child welfare. After a basic training in all aspects of childcare, Nurse Kent was to gain practical experience in outpatients. For approximately three days each week she worked at the hospital on all shifts, fitting in royal duties on the remaining days and a social life in the evenings. Keeping the two lives in tandem was not always easy. After attending Trooping the Colour in June 1957 she smiled from the balcony of Buckingham Palace then rushed to put on her uniform for the Thursday afternoon shift. Like her cousin, Princess Margaret, Alexandra enjoyed dancing in nightclubs and managed to do so far less publicly, sometimes not getting to bed until 4.00 am. Inevitably there was going to be a limit as to how long she could maintain what amounted to two demanding careers and any semblance of social life. As she approached her twenty-first birthday both media and Royal Family began speculating over Alexandra's choice of husband. On the surface she seemed too busy for boyfriends, yet she had already met the man she was going to marry.

Twenty-first birthdays are a milestone in anyone's life, royal or not, and the Kent family were no exception. Princess Alexandra was as actively involved in her brother Edward's as her own. Prince Edward's, on 19 October 1956, had involved several days of celebration. Firstly a private family lunch at Kensington Palace, followed a couple of days later by another lunch for the staff at Coppins. On the birthday itself there was a family tea and that evening a formal dinner and ball. All, however, did not run smoothly. When staff rolled back the carpet in preparation for the dance it was discovered that the wooden floor had warped due to hot water pipes underneath. Alexandra was close to tears. Bysouth the butler quickly ordered a sanding machine and the floor was levelled off within hours of the first guests arriving. While guests danced that night to The Joe Loss Band, including the Queen and the Queen Mother, three journalists managed to gatecrash the party by posing as 'friends of the Duke' who had mislaid their invitation cards. They were quickly evicted by police, one reluctant female reporter after a chase, and the party went ahead as planned. Security, however, was noticeably tightened and the Queen's Press Secretary, then Richard Colville, issued a statement:

The Queen and the Duchess of Kent were seriously disturbed by these incidents, and Her Majesty considers that it is not too much to ask that she and other members of the Royal Family should receive the same privacy in their homes as is enjoyed by others. On the occasion in question their privacy was not only invaded in an improper manner, but the methods by which this was achieved bordered on deceit.

Strong words and almost certainly those of Colville. In his authoritative biography of the Queen, *Majesty*, the author Robert Lacey says that Richard Colville distrusted all the media and saw his job as keeping them out of the Queen's private life. If a journalist asked anything more than the details of the bouquet the Queen was carrying, he would shut up like a clam, says Lacey.* Many felt that the incident at Coppins marked a watershed in the Royal Family's relations with the Press. They became less trusting after this blatant encroachment on their privacy, the Press more devious in their pursuit feeling that the Royal Family must have something to hide. Perhaps irritated that the entire British Press had been tarred with the same brush after the actions of just three unscrupulous journalists they became less reverential in tone.

One minor change to Prince Edward and Princess Alexandra at the age of twenty-one was that they became 'Royal Highnesses'. Until that age the staff at Kensington Palace, for example, had been told to refer to the Duchess of Kent's daughter as 'Princess Alexandra', but on reaching twenty-one it was amended to 'Your Royal Highness'. Even coming-of-age for Alexandra could not be treated as a private event but had to be of *royal* significance. At eighteen she was allowed to use a monogram on her writing paper for the first time. Princess Marina's was an 'M' beneath a coronet; Alexandra chose to adopt the symbol used by her great-grandmother, Queen Alexandra, a pattern of two 'A's intertwined beneath a coronet:

* Robert Lacey, *Majesty* p. 260.

Princess Marina   Princess Alexandra

Queen Alexandra had herself chosen the monogram because her husband, Edward VII, was christened Albert after his father (he was known as 'Bertie' throughout his life by family and friends), and the double 'A' obviously stood for Alexandra and Albert. By sheer coincidence, when Princess Alexandra married Angus Ogilvy the monogram remained appropriate.

Because of her birthday on Christmas Day, Alexandra was allowed to celebrate her twenty-first birthday two weeks later with a ball at Kensington Palace on 6 January, 1958. Perhaps less stately than her brother's party, Alexandra had the Sid Phillips Jazz Band instead of the royal favourite, Joe Loss. With a similar number of guests as her brother's party, around 200, Kensington Palace was chosen not only because of its tighter security but as it was more accessible than Coppins in the event of snow. By sheer coincidence the uneven floor had to be sanded into shape before the dance could take place. Even at this most private of parties royal status could not be cast aside and precedence dictated the order in which dancers were led to the floor. It was on occasions such as these that Alexandra particularly lamented the loss of her father. Hidden amongst the guests was Angus Ogilvy, but as the Princess danced with so many partners that evening her dance with him was credited with no special significance.

Just two months after her twenty-first birthday party Princess Alexandra contracted glandular fever. Although her symptoms were not debilitating, a slight fever, a faint rash, a sore throat and swollen lymph glands, it is nevertheless an infectious disease. As children are particularly susceptible Alexandra feared that she might pass it on to those in the hospital, indeed some must have wondered whether she caught it from the hospital in the first place. It marked the end of Alexandra's nursing career enabling her to concentrate on full-time royal duty.

Princess Alexandra was to suffer through having been born in less enlightened times when there was greater opposition to Princesses having a career. Today the daughter of the present Duke and Duchess of Kent, Lady Helen Windsor, has been allowed to follow her own choice of employment, as has Princess Margaret's daughter Lady Sarah Armstrong-Jones. Had Alexandra been born a generation later there might have been a wider choice of career opportunities open to her.

Princess Alexandra was exceptionally tired as a legacy of glandular fever and after a period of recuperation she returned to Great Ormond Street Hospital for just a few more weeks, leaving in August 1958. Later she joked that she had always been terrified of dropping a baby on its head. She still, however, looks back on the experience with affection and laments the loss of freedom it provided. It may have been difficult work, but it was a sortie into the real world where being royal was completely inconsequential. When she walked out of the hospital for the last time and packed away her pink nurse's uniform, it really marked the end of a liberty she would never again experience. When she next visited a hospital it would be officially, as a member of the Royal Family, with all the protocol that entailed. When she next spoke to parents and children in hospitals it could never now be in the relaxed manner that they had confided in Nurse Kent. There would always be an invisible barrier separating the two worlds.

Although onlookers considered Princess Alexandra's period of nursing as a waste of time, besides being of practical use to the hospital she had herself gained immeasurably from the experience. Whereas her clumsiness had once been a family joke, in the hospital there was no room for inaccuracy or mishaps, despite Alexandra's joke about dropping babies. Although it may not have been a conscious move on her part, she certainly left the hospital seeming much less gauche and far more disciplined than before. She knew how to stay calm in a crisis, and her medical experience, however basic, was indirectly good training for her future patronages. When she became Patron of the Cystic Fibrosis Research Trust, for example, and the National Heart Hospital, and made official visits to medical and research centres, she was not in an alien environment. A number of the organizations with which she is associated today are concerned with health and over the years the Princess's medical knowledge has extended so that she has a very sound understanding of their work.

Long-term plans had been made for Princess Marina to visit Latin-America in February 1959, undertaking engagements in Mexico, Chile, Peru and Brazil. Now that Princess Alexandra was no longer committed to a hospital schedule, in the Autumn of 1958 she asked if she could be included in the plans and accompany her mother on the five-week tour. Not only would this provide yet more overseas experience, it would also offer an opportunity to rid her mind of regrets at the curtailment of her nursing career. Princess Marina agreed, and the itinerary was expanded.

On 11 February they flew to Mexico City, which quite literally took their breath away because of the altitude. The schedule was heavy, the pace brisk, but as with the earlier tour of Canada it was very much a working holiday for Alexandra. From Santiago to Rio de Janeiro, the Basilica of Guadalupe to Copacabana beach, rodeos to Aztec sacrificial altars, the Princess experienced it all with wide-eyed excitement. Away from the cold of the British winter to the heat of South America, there must surely have been times when Alexandra found the stimulation of royal tours far greater than bandaging cuts in a London hospital. Princess Marina, now fifty-two, also appreciated the companionship and the sharing of duties, although she still had the determination not to be completely upstaged by her daughter, climbing the 220-foot pre-Aztec pyramid in Teotihuacan to prove 'I'm not as old as all that!'

By today's standards when royal tours are considerably shorter, Marina had a full programme with very little time for private outings of their own. For Alexandra it was almost a baptism by fire, the itinerary running to many pages. It included a lunch in their honour with President Lopez Mateos of Mexico, a reception for expatriates now living in Mexico, dinner with British and Commonwealth Ambassadors, a Press reception, and memorial service at the Mexican Independence Monument, visits to the University of Mexico City, the British Industrial Centre, they attended a ball to raise money for the blind, toured markets, factories, workers' homes, exhibitions, had a dinner with President Manuel Prado of Peru, attended a Peruvian State Banquet, visited hospitals, an orphanage, a college, a school, were given the keys to the City of Lima in a special ceremony, met President Jorge Alessandri of Chile and dined at another State Banquet with President

Kubitschek of Brazil, made extensive tours of every city and town they visited, danced at a Brazilian Embassy Ball, were shown round a factory making cellulose and watched a Chilean newspaper printers at work, were invested with the Collar and Cross of the Order of St Michael and St George (Chile); the Grand Cross of Diamonds and Order of the Sun (Peru), and the Order of the Aztec Eagle (Mexico). The list is seemingly endless and is exhausting simply to read. They flew back home to England on 15 March, Princess Alexandra looking distinctly thinner, although she had suffered from gastro-enteritis at the end of the tour.

There could have been no better training for Alexandra than the Latin-American tour for on it she seemed to have put into practice almost every skill that a royal visit requires, from planting trees and unveiling plaques, to entering into conversations with people in a foreign tongue. The greatest shock for the Princess was the adulation she received on the tour, unexpected and not encountered by her before. In Chile, for example, the streets and squares were packed to capacity, yet surely most of them could have no conception as to who they were. At the President's palace there was a deafening, relentless chanting outside. 'What are they all saying?' asked the Princess. 'They're shouting *Alexandra*,' she was told. Even Marina was seen to be fighting back the tears. This kind of excitement was expected for Cousin Lilibet, but Alexandra had never dreamt that she could evoke such emotion. Ironically the last British royal to have made such a tour had been Alexandra's own father in 1931.

The British Government heralded the tour a success. The object had not simply been to promote goodwill, more importantly it was intended to increase trade with Latin America. Prior to the Second World War, Britain's investments in this region had been in excess of £700,000,000 and trade flourished, but by 1945 financial interests had dwindled considerably and Latin America let go of the ties with London and turned instead to New York. Through the Kent Princesses' tour old acquaintances were renewed and interests rekindled. On their return one British newspaper said, 'The tireless Kents have done their part of the job. Now it's up to the City and to British businessmen to follow up the advantages they have created. The keys are in the doors.'

Princess Alexandra knew now that she had found her niche. Although she was happy to join the rest of the Royal Family in the round of duties in Britain, she saw that her enjoyment of overseas travel could be put to good use. She was now sufficiently experienced to begin solo tours and was quite prepared to fly the flag and become an ambassador for Britain.

6

Going Solo

'Had it not been for the war I would have spent my childhood in Australia,' said Princess Alexandra in a speech, and when a member of the Royal Family was invited to attend centenary celebrations in Queensland not only was she the obvious choice but she positively relished the idea. At just twenty-two years of age she must have been one of the youngest Princesses to have made such an extensive overseas tour on her own, but Alexandra appeared to have no qualms and spent many weeks beforehand reading every book she could find about the country and interrogated the Queen about her visit five years earlier.

While the prospect of a major solo tour must have seemed daunting, its success or failure resting fairly and squarely on her shoulders, the Princess felt sufficiently experienced to cope and looked forward to the challenge. Whereas Princess Marina had proved an excellent trainer in the past, her presence had inevitably been restricting to Alexandra and she must always have been conscious of her mother's watchful eye on her. What onlookers had not known was that Princess Marina would whisper instructions and reprimands to Alexandra in French if she saw something she disapproved of. In Australia, Alexandra knew that she would be free to be herself and let her own personality shine through, and if there were any lapses in protocol she could get away with it. The keynote of informality that she was about to introduce was to have a profound effect on the whole Royal Family's approach. 'I am a human being first, a member of the Royal Family second,' she insisted and she was determined to display the human face of royalty. The no-nonsense Australians were to love her for it.

The six-week tour began on 8 August 1959, the Princess flying via Vancouver, Honolulu and Fiji, landing eventually in Canberra. Who can imagine what went through her mind that night as she stayed at Yarralumla, the Government House, which was originally intended to be her home. Surrounded by furniture that her own father had selected in 1939, she slept in the room that was intended to be hers twenty years before. It was an uncanny experience. Not many days were to pass before the Australian Press were suggesting that she should marry and emigrate permanently. 'There are too many royals congregated in England,' they claimed. The Queen should spread them out around the world. 'Princess Margaret should marry an American,' they declared, 'and Princess Alexandra an Australian.' The thought must certainly have crossed Alexandra's mind, and even today there have been demands made for the Prince of Wales or the Duke of York to be made Governor-General.

Travelling with the Princess were Lady Moyra Hamilton, her lady-in-waiting; Philip Hay as Private Secretary, and Wing-Commander H. B. Kelly (known as Brian to the Princess) as medical supervisor. For one who had suffered mumps in Paris, enteritis in Chile, it was not long before Brian had to treat the Princess for laryngitis in Sydney. The schedule, as with her Latin-American tour, was not unexpectedly heavy with over 100 engagements planned in twenty-two towns and cities in Queensland, New South Wales and Victoria.

At first there was discontent, the Australians feeling that too much had been planned and the Princess's visits would be 'flying' and few would get a chance to see her, let alone meet her. As if to prove that she would not spend her time surrounded by dignitaries, Alexandra broke with tradition and held a press conference in London for Australian journalists to reassure them that she intended to meet with as many people as possible 'especially the young', but insisted the tour was 'mainly concerned with the Queensland centenary celebrations, so I mustn't play the giddy goat'. The words sounded almost like an instruction from Princess Marina. Nevertheless the press conference was informal, the Princess relaxed, and reporters felt bold enough to ask irreverent questions.

'Why are you taking two swimsuits?' one asked, although it is not recorded how he knew.

'Have you been warned the warmer sea might shrink the material?' quipped another.

'Oh, will it?' replied Alexandra with mock horror, 'In that case I shall have to do some slimming as well as swimming.'

The reporters left in high spirits after this departure from the usual formal press briefing and looked forward to the tour as much as she did. Astutely she looked upon her press contingent as part of the team and realized the importance of having them on her side.

At first it looked as if the tour was going to be too formal, especially when the Princess had to shake over fifty hands on arrival, then dine with the Right Honourable Sir Robert Menzies, the Prime Minister. But Alexandra was prepared to play to the crowds and having arrived shortly after Wattle Day that August, she gave a tribute to her hosts by deliberately wearing a 'wattle' dress in the colour of their National Flower. It did not go unnoticed. After a Governmental Banquet and ball in her honour she stepped out on to the balcony three times in the bitter wind to wave to the people, and in Sydney deliberately drove in an open car in spite of the pouring rain. 'They've waited in the rain to see me,' she said. 'It's the least I can do.'

Her aim throughout the tour was to meet as many people as possible and prove that she was not remote. She rewrote prepared speeches into plain English, lest she should sound too imperious. Driving through the streets of Brisbane she made what was to be the most revolutionary decision of the tour. Thousands had lined the streets to watch and they all stared at her in reverential silence. Suddenly in an unplanned move she walked over and began chatting to people, first to children, then to someone in a wheelchair. People reached out and she shook their hands. The cheers grew louder as she progressed down the street until an eight-mile line of people all roared with enthusiasm. On that August day in Australia Princess Alexandra had invented the impromptu royal walkabout that has now become a feature of the present generation's visits. It was exactly the kind of move that the Australians appreciated and warmed to.

Two days later after a service in Brisbane Cathedral, Alexandra tried it again. She stepped off the red carpet and first walked towards a group of choirgirls to thank them for their performance, then she carried on down the street, often waving both hands in the air. It was on returning to the car, by which time she was now on the wrong side, that she got in and sat on the Governor-General Sir Henry Abel Smith's top hat, crushing it completely. Unable to conceal her laughter she held it up to the cheering crowds, politely offering to replace it at the same time. This one incident made the news in almost every Australian newspaper. If anyone had the idea that this Princess would be stuffy and unapproachable, nothing could have dispelled the myth more quickly. Alexandra must have thanked her lucky stars that Princess Marina was 40,000 miles away.

From then onwards Alexandra's visit was treated like the second coming and she entered into the spirit. She made her official car pull up whenever there was a crowd waiting to see her on the tour, once even making the car stop at a place where one single schoolgirl stood waiting. Unconfirmed reports say that the Princess handed over some chocolate or sweets. At the Brisbane National Agricultural Show she broke away from her group and wandered freely amongst the crowds, much to Lady Moyra's horror. Once she had to be rescued as so many people crowded round her and she was in danger of being crushed. What is significant at this time was the obvious lack of worry over security. When details of her entourage were given out to the Press there was no mention of a private detective or personal bodyguard, it was just assumed that the local police force would be sufficient. As indeed it was. It is lamentable to Princess Alexandra that such spontaneous informality is now almost impossible, the security risks being too great. Not only do the Royal Family now need constant protection, a walkabout has to be planned well in advance and if the Princess is talking to the general public there will be armed marksmen on nearby roofs, and eagle-eyed policemen watching the crowds. The fear of kidnap or terrorist attack is never far away; in 1959 the Australian people had nothing more than words of welcome to throw in Alexandra's direction, along with innumerable bouquets. *How times have terribly & sadly changed.*

At the age of twenty-two, although she enjoyed visits to nightclubs back in London, her escorts were restricted to suitably eligible aristocrats and if she returned home late to Kensington Palace then her mother got to hear about it. Alexandra's antics seldom made the gossip columns because Princess Margaret's did, but her mother still expected her to bear her royal status in mind. In Australia Princess Alexandra let out the years of suppression and enjoyed the parties given in her honour to the full. She joined a party with the men employed to handle her luggage on the tour, staying for two hours; she invited the men of the Royal Australian Air Force who formed a guard of honour to another, dancing with each in turn, and when some young farmers in Canberra teasingly flirted with her they later received invitations to a ball and she made a point of again dancing with each. She broke down the social barriers and the tour became more enthusiastic as it progressed. In Melbourne she received a ticker tape welcome and found it impossible to control her tears.

Today Princess Alexandra has been overshadowed by the Prince and Princess of Wales, who now receive a similar welcome, but in 1959 Princess Alexandra's informality was a novelty and she enjoyed the film star reception she received. 'I will be back here some day,' she kept repeating, 'I *must* come back, I have loved it all.' Her sincerity was never doubted.

In typical fashion the tour was not without its mishaps. She was hit in the face with a misdirected streamer and was almost knocked over by her car when it moved forward unexpectedly, but she now had the composure that she once lacked and remained unruffled. 'She had a formal job to do: shaking hands, making speeches, touring towns and villages, eating long dinners, dressing up in full regalia for evening receptions and balls,' said the Melbourne *Daily Herald*. 'She did these things efficiently and charmingly, with a smile – in her eyes as well as on her lips – which suggested she really enjoyed it ... when she left Melbourne she wasn't ashamed of showing that the vast crowds shouting, "Come back soon, Alex," had reduced her to tears. Princess Alexandra had a goodwill job to do. She did it brilliantly.'

When she left the country there were calls for her to be created Duchess of Australia.

On the return journey she stopped off in Siam (now Thailand) at the invitation of the King and Queen, and was driven out to see the jungle in Cambodia. Along the route she was astonished to see literally thousands of soldiers lining the road, most carrying guns. Her own vehicle was preceded by an army minesweeper. It was the first obvious sign of security she had seen on her travels. Only later did she learn that the wife of a British diplomat had been robbed at gunpoint in the area, the police had shot and killed one of the men but other armed bandits were known to be hiding in the jungle. They did not intend to take any chances with Princess Alexandra. Before flying home she made a brief visit to New Delhi at the invitation of President Prasad of India and went shopping for gifts with Mrs Indira Nehru, wife of Prime Minister Pandit Nehru and mother of Mrs Indira Gandhi. She eventually returned to London Airport, where she was met by Princess Marina, swathed in furs as protection against the cold night, and her younger brother, Prince Michael. As she walked between them Alexandra looked radiant in a white two-piece suit and hat that enhanced a glowing complexion. For once Marina looked dowdy in comparison.

In November the Queen gave a welcome-home party for Princess Alexandra at Buckingham Palace and later a lunch was held at the Guildhall by the Lord Mayor of London in her honour. Alexandra's first solo overseas tour had been an unqualified triumph, and it was a phrase that was used time and again when reporting on the Princess. When King Bhumipol Adulyadej and Queen Sirikit of Thailand later came to England on a State Visit, as Princess Alexandra had met them already it was she who was sent to Gatwick Airport to greet them on their arrival. This was to mark the beginning of one of Alexandra's roles today, for it is invariably she who is sent to meet visiting dignitaries and Heads of State at the airport and escort them to Buckingham Palace.

Due to Alexandra's success, the Queen realized that she now had a proficient member of the family firm to represent her overseas. There was a limit to the number of overseas visits she or Princess Margaret could make in a year, and the Queen realized the advantage of having a young, glamorous Princess to enhance their image at a time when Princesses in their twenties were very thin on the ground. What impressed the Queen was her cousin's enthusiasm and enjoyment of overseas travel, which some members of her family regarded as a chore. Alexandra saw it as an opportunity, and was happy to volunteer for the next tour to Nigeria to attend their Independence Ceremony in 1960, and quite openly announced in a speech her appreciation of being able to visit Africa, a chance that 'few people of my age are given'.

It always seems rather incongruous that members of the Royal Family should attend Independence ceremonies, such as that in Nigeria, which mark the *end* of British rule, but it was as the Queen's deputy that Alexandra watched the Union Flag being lowered at six minutes past midnight on 1 October 1960. She read a message from Her Majesty and later opened the Nigerian parliament in Lagos. In tiara and full-skirted floor-length evening-dress, photographs of her at the State Opening could easily be mistaken for the young Queen Elizabeth. It was an image far removed from the plump schoolgirl in navy blue uniform at Heathfield a decade earlier.

Again the visit was a triumph, Princess Alexandra captivating the Nigerian people by her 'human' touch. Rain, or 'Queen's Weather' as it is known amongst the Royal Family, attempted unsuccessfully to dampen Alexandra's enthusiasm on many visits. In Siam the dye had actually come out of the wet red carpet, staining her shoes, and the heavens opened once more in Lagos. The Princess insisted on travelling in the open-topped Rolls Royce as planned to wave to the cheering crowds. Soaked to the skin she did not realize that the pink dye from her hat was running down her face. In sunshine, however, she sat through a Royal durbar organized by the Sultan of Sokoto. Wearing a diamond tiara and full-length blue silk evening gown, she was the personification of a fairy-tale Princess.

Like the Queen, it quickly became apparent on royal tours that Princess Alexandra had done her homework. At a reception hosted by Sir Abubakar Tafawa Balewa, the Nigerian Prime Minister, it was noted as people were introduced to her from many parts of the African continent that she knew where each had originated from simply from their style of dress. Not only had it taken considerable research to discover such information, it was impressive that she could memorize regional variations of costume so proficiently. Such small details were becoming a trademark of her visits. Instead of going to a new country and learning as she went along, and certainly her hosts were fully prepared to brief her in every detail, Alexandra enjoyed studying the background information before she left England. It added to the excitement and gave her confidence that she would be less likely to make a fool of herself. Also it resulted in her being able to ask serious questions out of a genuine desire for knowledge rather than resorting to trite pleasantries.

Once again she returned home with praises heaped upon her and was honoured with yet another Lord Mayor's luncheon, this time at the Mansion House. Not only was she now in demand to make official visits to other countries, she was starting to receive private invitations to travel and in the New Year of 1961 joined the King and Queen of Thailand on the Eggli Slopes of Gstaad in Switzerland for a skiing holiday. Staying at the appropriately named 'Palace Hotel', she appeared each day in black ski-pants, a sky-blue quilted jacket with a hood and striped mittens, and looking like any other tourist, was able to enjoy the sport and show off her skills on the slopes. The holiday was, however, cut short after she accepted an invitation to a ball, only to discover that tickets were being sold at exorbitant prices simply because she would be there as a star attraction. Not prepared to be a part of what appeared to be a commercial venture the Princess tactfully departed before the event. Within weeks it was announced that a tour of the Far East had been planned for October 1961, to include Hong Kong, Japan, Burma, Honolulu and Wake Island in the Pacific Ocean near Hawaii. For the globetrotting Princess there would soon be few areas of the world left to visit. While in the Far East she requested that a return trip to Thailand be included in the itinerary so that she could renew acquaintance with the King and Queen and personally apologize for her hasty departure from Switzerland earlier in the year.

Now following the familiar routine, the Princess spent the summer, when not involved in British engagements, doing her homework. She began learning key phrases in both Chinese and Japanese that could be slipped into speeches. In her bath each morning, where she had total privacy, she practised using chopsticks so that she would be able to eat in the traditional manner at dinners in her honour. At the Café de Chine in Hong Kong she successfully managed fourteen courses with chopsticks and made a speech of thanks in Chinese, so her endeavours were obviously not wasted. Part of her planned itinerary caused a certain amount of controversy when it was revealed that she would meet with Emperor Hirohito in Japan. No member of the British Royal Family had met the Japanese Imperial Family since the war. In 1941, under the influence of Prime Minister General Tojo (who authorized the attack on Pearl Harbor and established a military dictatorship in Japan), Hirohito had agreed to war against Britain and America. He was stripped of a knighthood that had been conferred on him by King George V and there were demands from around the world that he be tried as a war criminal. Ultimately, however, he had wanted peace and agreed to the allied demand for unconditional surrender on 15 August 1945. Once Alexandra had shown him royal acceptance, Hirohito later made a State visit to Britain himself when the Queen re-knighted him with the Order of the Garter. It was the Princess's first experience of controversy, and when meeting the Emperor's family in Tokyo she was faced with another potentially dangerous situation.

The Crown Prince Akihito (who succeeded his father as Emperor in 1989) took Alexandra on a wild duck hunt in Saitana, where birds were being caught in small nets and usually broke their necks or wings in the process. For once Alexandra was not smiling and showed her distaste by refusing to be photographed lest it should be misconstrued as condoning the sport. The one photograph that was taken shows her giving a duck its freedom.

The principal reason for the visit was to mark the fiftieth anniversary of the establishment of Hong Kong university and in a ceremony Princess Alexandra was awarded an honorary degree – a PhD in Law. She had been briefed that in Japan she was not supposed to laugh loudly as the people found it offensive, but in Hong Kong she discovered the rule of etiquette did not apply. After being given her cap and mortarboard as symbols of her doctorate, she stepped forward to make a speech. As she did so the cap fell forward over her eyes just as she was saying how she had always wanted to *see* Hong Kong. The laughter and cheers were deafening. It was as if a guardian angel was deliberately introducing a note of informality into every visit. Princess Alexandra would insist that she was simply being herself, but the British Press hailed her as 'Alexandra the Greatest'; to the Japanese she became 'the Pearl Princess'.

As so often with the Royal Family, it was usually the tritest, seemingly insignificant actions that brought Alexandra the greatest attention and with it success. At the theatre in Tokyo she acknowledged the audience after the performance and waved to all parts of the auditorium,

In the garden at 'Coppins', baby Alexandra plays happily with her parents, the Duke and Duchess of Kent, and brother Edward, in the peaceful summer of 1938, unaware of the tragedy that War would bring.

20 November 1947, at the wedding of her cousins Princess Elizabeth and Prince Philip of Greece, still a month short of her eleventh birthday, Princess Alexandra made her public début as a bridesmaid. Seen here with Princess Marina, Prince Michael and Prince Edward, now Duke of Kent.

Dressing like mother. Throughout her teenage years Princess Marina and Princess Alexandra could easily have been mistaken for sisters.

Wearing a yellow nylon blouse, Princess Alexandra on the eve of her departure to Mademoiselle Anita's Finishing School, Paris, in 1953. The ugly duckling was soon to emerge as a swan.

In elegant silk organza, this twenty-first birthday portrait taken at Kensington Palace proved that the once dowdy teenager had blossomed into womanhood.

Having gained in confidence, in 1960, Princess Alexandra was included in the World's Best-Dressed Women List for the first time. Here she accompanies her great-aunt Princess Alice, Countess of Athlone, at the wedding of Princess Margaret.

Engaged at last. After an eight-year romance with Angus Ogilvy, the marriage date is fixed. Posing here for Cecil Beaton, Princess Alexandra shows off her sapphire and diamond engagement ring.

The Glass Coach takes the bride and groom from Westminster Abbey to St James's Palace, 24 April 1963. While Alexandra smiles radiantly, Angus appears disconcerted by the cheering crowds.

The public get their first glimpse of Miss Marina Ogilvy as the family depart for the christening at St James's Palace, 9 November 1966. Angus carries their son, James.

The Ogilvy family at home. In the drawing room at Thatched House Lodge shortly before Princess Alexandra flew to Canada for the Centennial celebrations in 1967.

A formal portrait of Princess Alexandra wearing the tiara she had made from her own jewels in 1962, and the necklace that was a wedding gift from her husband.

Anxious to keep her home life private, Princess Alexandra appears strangely ill at ease in this informal family group taken at Thatched House Lodge, 1980. While James, sixteen, and Marina, fourteen, share a joke with their father, Princess Alexandra maintains the royal dignity.

Five years on, again in the garden of Thatched House Lodge, yet the Princess seems even more isolated and uncomfortable at the intruding camera in her family life.

Alexandra the natural Princess. Friendly, approachable, in the Nineties she remains at the top of the royal popularity stakes after four decades of public service.

including those in the top tier in the cheapest seats. It is exactly what she would have done in England and did it unthinkingly in Tokyo, not realizing that in Japan the poorest were usually ignored. Even she could not believe that such a trivial action on her part was to make headlines in Japanese newspapers.

On a visit to the Sham Chun River at Lak Ma Chau she wanted to take a photograph across the river of a typical Chinese scene – workers gathering rice in the paddyfields. As she produced her own small camera, a *Daily Mirror* photographer proffered his own more soph-isticated piece of equipment with a zoom lense and she took a picture. Diplomatically she then took another photograph with a camera be-longing to Robert Haswell of the *Daily Express*. No newspaper could now claim that they had an exclusive, but both printed pictures 'as taken by Princess Alexandra' the following day. The goodwill that these simple actions prompted served only to increase Alexandra's popularity with the Press and enhanced her reputation. Always it seemed she gave value for money. She water-skied, tasted pickled snake, had tea with a Chinese family in their skyscraper home, was prepared to dress up in oriental costume and bought kimonos as Christmas presents for her fam-ily back home. Alexandra was very much the pioneer of a new style of royal tours when they began to change course in the 'swinging Sixties'.

By the very nature of her role the Queen had to remain aloof; Princess Margaret had neither the temperament nor the motivation to show the relaxed face of royalty, but at twenty-two Alexandra had the energy and the zest to blow a breath of fresh air into the Royal Family's image and trod a path that others would follow. When she left each country, as in Australia, she repeated, 'I've loved it all, I can't wait to come back!' Thirty years later she still returns to these countries with renewed vigour.

On the last lap of her Far East tour Princess Alexandra went to Egypt and Burma. In Rangoon two incidents were to stay in her mind. In this city of two cathedrals, a plethora of mosques and temples, she was overwhelmed at the sight of the Shwe Dayon Pagoda. At 375 feet the Pagoda was more than double the height of Nelson's Column and over fifty feet taller than Big Ben in London, and contained over twenty tons of gold. She made a donation towards the upkeep of the temple that had taken her breath away.

Only one event in Rangoon seemed to dampen Princess Alexandra's spirits. She lost a small teddy bear that travelled with her in the luggage, which she referred to as her lucky mascot. Despite an extensive search it was never recovered. Only Lady Moyra Hamilton realized the cause of Alexandra's distress. The bear had been a gift from Angus Ogilvy.

7

Royal Romance

On 17 January 1991, Princess Alexandra may have become Queen of Norway. Until the age of twenty-five her name was consistently linked with two men. Prince Constantine of Greece and Prince Harald of Norway. Had she chosen Prince Harald, as so many expected she would, following the death of King Olav in 1991 Alexandra would now be Queen. By a strange comparison, Olav himself proposed to Princess Marina in April 1957, and had she accepted she would have become Queen of Norway in September of that year. Both Princesses of Kent turned down the royal suitors. Marina chose not to remarry, Alexandra already had a secret romance.

Once again Princess Alexandra benefited from her cousin's misfortune. Even before her much publicized relationship with Group Captain Peter Townsend, Princess Margaret's name was linked by the Press with an astonishing number of men. All were 'just good friends' and many remain close four decades later, but shared the distinction of being married off to the Queen's sister. The Earl of Dalkeith, the Marquess of Blandford, Prince George of Denmark, Prince Nicholas of Yugoslavia (Princess Alexandra's cousin, killed in a car crash in 1954), Prince Bertil of Sweden, Prince Christian of Hanover, Simon Ward the Earl of Dudley's son, Lord Ogilvy (Angus Ogilvy's brother), King Michael of Rumania, Mark Bonham-Carter, Colin Tennant, Jocelyn Stevens, the list is endless, almost inexhaustible. In the shadow of this frivolous royal speculation that was to surround Princess Margaret, followed by her controversial marriage to commoner Antony Armstrong-Jones, Princess Alexandra was able to pursue her romantic attachments relatively free from publicity. With Princess Margaret as the Aunt Sally, considered a fair target for journalistic sniping, Alexandra was able to remain out of the firing line.

Princess Alexandra's name is almost synonymous with discretion, and so clever was she at retaining a low private profile that she managed an eight-year courtship with Angus Ogilvy and even then the announcement of their engagement at the end of 1962 came as a shock to most. Alexandra had one big advantage over Princess Margaret. Whereas after Elizabeth's marriage in 1947, Margaret was the sole target of Press interest for thirteen years until she herself married, Princess Alexandra had the convenience of an elder brother to hide behind. As Duke of Kent and an extremely eligible bachelor, the focus of attention was inevitably targeted towards his girlfriends. Whoever he chose would instantly, on marriage, become Duchess of Kent. Whether he liked it or not he was dubbed 'the Playboy Prince' and he had only to dance with a girl for her name to be instantly linked with his in the Press. Julia Williamson, Carol Pease, Valerie Lawson, are names once tipped to be his bride. Even some of Alexandra's Heathfield friends found themselves paired off with the Prince. His love of fast cars only added to the media image and when guests at a party in Chelsea were thrown into the River Thames, Kensington Palace were forced to issue a statement saying that although the Duke had been present, he was not involved in the incident.

It was while stationed at Catterick Camp with the Royal Scots Greys, that Edward was invited for Sunday lunch on 28 October 1956, at Hovingham Hall, the home of Sir William Worsley, Lord Lieutenant of Yorkshire. The date is significant for it marks his first meeting with Sir William's daughter Katharine. A few weeks later they met again at a private dance at Stockeld Park, and then arranged to attend a hunt ball together in fancy dress, going in the costumes of a Tudor prince and a shepherdess. Probably unintentionally, their costumes symbolized the difference between them. Royalty and commoner. A significant variance in their backgrounds that was later to place a stumbling block in their path.

Edward was invited to Hovingham Hall to spend the Easter of 1957. Romance between them had begun. That Whitsun, Edward drove Katharine to Coppins to meet Princess Marina and Princess Alexandra for the first time. Alexandra and Katharine struck up an instant rapport. She was to become like the sister Alexandra never had. Princess Marina had greater reservations. At first she looked upon Katharine as just another girlfriend. She wanted her son to marry a Princess especially as she had so many European relatives and she would prefer a wealthy Princess to rid the Kent family of its 'poor relation' image. As nice as Katharine Worsley was, it was not the alliance Marina had hoped for. When the relationship became serious and Edward told his mother that he wanted to marry, he faced unexpected opposition. 'Breeding will out,' was Marina's phrase, and she told her son that he was much too young to marry and must wait. At heart she believed that in time he would come round to her way of thinking and fall for one of 'his own kind'. Like his sister, Alexandra, the Duke had a stubborn streak and was not to be swayed. Princess Alexandra refused publicly to take sides, but there is no doubt that her sympathy lay with her brother. She had always insisted herself that she would marry only for love. Princess Marina knew of many relatives with arranged marriages that had been successful and saw no reason not to give her children a gentle push in the right direction – towards Europe. Each of her children were to make up their own minds. Both Edward and Alexandra married commoners, and Prince Michael was to be just four days away from his thirty-sixth birthday when he eventually took the step. Although from Europe, his bride was an Austrian Baroness, a divorcee and he had to renounce his rights of succession to marry her. The fact that she was also a Roman Catholic only added to his problems. By this time Princess Marina was not alive to see it.

Another point that counted against Katharine Worsley was her age. At two-years, eight-months *older* than Edward, Princess Marina felt that when her son married it ought to be to someone of his own age and she used it to add weight to her argument that he was too young to marry anyway. Also she felt that the outwardly shy Katharine would not cope easily with life as a member of the Royal Family and her duties as Duchess of Kent. Is it possible that Marina would have raised objections to whoever her son chose? Not only from a maternal point of view did she want what she considered to be the best for her son, but on the day he married she would relinquish the title 'Duchess of Kent' that had been hers since her own wedding day in 1934.

Princess Alexandra offered what little advice she could. She told her brother that if he truly loved 'Katie' then he would have to stick it out. He introduced her to as many members of the Royal Family as possible in an attempt to get the majority on his side, and at one point even considered going over his mother's head and asking the Queen for permission to marry. Under the Royal Marriages Act the Queen had to give her consent to heirs under the age of twenty-five. Princess Alexandra pointed out that the Queen would never go against Princess Marina's wishes and that such a move would only place their cousin in an embarrassing situation. The final nail in the coffin seemed to come when Edward learned that his regiment was to be posted to Germany for two years.

Princess Marina took advantage of this situation. She gave them an ultimatum. If they did not see each other for twelve months then they could seek the Queen's permission to marry. On 14 October 1958, Edward went with the regiment to Hanover. They kept their side of the bargain and the couple did not meet again until November 1959. As with Princess Margaret's enforced separation from Peter Townsend, it was believed that in twelve months they would drift apart. Marina felt, perhaps, that Katharine might find somebody else, somebody whose position would present less problems. Absence, however, only served to make the heart grow fonder. Princess Alexandra was able to offer comfort to both. When they did meet again at Kensington Palace, Edward was so excited that he fell down the blue-carpeted steps onto the hard parquet floor and broke a bone in his foot.

By the time they met with the Queen, Princess Margaret and Antony Armstrong-Jones had already decided to marry. In the complicated workings of royal life, the Queen had made them delay their engagement because she was herself expecting a baby. As public interest now centred on the birth of the Queen's third child, she did not think it fair that her sister should have to compete. Secondly, the Royal Family try to avoid long engagements in the knowledge that the resulting wedding fever builds up to an almost unbearable pitch. Subsequently, Prince Andrew was born on 19 February 1960, and Princess Margaret's engagement was announced a week later on 26 February. The Queen told Katharine and Edward that although she consented to their betrothal in principle she could not allow them to marry for at least another twelve months. She did not want there to be two royal weddings in the same year. While Princess Margaret's love life worked in Princess Alexandra's favour, it seemed to go against her brothers. Eventually Princess Margaret married Antony Armstrong-Jones on 6 May 1960, in Westminster Abbey; the Duke of Kent married Katharine Worsley on 8 June 1961, in York Minster. It had taken them nearly five years.

Forever conscious of the problems that her brother had encountered, Princess Alexandra realized that the royal path of true love cannot run smooth. Although she dallied with titled young men, it seemed suspiciously like keeping Princess Marina happy. Knowing the problems it cannot have been easy for her to tell her mother that she, like Eddie, was in love with a commoner. Ageism again risked rearing its head for Angus Ogilvy was not only eight years older than Alexandra, no-one could deny that he looked even more.

Although not royal himself, Angus Ogilvy's family have long been associated with royalty. His father, the 12th Earl of Airlie, had been a lord-in-waiting to King George V and for some thirty years was Lord Chamberlain to Queen Elizabeth (the Queen Mother); his grandmother, Mabell, Countess of Airlie, was a lady-in-waiting to Queen Mary for half-a-century. Historically, both he and Princess Alexandra share a common ancestry with Mary Queen of Scots. It is popularly believed that the couple met for the first time at the Eton Beagles Ball in 1954, but their paths undoubtedly crossed before then. Some sources suggest that they must have met at Birkhall, the Queen Mother's home on the Balmoral estate, because Angus and his elder brother David socialized with Princess Elizabeth and Margaret. The Airlie family were frequent guests at royal weddings and christenings, which Princess Alexandra attended, and the chances are that they could have met at Marlborough House. Here Alexandra would visit her grandmother, and Angus his.

In Coronation Year Princess Marina invited Angus for lunch at Coppins. She was about to embark on a tour of the Far East with Edward, and as Angus had previously spent seven months in Malaya doing his National Service she probed him about the country. Princess Alexandra was also present when he described her as 'a charming child'. Not necessarily indicative of a romance, but when Prince Charles met Lady Diana Spencer for the first time he described her as 'a very jolly and amusing sixteen-year-old'. Angus and Alexandra met again at a house party given by Lady Zia Wernher at Luton Hoo in Bedfordshire, where the Queen and Prince Philip always spent their wedding anniversary. Each time they met Alexandra had blossomed into womanhood just a little more. Although they danced together at parties and chatted animatedly, royalwatchers did not consider it significant. There was a family connection, and besides, an eight-year age difference ...

Once she had reached the age of eighteen Alexandra's name was inevitably linked with a variety of eligible young men. Fair-haired and hazel-eyed, attractive and in the line of succession to the throne, she was an obvious target for speculation. When she went to stay with her lady-in-waiting's family at Baron's Court, Omagh in Northern Ireland, after the third visit there were rumours of romance with Lady Moyra's brother, James, the Marquess of Hamilton, heir of the fourth Duke of Abercorn.

When this proved to be without foundation, attention turned to James's friend, Lord O'Neill, of Shane's Castle, Antrim, Northern Ireland, and on the surface Alexandra appeared to have formed a very close attachment. They were seen dancing at a nightclub in London, eating *à deux* in a restaurant, and he was even invited to stay at Coppins. As late as the summer of 1961 he and Alexandra were guests of Charles Morrison* on the island of Islay in the Inner Hebrides. This was quite deliberate on Alexandra's part for Raymond O'Neill acted as a decoy, and was good at the job. Certainly he was privy to the Princess's secret and you only have to look at the newspapers at the time to see that his touch of the blarney effectively kept the Press on the wrong trail.

On one occasion he told an inquisitive reporter 'it's all in the air ... there's no question of an engagement.' Later he 'revealed' that he was 'hesitating about marriage to Alexandra', adding, 'I don't want to become like Philip, a prisoner of protocol. I don't want to be obliged to walk two steps behind my wife, clasping my hands like a clever little boy. Alexandra loves me very much, but I don't want Buckingham Palace as part of my dowry.' We shall never know whether or not Alexandra wanted him to get into the role so deeply, but his performance had the desired effect. He had very cleverly implied that they

---

* Charles Morrison's father, Baron Margadale, owned the island. His sister, Lady Mary Morrison, has been a Woman of the Bedchamber since 1960.

might get engaged, but gave himself a get out clause. When they did not become engaged it would be assumed that he had not accepted the protocol. Conscious that they were being watched as they stayed on Islay, Princess Alexandra took hold of the Irish Lord's hand. It worked to their advantage also that just before the Islay visit a reporter had mistaken Viscount Ednam (the present Earl of Dudley) for Lord O'Neill. Lord Ednam was about to marry for the second time and was buying a wedding ring; the case of mistaken identity (despite the fact that Ednam is thirteen years older than O'Neill) spread the rumour that Alexandra was about to marry.

Another supposed suitor was a David Bailey. They were known to have spent a weekend in Wiltshire with mutual friends, and he was seen to drive her home. What was not revealed was Bailey's great-grandmother was Mabell, Countess of Airlie, and a relative of Angus Ogilvy. Matters were made worse when Bailey's car was broken into and it was revealed that two suitcases belonging to the Princess had been stolen. Fortunately these were discovered the following day and, no doubt to Alexandra's acute embarrassment, the entire contents were listed in the newspapers. Whilst ignoring the personal items, the most revealing fact about Alexandra to come out of the event was that in her weekend suitcase she had packed a Bible, a prayer book and a Russian icon. Obviously indicative of a deep faith and not the first items one would normally expect a young girl to have in her luggage. It enhanced her reputation. When David Bailey got engaged himself, Alexandra watchers struck him off their list.

Ever hopeful, Princess Marina introduced Alexandra to a number of young eligible royals. In Holland she was photographed with Prince Karl of Hesse. As early as 1955 and as late as March 1960 when they were photographed at a house party together, Crown Prince Harald of Norway was the perennial favourite. One American newspaper in 1955 even went as far as to claim that their engagement would 'shortly be announced'. It wasn't. Prince Harald, the only son of King Olav, was Alexandra's second cousin (Edward VII was great-grandfather to them both) and was born just two months after her in February 1937. Like Alexandra, Harald had been sent to school, and they had many interests in common such as a love of skiing, but they were never romantically involved. Like Alexandra, Prince Harald eventually married a commoner after a nine-year courtship, and like the Duke of Kent, he had faced fierce opposition to his marrying a non-royal.

Princess Marina had her own personal choice for Alexandra. Prince Constantine of Greece. Not only was 'Tino' a good match, she thought, but there were obvious links with her homeland. Her own marriage had been the union of a Prince of Kent to a Princess of Greece, so why not now a Prince of Greece to a Princess of Kent? Princess Marina's father and 'Tino's' grandfather were brothers, he and Alexandra are cousins. Constantine was to succeed his father, King Paul, in 1964 but was to flee Greece in exile just three years later. Although Princess Alexandra enjoyed his company, she did not view him as a prospective marriage partner and it was noticeable that they deliberately avoided each other at family functions, perhaps reacting against Marina's matchmaking. He eventually married Anne-Marie, Queen Margrethe II of Denmark's younger sister. They called their first daughter Princess Alexia.

What Princess Alexandra found attractive in Angus Ogilvy was his maturity. Possibly she was seeking a father figure, having lost her own at such a young age. All the men that she associated with seemed to be much younger than she was, and she equated them on the same level as her brother Michael and his associates. Those that were her age or a couple of years older seemed like Edward and his friends. One of Edward's friends in fact was James Ogilvy, a younger brother of Angus, but she did not consider him romantically. 'I'm too old for marriage,' Angus had said publicly in 1962, but Alexandra did not agree. Princess Marina had not married until she was twenty-eight and Alexandra was in no hurry.

When once asked about her ideal husband, Alexandra had said that he must be 'rich and good-looking'; Angus had what she considered to be rugged good looks and was already the director of some fifty-six companies. His family owned two estates, both with castles, he being born on 14 September 1928 at Cortachy Castle, Kirriemuir, Scotland. Alexandra may have had royal parents, but even she was not born in a castle. Angus had one up on her. They shared many of the same friends, both often being invited independently to the same parties, and had many mutual interests. A love of classical music, tennis, riding, cinema, theatre and books. Angus once enjoyed Alexandra's love of skiing, but severely injured his back in a skiing accident from which he has never fully recovered. Most important of all they shared the same sense of humour, often giggling over each other's clumsiness.

Angus had once worked as a waiter at the Savoy Hotel, but was dismissed when he dropped a plate of food on a distinguished customer. He had also been involved in a few minor car accidents and once skidded on some ice with Alexandra inside the car. The vehicle turned over on its side, but neither was hurt. Alexandra did not dare tell her mother. She had herself once steered her car into a stationary vehicle. When the driver saw who she was he was so shocked that he apologized and blamed himself for the accident.

The courtship between Angus and Alexandra was conducted discreetly and in relative obscurity. They would go with a group of friends to the cinema, the Princess lost in the crowd and unrecognized. Afterwards they would go to Lyons' Corner House for tea and fish and chips. In 1955 the Princess began visiting Angus's small flat at 17 Park West Place, just a short drive from Kensington Palace where they would sit on the floor listening to records. Later he bought a grander house, 10 Culross Street, off Park Lane, less than half a mile away. Perhaps in preparation for the royal way of life he had his own manservant, Stephen Leake. Occasionally at house parties Princess Alexandra might have been seen publicly with Lord O'Neill, but invariably Angus was a guest in the background. When Alexandra attended a rugby match officially in Richmond, few knew that just a couple of days earlier she and Angus had been incognito to another match so that she could learn the technicalities. As his own family had given the monarchy long service, Angus was no stranger to the royal way of life, unlike any other commoner marrying into this extraordinary family who faces a difficult period of adjustment. Already he was involved in a great deal of charity work, for example, he was a member of the finance committee for the National Association of Youth Clubs. That is not to say that he did not have doubts about marriage to Alexandra, money being one of his greatest concerns. He was no stranger to the inside of royal homes, which however threadbare made his home look modest in comparison. He assumed that he would be unable to keep Alexandra in a style that befits a Princess. Alexandra made no bones about the fact that she had learned to be thrifty, often bought clothes from Marks and Spencers and chain stores, and had been taught many tricks of economy from Princess Marina. They were perhaps comforted by the fact that Princess Margaret had paved the way by marrying a commoner, Antony Armstrong-Jones, a photographer who almost certainly had less money than Angus and had a wife who would demand a higher standard of living.

Angus Ogilvy proposed to Princess Alexandra in October 1962 in the romantic setting of Birkhall, the bow-fronted house on the Balmoral estate so beloved by the Queen Mother. Alexandra accepted without a moment's hesitation. It was a weekend of deep discussion, particularly as to how they could intermix their two very different lifestyles. Angus was a free agent and did not want to be burdened by security, protocol, or be forced to give up his business life. Neither did he want marriage to put pressure on Alexandra's already heavy workload, nor should she feel that she should reduce the number of engagements, which she obviously enjoyed. They agreed that they could manage like any other newly-married couple with full-time careers and would face each problem as it arose. It is said that whilst Alexandra rushed over to Balmoral Castle to seek the Queen's permission, Angus went at the same moment to see Princess Marina. Obviously the conversations were private and unrecorded. Some sources, unconfirmed, say that Princess Marina did not give Angus an instant answer but made him wait several days. Certainly Angus did not tell his parents or brothers until the following weekend that he was to marry Alexandra and one would have expected him to telephone that same day.

Princess Marina may well be one of the reasons why Princess Alexandra married later in life than she might have done. She had known Angus a long time and could have moved events to a swifter conclusion had she so wished. Alexandra was concerned for her mother's future. On the Duke of Kent's marriage in June 1961 she had relinquished her title 'Duchess of Kent' that had been hers since her wedding day and became known only as 'Princess Marina'. In March of that year she gave up Coppins, which had been her home for twenty-two years, the late Duke having left the property in trust to Edward. Although he had legally been owner of the property from the age of twenty-one there seemed no reason for Marina to leave, but when he married she knew she could no longer stay. This meant she now lived solely at Kensington Palace, the only advantage of giving up Coppins being that it considerably eased her financial position. Alexandra knew, however, that with Prince Michael now in the Army, when she married and moved out Princess Marina would be alone. This must have had some bearing on Alexandra's delay.

The engagement was eventually announced on 29 November, 1962, a not insignificant date for it was the anniversary of Marina's own wedding. At 5.15 pm Kensington Palace issued a statement:

'It is with the greatest pleasure that Princess Marina, Duchess of Kent, announces the betrothal of her daughter Princess Alexandra to Angus Ogilvy, second son of the Earl and Countess of Airlie, to which the Queen has gladly given her consent.'

Although Princess Marina had relinquished her title to her daughter-in-law, and had publicly made a statement to that effect, it was surely no oversight that it continued to be used on official statements such as the above. Technically she should have been the Dowager Duchess of Kent, but found the title too ageing. Alexandra displayed an engagement ring with one large sapphire flanked by two diamonds, and the following day she and Angus posed for photographers in the garden at Kensington Palace. Wearing an elegant dark velvet two-piece suit with a fur-trimmed skirt, the Princess looked relaxed; her fiancé in a double-breasted pin-striped suit, with a triangle of white handkerchief just showing at the pocket, looked every inch the businessman. Uncertain, perhaps, as he faced television cameras for the first time as to what he had let himself in for. As they were photographed leaving St Peter's Church, Iver, after evensong five days later, Alexandra was wearing a coat and hat that, although her own, could easily have been worn by her mother; Angus the same suit as in his engagement photographs, it was as if Alexandra was deliberately trying to make the age gap between them less apparent. Photographed at Airlie Castle with Angus's parents, Alexandra and Marina, both dressed in tweeds, could have been younger and elder sister. It was a complex Alexandra would have to come to terms with.

The date of the wedding was arranged for 24 April, 1963, giving them just five months to make all the preparations, including their future home. Once again Alexandra became a pioneer by becoming the first member of the Royal Family to place a wedding gift list at Harrods. Some members of the family shook their heads in disbelief.

Typical of the financially embarrassed Kents, thought others, who had assumed that when, in 1960, Princess Marina sent items to auction, it had been to raise money for Alexandra's wedding, the bride's family traditionally being the ones to pay. The wedding present list not only included anticipated items, such as glasses and decanters, table silver and a Wedgwood dinner service (Celadon pattern), towels and bed linen, cooking utensils and white picnic table, but some unexpected items for a Princess. An ironing-board and sewing-machine, for someone who would never actually need to iron or sew, and a roulette wheel! Not usually a priority for a newly-married couple.

Other gifts naturally came in from European aunts, uncles and cousins, and the Princess was to receive many gifts from the charities with which she was associated. The Guide Dogs for the Blind Association, for example, bought four silver salt pots; the Royal Commonwealth Society for the Blind gave a gilt-framed mirror. Not, obviously, from charitable donations but from the pockets of the staff. The staff at Kensington Palace clubbed together to buy the couple a white garden table, and Alexandra wrote to each personally to thank them, as indeed she wrote to every individual who had taken the trouble to buy her a gift.

'I want to let you know,' she wrote, 'how warmly I appreciate your kindness in joining together to send me such a wonderful wedding present. I would like you all to know how greatly touched I am by your very kind thought for me and how delighted I am with your lovely gift. That charming table will not only be a great joy in our garden here but also a very happy reminder of you all and of your kindness. With my most grateful thanks and best wishes to you all, ALEXANDRA.'

The people of Scotland contributed a Chippendale writing desk, an antique silver coffee pot, and some paintings of the Airlie estates, from others a grandfather clock and four silver candlesticks – all of which still give the Ogilvys pleasure today. The choice of home for the newly-married couple was obviously of the utmost urgency. For reasons of security the couple could not live in Angus's Culross Street house, to move to Scotland would have proved too inconvenient for both, and Angus did not want to reside at Kensington Palace with his mother-in-law. Already they had seen the problems created for Antony Armstrong-Jones, who on marriage to Princess Margaret lived with the Queen Mother at Clarence House. There the staff frowned if he was informally dressed at dinner, or rolled up his sleeves even, and Angus knew that was not the way to begin married life. Whilst he got on well with Princess Marina he did not particularly want to face her across the breakfast table every morning, or indeed have his wife under the rule of her mother. Eventually they decided to take a five-year lease on a house in Richmond Park belonging to the Duchess of Sutherland. Standing in 2,000 acres of royal parklands and deer forest, Thatched House Lodge was early Georgian and had once been the home of Sir Robert Walpole, 1st Earl of Orford, chief Whig statesman and considered to be the first Prime Minister. Just as Alexandra's parents had leased 3 Belgrave Square as their marital home until they found Coppins, it seemed an ideal start for a newly-wed couple. It was sufficiently close to central London for the Princess to continue her duties as before, many of which were throughout Britain anyway, yet the couple appreciated the fact that they would be surrounded by rolling countryside. On a clear day you could see across the Sussex Downs. Angus, who then had an income of some £60,000 per annum bought the lease on a mortgage for around £150,000. The lease was eventually extended and it is still their home today. They have approximately four acres of land, their own heated swimming pool, and five reception rooms with sufficient space for entertaining guests. Their need for practical wedding gifts and furniture were perhaps of greater necessity to them than to other members of the family. Her brother Edward, for example, had received Coppins, complete with furniture when he married. Alexandra and Angus were virtually starting from scratch.

Another important concern of Alexandra's was naturally her wedding dress. For this she went to designer John Cavanagh, who had made many of her outfits for the overseas tours and had created Katharine Worsley's tight-waisted, full-skirted dress, surrounding her in a mass of flowing lace that was to cause her to be dubbed the 'Cinderella Princess' – the ordinary girl who had found her Prince Charming.

Princess Alexandra had very different ideas as to how her bridal gown should look. Ingrained in her mind was Mademoiselle Anita's dictum, no frills or flounces and together she and Cavanagh drew up a stunningly straight style, that showed off her feminine curves but was beltless and apparently seamless. She knew that with her height a full skirt would only make her look enormous. The basic design was inspired by a length of Valenciennes lace from Princess Marina which she had worn on her own wedding day. It came with the gift of a veil, last worn by Princess Patricia of Connaught at her wedding to Commander Alexander Ramsay in February 1919. A granddaughter of Queen Victoria, hers was the first royal wedding to take place in Westminster Abbey since Tudor times and the ceremony encouraged others to follow suit. If eyebrows were raised at Alexandra marrying a commoner, one wonders at the reaction to Princess Patricia who on marriage renounced her titles and thereby *became* a commoner. Although her bridal veil was too fragile to wear, Princess Alexandra liked the typically English design, a pattern of acorns and oak leaves. John Cavanagh had this sent to France and the lace was copied for the dress. Just eighty yards were woven and all were incorporated into the dress. It had a twenty-one-feet-long train of magnolia-tinted lace, which John Cavanagh persuaded her to wear as a veil, secured by the diamond fringe tiara that had been made in the Russian style for Princess Marina's wedding. Marina's own gift of lace was also incorporated into the train. The Princess chose to wear no jewellery of any kind, not even earrings, so that when she returned from the altar the wedding band on her left hand would be given greater significance.

Two days before the wedding itself the Queen held a State ball in the Waterloo Chamber at Windsor Castle for the couple. She had taken an exceptional interest in the plans for Alexandra's wedding and paid for the glittering ball with some 2,000 guests herself. Perhaps as it also happened to be the day after her own birthday made the party all the more enjoyable. Those present likened it to one of the grand Victorian balls that had long been impractical to organize. The amount of food and drink consumed by the guests is staggering. Over 1,500 bottles of champagne, 2,000 bottles of beer, more than 10 cases of gin, 80 lbs of smoked salmon, 500 ounces of caviar, 15 legs of pork, and more than 200 chickens. The Queen was said to have seen little change out of £25,000 at the end of the evening. No doubt the Queen was aware that Marina was financially unable to celebrate her daughter's marriage in such style, maybe too she felt that Alexandra had missed out on so much over the years because of her father's early death. The next day, however, there was inevitable Press criticism at such extravagance even if it was the Queen's own money. The *Court Circular* that day gave an impressive list of senior guests from practically every Royal House in Europe. As obscure as the Margrave of Baden, the Prince of the Asturias, and a Princess of Hohenlohe-Langeburg. 'Is this a marriage between two popular young people,' asked the *Daily Express* editorial, 'or a campaign for Europe's busted down, pensioned off, purpled off, forgotten but not buried royals?' The article continued, 'Why should Alex and Angus's romance degenerate into a rollicking group for royal exiles, pretenders and pensioners?' Those in the know were aware that Princess Marina had been responsible for organizing much of the guest list. Alexandra would no doubt have preferred a simpler affair for her own small circle of friends. For Angus the prospect of being centre stage amid so many crowned or ex-crowned heads, from King Umberto of Italy to Queen Eugenie of Spain, must surely have been a terrifying one. So nervous was he that *en route* he crashed his car into the back of a van near the Royal Albert Hall and cut his head. He was at the point of exhaustion by the time the ball eventually ended at four o'clock the following morning.

On the eve of the wedding itself central London was filled with revellers in party mood. Many had been camping along The Mall for over twenty-four hours and as the Press went to interview them it was apparent that they had not only travelled from all parts of the United Kingdom, including a large contingent of Scots because of Angus, but there were crowds from Australia, New Zealand, South Africa, indeed representatives from all the countries where Princess Alexandra was popular.

Wednesday 24 April dawned grey and dull with the threat of rain in the air. Thousands nevertheless lined the route for the car procession to Westminster Abbey. The Lord Chamberlain's office had decreed that this was a Civil marriage, not a State wedding, and so Alexandra did not warrant a horse-drawn carriage to the Abbey. The same office drew up a detailed itinerary:

10.30 am   The Queen and the Duke of Edinburgh will leave Windsor Castle, accompanied by the Prince of Wales.

11.15 am   Non-royal guests will arrive at the entrance to Westminster Abbey.

11.15 am   The Bridegroom, with Mr Peregrine Fairfax (the best man) will leave 10 Culross Street and arrive at the Cloisters Entrance in the Dean's Yard at 11.30 am.

11.20 am   Bridesmaids and pages leave Buckingham Palace.

11.25 am   Members of foreign Royal Families leave Buckingham Palace.

11.33 am   Members of the Royal Family leave St James's Palace.

11.38 am   Queen Elizabeth the Queen Mother and foreign Sovereigns leave Clarence House.

11.30 am   Princess Marina, accompanied by the Duchess of Kent and Prince Michael of Kent leave Kensington Palace.

11.45 am   The Queen, Duke of Edinburgh and Prince of Wales leave Buckingham Palace.

11.43 am   The Bride, accompanied by the Duke of Kent, leaves Kensington Palace.

Princess Alexandra travelled in an open-topped Rolls Royce with her brother, the Duke of Kent, who was representing their late father. Neither seemed able to hide their nerves, although Alexandra managed to smile and wave at the crowds as the sun broke through the clouds. As Big Ben in the distance struck twelve, Princess Alexandra stepped from the maroon car and entered the Abbey to a trumpet fanfare and processed down the aisle to a choral version of *Holy, Holy, Holy*. The marriage ceremony itself was conducted by Dr Michael Ramsey, Archbishop of Canterbury, and the Revd Tees, Vicar of St Mary Abbots Church in Kensington where Princess Alexandra worshipped. There were five bridesmaids, headed by Princess Anne, and two page-boys. The traditional Service of Matrimony had been chosen and Alexandra promised to 'obey' her husband. With a love of classical music, Alexandra and Angus chose to leave the Abbey to *Widor's Toccata* from Organ Symphony No. 5 in F minor, and at the Queen's insistence returned to St James's Palace for the reception in the Glass Coach, used by royal brides since 1910.

The reception itself was small, compared to the earlier Windsor Castle ball, with less than 500 guests. The wedding cake was some five-feet high and decorated with Alexandra roses and tartan bagpipes. Incorporated in the design was Alexandra's monogram of entwined 'A's' and both their armorial bearings. A civil wedding it may have been, but there was no escaping the royal protocol. After cutting the first slice of cake and posing for photographs, Angus turned to his wife and said, 'Now you do the rest'. He was tired of posing and went to one side for a cigarette. This was to be one of the rare occasions when he was forced to share the limelight and he had had enough.

In preparation for the honeymoon Alexandra changed into a fuchsia pink two-piece suit with matching hat and cream gloves and drove to London Airport for the first stage, which was to be five days at Birkhall where Angus had proposed. Whilst the wedding had gone smoothly, with few mishaps other than Alexandra nearly losing her veil several times as it was so long and precariously balanced, problems were to arise on the honeymoon.

As their plane of the Queen's Flight approached high ground in Scotland, and one wonders if Princess Alexandra must have thought of her father on this her wedding day as she was flying on almost the exact route he had taken on his final flight, fog covered the hills and the plane had to be diverted. Instead of flying direct to Aberdeen – the nearest airport to Balmoral – the pilot had to go further north and land at Lossiemouth. Directly opposite Lossiemouth in a straight line is Berriedale from where the emergency services were alerted that the Duke of Kent's plane had crashed at Eagle's Rock nearby. It was an uncanny coincidence.

While a car was being arranged to drive them the eighty-five-mile journey to Birkhall, Alexandra and Angus made an unplanned visit to the home of the station commander of RAF Lossiemouth where they had sandwiches and watched a repeat of the wedding on television. Alexandra squealed with delight and embarrassment, hardly able to watch. It brought back memories of Heathfield when she could not bear to watch herself in the film of Princess Elizabeth's wedding. It was after midnight when they eventually arrived at Birkhall.

Once safely ensconced at Birkhall they faced another problem. A Press photographer. Not the usual hordes that had followed them on their wedding day or waited for them when they went to Crathie Church on the Braemar Road a mile from Balmoral. Just one particular photographer. Raymond Bellisario, who was well known for his candid shots of royalty. Princess Margaret and Antony Armstrong-Jones had long been particular targets of his and when Lord Snowdon once accidentally crashed into Bellisario's car he said it was worth the £20 fine. He was not unknown to Princess Alexandra, but he had seldom caused problems for her as she generally kept photographers happy anyway by agreeing to pose when requested. On this occasion, however, it was the candid type of photograph that Bellisario was after. Royal lovers on their honeymoon. He was not to be disappointed. Hidden in the undergrowth on the banks of the River Muick south of Birkhall, Raymond Bellisario watched. Whether it was a lucky guess or, more likely, he had received a tip off, it was the spot where the newly-married couple had chosen to picnic. They could easily have gone northwards to the River Dee, they might have walked into the heather-clad hillside of 'Greag Phioboadh' or into Ballater, yet they chose to walk towards Loch Muick. Surely the photographer must have known. Alexandra and Angus spread out their rug and opened a picnic hamper, obviously enjoying each other's company and oblivious to the fact that they were not alone. With a 400mm telescopic lens focused on them, Bellisario clicked away to his heart's content. The resulting pictures, although some were later published in Europe, were considered to be 'of too personal a nature' for the British Press.

Princess Alexandra was livid when she heard about the photographs and demanded that the negatives be destroyed, but Bellisario refused. His candid shots had consistently caused offence to the Royal Family and this honeymoon set were no exception. In the early Seventies, to their relief, Bellisario moved to South Africa, no doubt having made a good income out of the family whom he despised. A self-confessed Republican, he had no qualms about exploiting royalty. One single exclusive photograph if of sufficient interest can net a photographer £50,000. Before giving up his 'royal' career, Bellisario published a book, *To Tread On Royal Toes*, which he boldly sent to the Queen as a wedding anniversary gift. It was promptly returned by her Private Secretary saying that the Queen did not wish to accept it.

Bellisario's intervention on the honeymoon was one more hard fact of life that Angus Ogilvy now had to accept. Try as he might to insist that he was only a businessman, he was married to a Princess of the

Realm and like it or not there would be consequences. After a relaxing few days in Scotland the couple flew on to Spain as guests of the Duke of Alba and stayed in his private holiday villa near Marbella on the Mediterranean. Once again the problem of Press intrusion arose, one photographer hiding in a tree and refusing to leave even when police began chopping down the tree. Sensing a story, other local photographers appeared, until at one point the Princess was frightened to step outside the door. As in earlier years, when for example she had been hounded by a photographer in Venice and to Princess Marina's disgust had agreed to pose for him, Alexandra felt that the simplest solution would be to let them take the photographs they wanted and then they would go away. The theory worked. Angus told a group of photographers that they could take pictures when they went shopping. They did not actually agree to pose, but the cameramen knew that the seemingly off-guard shots sold the best anyway. Out of all the pictures taken that May, the most popular of all was one taken of Alexandra picking a four-leafed clover. This innocent scene was shot by Raymond Bellisario.

Although photographers were a minor irritation, one incident was to have repercussions throughout their married life. Swimming in the Mediterranean sea, Angus was hit by a speedboat. Whilst he did not appear to be seriously injured, the force of the blow exacerbated the back injury he had sustained as a skiing instructor in the Army when in Austria – which had also necessitated the removal of his kneecap and subsequent insertion of an artificial patella. It was to result in a lifetime of pain.

At the end of May the couple left Spain and returned to London, planning to spend a few days at Angus's house in Culross Street while Thatched House Lodge was made ready for them to take up residence in the second week of June. First they called in to Kensington Palace to see Princess Marina and collect Alexandra's belongings. It was there that the telephone call came to tell them that a fire had broken out in their temporary home. It was an unwelcome start to married life.

8

The Private Side

Princess Alexandra gently shook her head. The decision was final, but it was a question that the Queen had to ask. Her Majesty took her favourite cousin quietly to one side and asked her if she would like her husband to receive a title, but Alexandra was adamant. He already warranted the prefix 'Honourable' as the son of an Earl and Angus saw no reason to accept a peerage for no better reason than that he had married a Princess. Some twenty-five years were to pass before he agreed to a Knighthood, and only then because it was given in recognition of his long years of service with Cancer Research, the British Rheumatism and Arthritis Association, and similar worthy causes.

At Kensington Palace, Princess Marina had contemplated her son-in-law's position. Should he receive a Dukedom, like Prince Philip, or an Earldom, like Antony Armstrong-Jones? Even the Press jokingly speculated. 'Lord Ben Nevis? Count Killiecrankie?' asked the *Evening Standard*. It shocked Marina that not only had Angus refused a title but Princess Alexandra was to take the unprecedented step of including 'Mrs' in her title. It was a determined bid on her part to show that being the wife of Angus Ogilvy was as important to her as being royal. In 1960 Princess Margaret had equally married a commoner, but did not even consider being 'Mrs Jones'. It was not until her husband's elevation to the peerage in November 1961 that she began using 'Countess of Snowdon' as a suffix. Unlike Alexandra, Margaret found 'Mrs' incongruous with 'Princess'.

Marriage and the move to Thatched House Lodge in June 1963

meant independence for Alexandra. No longer was she under the watchful eye of her mother. She was also in control of her own small retinue of staff for the first time. Marjory Dawson, her maid, naturally remained with her, but she had to employ new people to cook and clean for them, plus gardeners to tend their four acres of land. As ordinary as Alexandra seemed, and indeed tried to be, any home she had lived in was always staffed. It was a way of life to her. Even on her honeymoon, while at Birkhall she had a 'reduced' staff of eight. From Kensington Palace went two footmen and two maids, plus four resident staff. For royalty this meant 'being alone'; they had what was considered to be the minimum to cater for their needs. At the time of the Ogilvys' wedding in 1963 women's magazines were still writing reverently about the Royal Family, one declaring in tones of admiration that Princess Alexandra, if necessary, could actually wash and set her own hair, even applying her own make-up. Surely this cannot have been very sensational to discover. What magazines did not reveal was how royal staff (they are never called servants) at Kensington Palace would run baths for the Princes and Princesses, lay out the towels, put soap solution on to a sponge (face flannels were not used), take the top off the toothpaste (some royals even expecting the paste to be squeezed on to the brush), then put out clothes for the royal personage to step into. Although Princess Alexandra was perhaps better equipped to look after herself than some members of her family, she had nevertheless been brought up to look upon this royal way of life as normal. She had the personality to make staff feel appreciated, but like Princess Marina she expected high standards. If anyone neglected their duty or failed in the job they were employed to do, Alexandra gently but very firmly put them in their place. Her benevolent character meant that once she had told someone off, it was forgotten on her part and never mentioned again. Angus, it is said, was, and is, less forgiving. He treats their staff fairly, but cannot abide idleness.

Alexandra derived great pleasure from turning Thatched House Lodge into a home. From the outside the building is unimpressive, giving the impression of a once smaller house with a wing added on to each side to elongate it. Its panelled Georgian windows with wooden shutters were seemingly the only feature. Inside there are many original features. An oak-beamed entrance hall has a very impressive sweeping staircase. On the ground floor is a large drawing room, a small intimate family sitting room, a library, panelled dining room, kitchen, offices and a bright conservatory. The rooms are light and airy, with large full-length windows, several rooms have French windows that open out onto the lawns. What was originally a squash court is now a private cinema and there is a heated indoor swimming pool. When they first bought the house there were six bedrooms on the first floor, four of them with bathrooms, those on the west side of the house being used as a guest wing. Angus added dressing rooms to some of the bedrooms and eventually a nursery was created. On the top floor, in the attic area, were staff bedrooms, plus the house had some nearby cottages which proved to be suitable for staff. In addition there were garages and stables.

As the Princess stood at the bay window of their large first-floor bedroom, she looked out over rolling parklands and wooded country-side, yet the house is only some seven miles from London. Richmond Park is an area of 2,469 acres, administered by the Crown as a royal park, and is noted for its herds of fallow and red deer. Near Thatched House Lodge is a small thatched summer house and it is from this that the Lodge takes its name. Also in the park is White Lodge, once the home of a great-grandmother of Princess Alexandra's, Princess Mary of Cambridge (a granddaughter of George III). More impressive than Thatched House Lodge, it is faced with white Portland stone, hence its name. The red brick gateway of Henry VII's Palace of 1498, of even greater historical significance, still remains. Princess Alexandra was surrounded by reminders of her royal background. In White Lodge her Uncle David had been born (Edward VIII, later Duke of Windsor). If she was out walking she could follow 'Queen's Ride', an avenue named after Queen Caroline, wife of George II. There was no escape.

The first year of marriage was not the easiest for Alexandra. The first half of the year had meant coping with increased public attention and greater media intrusion than she had experienced before. She faced the task of establishing her first home, and Thatched House Lodge was not small by general newly-wed standards, plus it was necessary to adapt to the new role of employer. Mistress of a retinue of staff. She also faced the testing time that every couple experience of learning to live with someone else. Inevitably it takes time to adapt. Then, scarcely three months after the wedding, in July 1963 Alexandra discovered that she was expecting her first child. In line with all royal mothers to be at this time, she withdrew from public engagements.

Whilst Princess Marina and the rest of the Royal Family were delighted at the news, Alexandra was happier still when she discovered that her sister-in-law, the Duchess of Kent, the Queen and Princess Margaret were all pregnant at the same time. As each withdrew temporarily from public life and each steadily gained weight, they collectively became a royal support group. Princess Alexandra was the only one of the ~~three~~ *four* experiencing the process for the first time and it must have been a comfort to have advice always on hand. That Christmas, at Sandringham, Prince Philip complained that it was like an anti-natal clinic and there was much laughter when all met in a corridor. 'To the four little strangers we know are present!' came the toast over Christmas dinner.

In many ways it was a year of intrusions into Alexandra's once carefree life. Her husband and child by choice, the staff out of necessity, photographers by sheer force. Equally engagements which she so enjoyed were forbidden. A fanatical admirer declared he was in love with her and threatened to kill Angus. 'If someone blows you up, they blow you up,' Angus said resignedly, but it was of no comfort to his pregnant wife. Her emotions already in a turmoil through the physical changes in her body, the greatest distress came one evening in November.

Alexandra and Angus were having a quiet dinner on the ground floor, when a man came through the trees and across the lawn at the back of the house. Using the ivy cladding on the walls and a drain-pipe he managed to climb in through a bathroom window. It was a foggy night and in the secluded park security was almost non-existent. Certainly there were no burglar alarms at this time. No one knows quite how long the intruder was in the house, although it is believed that he may have searched the first floor. Whether or not he knew the layout of the house, he found Princess Alexandra's bedroom. The disturbing fact was that had he been a terrorist, or indeed the maniac intent on killing Angus, Alexandra could have been murdered or held hostage in her own home. It was after dinner when the Princess went into the bedroom and in the dining room below Angus heard his wife's petrified screams. On opening the door she had found the man standing over her jewellery case, in his gloved hands the sparkle of diamonds, the glint of gold. Within seconds he was through the window and vanished into the darkness.

Running upstairs, Angus found Alexandra in a state of shock. At six months pregnant there were concerns over the baby. Some twelve items of jewellery had been stolen from the dressing table and jewel case. The items were not only of substantial monetary worth, but they were of greater sentimental value. A ruby and diamond brooch that had been a gift from Marina's sister Olga; a gold watch inscribed 'From A to A' that Alexandra had given Angus when they married; some ruby studded cuff links that Princess Marina had given to Angus at the same time and a gold cigarette case with an inscription from the Queen and Prince Philip. Also three pearl necklaces, two diamond bracelets, pearl and diamond earrings – all irreplaceable. When Coppins had been burgled years earlier Alexandra had laughed because only a police whistle that Princess Marina kept beside her bed had gone, but this was a different matter altogether.

Her home felt sullied and she developed a fear of being alone. Alexandra always had an uneasy sense of what might have happened. If it had occurred just two days later Angus would have been away in Spain on a business trip. Although the police arrived within minutes there was little that could be done at the time, other than to advise on security for the future and to arrange greater protection for the Princess. Already Alexandra had restrictions on her life through being royal and saw this as a further erosion of her freedom. The relaxed atmosphere that she had experienced at Thatched House Lodge for five brief months had ended. Within days the installation of a sophisticated security system had begun. The Royal Parks Constabulary, responsible for policing the area, kept a closer eye on Thatched House Lodge and Princess Alexandra's comings and goings.

Several weeks later some of the stones from Princess Alexandra's jewellery began to appear on the market and a man was charged with receiving. Some of the items were recovered as a result, but the original burglar was never found. Months later when Alexandra had put the episode from her mind, further pieces were recovered in Sussex including Angus's cigarette case.

Not wishing to remain at Thatched House Lodge on her own, Princess Alexandra persuaded Angus to take her with him on his Spanish business trip. She was only pregnant, not ill, she insisted and a short break would be beneficial. Angus agreed and the couple flew on an economy flight to Madrid, booked under the names 'Mr and Mrs Butler'. On private visits Alexandra frequently changed her name. When she used to fly to Ireland to be with Lady Moyra Hamilton's family she went as 'Miss Kirby', and later when the Ogilvys went on a private holiday to Portugal it was as 'Mr and Mrs Kent'. On this occasion security was extremely tight and she was protected by the Spanish Civil Guard. Not only did this prevent photographers from getting shots of the now heavily-pregnant Princess, but it led on one occasion to Angus being arrested by the police when mistaken for an over zealous journalist. Although they laughed about it afterwards, Alexandra had to formally identify her husband before police would agree to release him.

Returning to England, in the weeks preceding the birth, Alexandra's rebellious streak reared its head again and she kicked back at the suffocating security that now surrounded her. Instead of being visited by her hairdresser she went personally to the salon. She and Angus went out to restaurants and were once seen queuing in a public self-service coffee bar. There were times also when Alexandra's cravings for fish and chips had to be satisfied, and it was not unknown for her to eat them out of newspaper. Once, when visiting a ship, Princess Anne was given fish and chips and revealed 'we never get these at the Palace'. Was Alexandra's taste for fish and chips as much a statement about royal restrictions – just as Princess Marina would order a fried supper of bacon, eggs and kidneys, only when she was alone at Kensington Palace? Or did the taste take her back to those pre-married days when a fish supper at Lyons Corner House, with Angus, was possible unrecognized, unprotected?

In keeping with Alexandra's run of bad luck, her baby due on 16 February 1964 was two weeks overdue. Not only that, being Leap Year, her son was born on 29 February. 'It's bad enough me having a birthday on Christmas Day,' she wailed. 'I didn't want my poor child only to have birthdays every four years!' The nine-pound-six-ounce baby was born in the thirteenth hour that Saturday and was thirteenth in line to the throne. Alexandra laughed about it being unlucky as she toasted his health with the Thatched House Lodge staff.

As an Ogilvy the boy was given sound Scottish names – James Robert Bruce – and was christened at Buckingham Palace on 11 May, by which time the arrival of Prince Edward had pushed him down to fourteenth in line of succession. Although Alexandra was an expert with babies following her training at Great Ormond Street hospital, in the royal tradition a nanny was employed to undertake the bulk of the work. Miss Olive Rattle joined the Ogilvy staff and took over the newly-created nursery and was given a bedsitting room of her own. The arrival of a nanny caused consternation in many an aristocratic household. They frequently caused resentment by seemingly behaving as though they were above the resident staff and on a level with their employers. Once established, they generally knew that the mistress of the house relied on them and that a change of nanny would be bad for the child and therefore considered themselves to be indispensable. Nanny Macphearson, employed by the Duke of Kent at Coppins to look after the Earl of St Andrews, was particularly unpopular. Fully aware of this, Princess Alexandra opted for the 'firm but fair' Nanny Rattle who came to her on the recommendation of a friend. Even so, she made her demands. The nursery was beautifully equipped, she said, *but* it lacked a rocking chair. So essential for a nanny to rock a baby to sleep, she urged. She hated to be any trouble ... Angus purchased a rocking chair that same day.

Mother and baby were both doing well and Alexandra was anxious to get back to the public engagements which had been denied her since 28 July in the previous year. The day before the christening she attended the 250th Anniversary celebrations of St Anne's Church in Kew, just a short distance from Richmond Park. Gifts for the baby came from the countries that the Princess had visited, koala bears from Australia, silk baby clothes from Thailand, and although the British Press latched on to the Leap Year birth, James was overshadowed by his cousins born in the succeeding weeks. Prince Edward was born on 10 March, Lady Helen Windsor (to the Duke and Duchess of Kent) on 28 April, then Lady Sarah Armstrong-Jones on 1 May. Just as Princess Alexandra had to celebrate her birthday amid the Royal Family's Christmas celebrations her son was to find his milestone birthdays celebrated with

110

his cousins. They all came of age within weeks of each other and so one major family party was given. In the years that James was eighteen and twenty-one, not being Leap Years he strictly had no birthday at all.

Now juggling all aspects of her life as wife, mother and Princess, it was not easy. From the time of their marriage Alexandra and Angus had always had breakfast together. As he drove into central London each day this frequently meant an early start, and often if she had attended an official dinner on the previous evening they would have gone to bed late. Angus resigned some of his directorships to cut down the heavy work schedule, retaining those with the Drayton Group, but this consequently led to an inevitable reduction in salary which they could ill afford. Although the Queen gave Alexandra an allowance out of her own Civil List to cover official expenses, it did not stretch to such items as the Princess's wardrobe for public appearances, and barely covered the costs involved ranging from postage (which the Princess has to pay herself, unlike the Queen whose letters can carry the royal cipher and no stamp) and travel. Whilst Angus and Alexandra enjoyed their Jaguar for private use, it was not suitable for a member of the Royal Family to arrive in at an official function. Besides private staff to run Thatched House Lodge – cook, butler/valet, Alexandra's personal maid, resident housekeeper, nanny, housemaids, gardeners, chauffeur, and odd-job man – she needed a private secretary, a lady-in-waiting and when necessary extra ladies-in-waiting and equerries. Angus had to subsidize Alexandra to keep her in the style of a Princess, which had been one of his concerns before they married. He began working longer hours and was determined also to keep his commitments with the charities he supported. As those marrying royalty all discover, the practicalities of reconciling a private and public life are seemingly impossible. The combination of financial worries, the pressures of work and almost constant back pain proved almost too much and Angus was eventually admitted to St Mary's Hospital, Paddington, and was treated for nervous exhaustion. When they did finally manage to fit in their first holiday since James was born, Princess Alexandra was called back to England. At the end of January Sir Winston Churchill, former Prime Minister, had died and she was required at the State funeral in St Paul's Cathedral. Once again her public life had to take priority, and even when the holiday was resumed she had to fly to Belfast for one day from their Swiss resort to launch a ship. Two months later her Aunt Mary, the Princess Royal, died, and private grief became public, again simply because Alexandra was royal.

Although from the outset Angus Ogilvy had made it clear that he would not undertake any royal duties himself, just as Captain Mark Phillips later decided to keep in the background, he always seemed to be measured against Princess Margaret's husband who chose to have a public life. Whilst Lord Snowdon was content to accompany his wife on engagements and fulfil his own diary of public appearances, but still maintain a private career as a photographer, the public found it difficult to accept Angus Ogilvy's decision. Part of the problem occurred because he occasionally was seen with Princess Alexandra officially, perhaps spending just one day at Ascot while she went on each of the four days; often he would be her escort if her engagement was a theatrical event or cinema visit. When he was then later missing, questions were raised. It was difficult for him to stay out of the picture totally. Likewise, on the birth of James there was criticism from certain quarters that Angus's refusal of a title had made his son a commoner. Princess Margaret's children were titled, even the children of Alexandra's brother were Lords and Ladies. Did this not seem unfair on James, people asked. Again, Alexandra insisted that like her husband, her children would not follow her lifestyle. Indeed, in 1987 when I wanted to interview James Ogilvy for a book he replied that it was 'with regret' that he could not comply because he would 'never be in a position to undertake official duties' and was trying to formulate his career 'without any publicity'.*

By this time he was well aware that if he had a title it would be an added burden, not a help. Princess Anne said of her own children that they stood a 'marginally better chance in life as plain Mister and Miss Phillips'.

For Princess Alexandra there was a division of loyalties, and although she intended always to place her children first, there were inevitably times when royal duties took priority. When the Ogilvy children were of school age the Princess kept the holidays free to be with them, but

* Private letter 19 January 1987.

this was not always possible. 'The time is coming shortly when if we don't see more of our children, we're going to pay the price at the other end, when they're older,' said Angus in an interview. 'But it's very difficult. You decide to spend an evening with the children, but then someone rings up and says "Will you please come to a film premiere? If you come it will help us raise another £1,500 and this could help 300 spastics." Well, who are more important, 300 spastics or your own children?'*

One exception Angus Ogilvy was to make to his rule of non-involvement with royal duties was that he agreed to accompany Princess Alexandra on overseas tours – always at his own expense. Not only did this provide him with an opportunity to arrange business meetings of his own in the countries that they visited, but it avoided the need for long separations from his wife. Out of necessity overseas tours are always of several days' and often weeks' duration. James would always remain at Thatched House Lodge with Nanny Rattle. In the Sixties it was not even considered that babies might be included on the tour and when the Queen and Prince Philip had earlier travelled throughout the Commonwealth they did not actually see their children for six months.

In September 1965 Alexandra and Angus went to Japan, Hong Kong, Tehran, Amman, and on a few days' private holiday with King Hussein of Jordan went sight-seeing in Jerusalem and Bethlehem. The Princess renewed her acquaintance with Emperor Hirohito and his family and toured the British Exhibition in Tokyo, which no doubt was advantageous to Angus as a British businessman with an interest in overseas trade. In 1967 they undertook extensive tours of Hong Kong and Burma, followed by one of America and Canada, also fitting in a private visit to Australia. History repeated itself once again when Princess Alexandra like her father before her was tentatively offered the Governor-Generalship of Australia. Once again there was an opportunity for Canberra to become her home. She declined the offer, not only because her husband's career was now firmly established in England, but because the Queen also needed her cousin to fulfil her duties in her homeland. If ever the Queen was indisposed, or Prince Philip, and on one occasion Princess Marina, it was Alexandra who

* Quoted in *The Kents* by Audrey Whiting (Hutchinson, 1985).

was called in to deputize. The Royal Family might well have increased in size but none of the recent additions were of any use on the round of royal duties and Alexandra was still very much in demand. 'It was such a relief when Princess Alexandra grew up and was able to help us,' Princess Margaret told author Andrew Duncan in an interview.★

It was after returning from Japan that Princess Alexandra discovered that she was expecting their second child, which was born on Sunday 31 July, 1966, weighing in at seven-pounds-eight-ounces. As with the arrival of James two years earlier, Angus was present throughout the birth. Although accepted now, it was much less common then. The baby was christened two months later in the Chapel Royal of St James's Palace and given the names Marina Victoria Alexandra. Marina after her grandmother, Victoria in honour of her great-great-great-grandmother Queen Victoria, and Alexandra because of her mother and great-great-grandmother Queen Alexandra. The Ogilvy family was now complete.

Princess Alexandra had a specific approach to bringing up her children. She wanted them to be fully aware of their royal background but neither to take it for granted nor take advantage of it. Holidays at Balmoral, Sandringham and Windsor Castle were a privilege to be enjoyed and appreciated, but were nothing more than that, just holidays. They were to learn to keep both feet firmly on the ground and ultimately they would have to make their own way in life, which would be influenced neither by titles nor royal connections. What Angus and Alexandra could do, however, was give the children a firm foundation on which to build their lives.

At Buckingham Palace the Queen had employed Miss Peebles – who had once taught Prince Michael at Coppins – to educate her children. Joining Prince Edward in the schoolroom in 1969 was to be Princess Margaret's daughter, Lady Sarah Armstrong-Jones, and it was decided that young James Ogilvy should join them. She taught them English, mathematics and geography using the same traditional methods that a governess had applied on Alexandra twenty years earlier. The advantage for James over his mother was that in the small schoolroom on the top floor of Buckingham Palace looking out over The Mall, he was not alone in his studies.

★ *The Reality of Monarchy* by Andrew Duncan (Heinemann, 1970).

Princess Anne, who had been taught by 'Mispy', revealed that she could not wait to get away to Benenden because private tutorage 'requires an awful lot of concentration'. James had the business brain of his father and excelled in arithmetic, which was never Alexandra's strongest subject. Like his mother, however, he was keen on music and learned to play the piano, and like Princess Marina had an artistic flair. Marina had been taught to paint when very young and continued to paint and sketch throughout her life. Particularly good at portraits, many of Marina's works had gone on public display including drawings of Alexandra and paintings of her husband. Like his mother, James became particularly keen on photography.

Since the time when Princess Alexandra had paved the way, in the Seventies it was accepted as normal that royal children should go to school and after being educated in the basics both Prince Edward and James Ogilvy went to Gibbs preparatory school in Kensington, not far from the Palace, then on to Heatherdown at Ascot, near Windsor. While Prince Edward went on to Gordonstoun and Jesus College, Cambridge, James was sent to Eton before gaining a place at St Andrews University in Scotland. Although James ended up with thirteen 'O' levels, three 'A' levels and a Bachelor of Arts degree, he took his parents' advice to heart about being down-to-earth and went to great lengths to experience a non-royal life.

Between Eton and going to university he embarked on a series of widely differing jobs, ranging from working in a bottle plant where he screwed the tops on bottles to lorry driving and bricklaying. Having won a prize for his photography while at Eton he later became a photographic assistant for a time to Geoffrey Shackerley (who not surprisingly took the official photographs at James's wedding in 1988) before deciding to set up his own magazine. Having no capital of his own he borrowed money from his father, on the proviso that it was paid back. The magazine *Freeway* was relatively successful, certainly not making a loss and Angus received his money back. It was not, however, the full-time career Angus had wished for his son and whether through persuasion or his own decision, James ceased publication before the magazine had taken off, at least with the satisfaction that he had made a success of it.

If James Ogilvy inherited any qualities from his parents it was certainly a seemingly endless supply of energy. The sheer variety of jobs he tried in a relatively short space of time display a craving for new experience. Were the pressures on him so great that he wanted to prove he could make a successful career for himself, or did he see the golden cage that surrounded his parents' lives binding them up in protocol so that he wanted to remove himself as far away as possible from the royal way of life?

In 1983 James Ogilvy briefly joined the Army, choosing the Scots Guards, his father's former regiment, and became a second lieutenant. He took only a short commission for the sake of experience, it was not to become a career. After being stationed in Hong Kong, one of Princess Alexandra's favourite countries, where he spent some of the time on patrol in the jungle, instead of returning straight to England, he used the opportunity to earn some extra money by taking various jobs on the way back. Princess Alexandra greatly admired her son's courage, neither of her children ever suffering through lack of confidence.

At two years younger than James, Princess Alexandra's daughter Marina is equally adventurous. Although less academically qualified, leaving St Mary's Convent School in Wantage with no 'A' levels, she surprised her family by joining 'Operation Raleigh' in April 1985. She shared her brother's iron determination and raised the necessary £2,800 herself to join the expedition by working as a sales assistant in Harvey Nichols department store for six months. The 'Operation Raleigh' expedition was Marina's own choice. 'I felt trapped and very low,' she told author Douglas Keay as her reason for going. She trained for twelve hours a day at RAF Gulford in Wiltshire and joined thirty other people on the community project at an island off the coast of Honduras, helped build a school in the jungle and undertook underwater marine surveys. In 1987 she did a counselling course to help young drug addicts and took a job in Scotland at the Outward Bound School in Wester Ross, instructing underprivileged children from inner cities on adventure holidays.

In the nursery at Thatched House Lodge in the mid Sixties, a cosy protected world where the children were nurtured, rode ponies in Richmond Park, took tea with Nanny in her starched apron and adopted the genteel manners expected of royal children, Princess Alexandra could have no inkling of the path that lay ahead for her son and daughter. Certainly not red-carpeted as her own world had been and a path from which at times they were to deviate. Princess Alexandra was to face the fact that both James and Marina would live openly with their partners before they married, which would never have been accepted had Alexandra and Angus wanted to cohabit, and that Marina would announce her pregnancy before her wedding. Theirs was to be a very different world. In the distant future lay a bizarre episode in which Marina would openly accuse her parents of trying to trick her into an abortion.

It was a very united Ogilvy family who posed for the late Norman Parkinson, grouped under an umbrella in what appears to be falling rain, but was in fact a hosepipe being squirted at them for effect. Theirs was the new relaxed face of royalty, in a decade that would culminate in the then revolutionary film *Royal Family* in which the emphasis was on the human side of the monarchy. For the first time the general public were able to see the Windsor Castle Christmas celebrations, Alexandra with a trolley of Christmas gifts, looking very nurse-like in a white short-sleeved dress, and Angus playing with James and Marina in toy pedal cars. One sequence of the film even showed James and Prince Edward, then five, learning to read with Miss Peebles in the Palace schoolroom. Inevitably Princess Alexandra was also seen in the trappings of royalty, wearing full evening dress and diamond tiara at a diplomatic reception in a more recognizable public guise. Despite the outward picture of contentment that the Ogilvy family displayed, there were events in their private lives as the Sixties drew to a close that were to have a traumatic effect on Princess Alexandra's secure world. First a private grief, followed by a public scandal that threatened their future.

On 18 July, 1968, Princess Alexandra was informed that her mother Princess Marina had fallen and hurt her knee and was to be admitted to hospital. Her left leg had always been weak and as she grew older it occasionally gave way, but now it required treatment and she was to be kept in hospital under observation for three days. By this stage in her life the doctors certainly knew the cause of Marina's gradual deterioration – an inoperable brain tumour that would prove fatal. It is said that they gave her six months to live, but Marina was never told. Princess Alexandra and her brothers were and it was an unbearable burden that they had to live with. Princess Marina put her problems down to old age.

'Poor little thing,' she said of her left leg. 'It hasn't done too badly. After all, it has supported me for sixty years,' and in two speeches that summer she made references to the fears she had of old age and the loss of independence that this would lead to. She had, nevertheless, continued with a busy schedule of engagements, which included her favourite event of the year, Wimbledon fortnight, which she never missed as President of the All-England Lawn Tennis Association (a position now held by Alexandra's brother the present Duke of Kent). Whil Marina was in hospital, Alexandra fulfilled the one engagement in her mother's diary, a visit to the Frimley and Camberley Cadet Corps.

It was a warm summer and spending time out in the garden of Kensington Palace helped Princess Marina to recover, although she cancelled a planned holiday in Florence with her sister Princess Olga. It was considered that the journey would be too exhausting, the air pressure when flying might aggravate her leg condition. More likely also is the fact that her doctors wanted her to remain in London in case anything should happen. The last time she had been seen in public was actually at Wimbledon presenting the ladies' singles trophy to Billie Jean King, who had just won it for the third year running. The Challenge Cup for the Men's Singles Championship had been won by Rod Laver, one of Marina's favourite players. She had been President for twenty-five years, seldom attended less than ten out of the twelve days in each Championship meeting, and always tried to arrive before play commenced. If not she would hide behind the scenes and not enter the Royal Box until the players changed ends, never wishing to disrupt play, and would stay until the end no matter how late the day's games finished. Had she known that this would be her last official engagement, few doubted that it was one she would have been proud to finish on.

Sunday 25 August marked the twenty-sixth anniversary of the Duke of Kent's fatal plane crash and Princess Marina went to a service that morning at St Mary Abbots Church to say a prayer for her late husband. Alexandra and Angus joined Marina at Kensington Palace for a quiet family lunch, and Alexandra apparently commented on how well her mother looked and particularly youthful for her age. Later in the afternoon they drove home to Richmond and Princess Marina sat in the garden with a friend and did a crossword in the Sunday newspaper, as she did each week. Word games always appealed to her and she particularly enjoyed playing Scrabble. In the early evening she watched a television programme in which Malcolm Muggeridge appeared – who had not always been flattering about the Royal Family – then bathed and had her supper on a tray, feeling too tired to get dressed again.

It was on going up to bed that her left leg gave way and she fell on the stairs. She insisted that she was all right and her staff assisted her up to the elegant bedroom suite with its white and gilt furniture, chintz fabrics and crimson carpet. When her maid woke her up with a tray of tea the following day, Princess Marina decided not to get up. 'I feel tired. I think I will go back to sleep,' she said.

Later that morning Princess Alexandra received a telephone call from Philip Hay, Marina's Private Secretary, to say that her mother had lapsed into a deep coma. As she was driven speedily to Kensington Palace, Alexandra must have known that this was the end. Possibly doctors had warned her that this was how it would be. At Kensington Palace Alexandra telephoned Marina's sister, Princess Olga, who flew immediately from Italy, arriving that Monday evening. The Duke of Kent and Prince Michael were also brought to the Palace. Through the night they sat at the bedside until the following morning when Princess Marina passed away without having regained consciousness. For one fleeting moment she opened her eyes and appeared to sense that her family were with her.

The greatest single influence in Princess Alexandra's life had gone. Her one consolation was that their last day together had been a happy relaxed occasion. A fond memory to look back on. A family friend who had also been there that day later said that being the anniversary of Prince George's death that very day, he had been foremost in their minds and seemed to be with them in spirit. As if he had come to fetch Marina, she said.

Alexandra took the loss badly. Princess Marina had been a dominant figure and they may always not have seen eye to eye. Even in the presence of strangers she would scold her daughter, and favoured royal photographer Cecil Beaton revealed in his diaries that while taking pictures at the Coronation, Marina had constantly nagged her daughter.

'Stay still, Alexandra ... Oh, you've ruined that picture now, Alexandra.' Yet, her passing left a void in Alexandra's life. As she had grown older Princess Marina had become like a sister to her and their relationship was at its best. Marina was by this time proud of her daughter, the way she looked, the manner in which she carried out her duties, the popularity she had brought the Royal Family, the stability she had achieved in her marriage at a time when they were all conscious that Princess Margaret's was on the verge of going disastrously wrong.

'I am indeed overwhelmed with pride about Alexandra possessing the wonderful gift of spreading happiness around her,' Princess Marina had said after Alexandra's highly successful tour of Australia in 1959. 'It has made her tour something greater than a triumph, and is very moving for me.' She knew that if Princess Alexandra was hailed as a success then it was a credit to her own abilities as a royal mother.

On 29 August, the anniversary of his own funeral, the late Duke of Kent's coffin was taken from the vaults of St George's Chapel, Windsor, where Marina had visited it so often, and taken to its now final resting place in the Royal Mausoleum at Frogmore. The following day Princess Marina, Duchess of Kent, was buried beside her husband. It was a short, private funeral service conducted by Dr Michael Ramsey, the Archbishop of Canterbury, who had married Alexandra and Angus in happier times. Also there was a representative of the Greek Orthodox Church from Marina's native land. Amongst the royal mourners was Princess Alexandra's uncle, the Duke of Windsor, whose abdication just two weeks before she was born had so profoundly affected the future of the Royal Family and, indirectly, the course of her life. Had he remained King, there would have been less responsibility for the then Duke and Duchess of York who would have been free to fulfil general royal engagements along with the Gloucesters and Kents. There would have been room for Princess Elizabeth and Princess Margaret to begin royal duty, but the demand might well not have been great enough for Princess Alexandra to be needed. She might well have married and lived a life of obscurity. As it was, the abdication caused a shortage of working royals and Alexandra was called into service.

Such thoughts were forgotten at the moving funeral service. Princess Marina had made her peace with her brother-in-law in 1965, and from that time until his death in 1972 Princess Alexandra always visited her uncle whenever she was in Paris. Whether her royal upbringing ever allowed her to accept the former Mrs Simpson as Duchess of Windsor, however, is another matter. When she sent them Christmas cards she would always write them 'To Uncle David and Wallace', misspelling 'Wallis' and certainly never calling her 'Aunt'. Surely Alexandra must have known the correct spelling, so was it a deliberate error, a statement of disapproval? At Marina's funeral the Duke sat behind the Queen, tears in his eyes, possibly his brother also in his mind. His funeral in 1942 had been too close to the abdication for the former Edward VIII to attend. His homage to Marina was certainly also out of respect for his late brother. In her autobiography, published in 1956, the Duchess of Windsor wrote that the Duke of Kent was her husband's 'favourite brother'. She expressed a wish that his tragic death might have caused a 'softening of hearts' amongst the Royal Family, but it was not to be.

On Princess Marina's coffin were two wreaths. One from Princess Olga in blue and white, the national colours of Greece, and a larger tribute in pink, yellow and red roses from Princess Alexandra and her brothers. Eight weeks later Alexandra had to face the further ordeal of a larger Memorial Service in Westminster Abbey as a Thanksgiving for Princess Marina's life. As it was televised, Alexandra had to keep her private emotions under control – 'You are a Princess,' her mother would have reminded her – and not give in to grief. Looking around the congregation she saw relations from the royal houses of Greece, Denmark, Russia, Yugoslavia, Norway and Britain; together they symbolized Alexandra's background.

The decade that had begun so well for Alexandra was ending unhappily. Shortly before Princess Marina's death, a planned visit to the Independence celebrations of Mauritius in the Indian Ocean had to suddenly be postponed due to political unrest. A state of emergency had been declared there and Princess Alexandra's life had been threatened. Alexandra was upset as she had never faced hostility of this kind. Mauritius was to remain part of the British Commonwealth and she wanted to unite the country but militants saw her as a symbol of colonialism. In 1969 she and Angus made the planned visit, albeit twelve months late, but still faced animosity. There were riots and protest marches, demonstrators waving placards at her saying 'Alexandra Go Home'. Security had to be strict for fear of an attack, which was alien to a Princess known for her informality and spontaneity.

Also in 1969 Angus not only suffered from ill health, including gastric problems, but encountered the first of a series of problems with the Lonrho company for which he worked. It was in 1961, two years before his marriage to Princess Alexandra, that he had first become involved with Lonrho, having been placed on the board by the financier Harley Drayton. His career in the City had actually begun as a humble clerk earning £3 a week, when at a family house party Angus was expounding his views about finance and out of the blue one of the guests, a Colonel Robert Adeane, offered him a job. Joining the Drayton Group, Angus's income increased dramatically overnight. Because he had once worked as a cattle-rancher in Rhodesia, when business tycoon 'Tiny' Rowland merged his interests with the London and Rhodesian Mining and Land Company (hence the name Lonrho from London and Rhodesia) in 1961, Angus seemed the perfect person to go out to Rhodesia and make something of the company.

Eventually Tiny Rowland's Lonrho empire was worth £4 billion and had over 800 companies in eighty-two different countries, but in 1969 there were problems in Rhodesia with sanctions. Five years earlier Ian Smith had become Prime Minister and on 11 November 1965 declared Rhodesia an independent state because he was opposed to sharing power with the African majority. This was condemned by the United Nations and the British Government imposed trade restrictions and an oil embargo, and a naval blockade was set up to prevent oil getting through. As Lonrho was trading in Rhodesia there were rumours that they were breaking sanctions and Angus Ogilvy was implicated. It is said that the then Secretary of the Cabinet, Burke Trend, suggested that Angus should resign. As far as Angus was concerned he had done nothing wrong and resignation would be tantamount to pleading guilty. He decided to remain with the company, but an eventual long drawn out enquiry by the Department of Trade, during which time both Angus and Alexandra had suffered with the strain of uncertainty, said in its report that Angus Ogilvy had been 'negligent in his duties' and he was severely criticized. 'A weak man,' was the phrase used to describe him.

In the report Angus found fifty-eight errors of fact and wild accusations based on assumption, but there was nothing he could do to gain recompense for the report was 'protected by legal privilege'. He might have been able to have ridden the storm and survived the scandal from a career point of view had it not been for the fact that his wife was royal. He could not cause the Queen embarrassment. As it was the whole episode received far more publicity than it would have done for any other company director quite simply because he was Princess Alexandra's husband. After the report in 1976 Angus took what he considered to be the only honourable course of action and resigned from all his directorships. Within weeks he was admitted to King Edward VII Hospital, officially suffering from pneumonia but no doubt the years of the 'Lonrho affair' hanging over his head had exacerbated his condition. Almost two more years were to pass before in 1978 the Director of Public Prosecutions exonerated Angus completely, but it was little comfort to Angus, whose income had suddenly dropped from an estimated £90,000 a year to £9,000. A piece of land that he and Alexandra owned in Perthshire, on which they had intended to build their own country retreat, had to be sold to raise capital.

It was more worrying for Princess Alexandra that Thatched House Lodge and their small staff would be impossible to keep. Once again the Kents looked like being tagged the poor relations, especially as in 1974 her brother had been forced to sell Coppins where they both had grown up because the running costs were too great. Both were thankful that Princess Marina was no longer alive to witness the situation. Princess Alexandra coped in the only way she knew, by throwing herself into her work.

$\rightarrow\!\!\!\rightarrow\!\!\!\rightarrow\!\!\!\rightarrow$ 9 $\leftarrow\!\!\!\leftarrow\!\!\!\leftarrow\!\!\!\leftarrow$

Princess Understanding

Princess Alexandra ducked as a large wooden chair was thrown fifteen feet with great force, just missing her by inches. A visit to the South East London Juvenile Court was proving perilous as a boy just sentenced to Wormwood Scrubs for theft vented his anger on the royal observer. Unnerved but unharmed, it was just another experience in Princess Alexandra's varied working life that has not always gone as smoothly as she would like.

As mentioned in chapter four, Alexandra's first British tour (of Lancashire in 1953 with Princess Marina) had not been an outstanding success, and although today she jokes that she ought to be called Helen of Troy because 'I must have launched a thousand ships', she still shudders at the thought of her first ship launch which was an unmitigated disaster. To the observer a ship launch seems the easiest thing in the world. You make a short speech, smash a bottle of champagne on the ship's hull, then press a button that will send the boat gliding into the water. Yet, when launching the frigate *Jaguar*, the champagne bottle simply bounced back at her and refused to break. Today at royal ship launches champagne bottles are surreptitiously weakened with glass cutters beforehand, but Alexandra was left to flounder. When she pressed hard on the launch button, the *Jaguar* remained motionless. Jokingly she pretended to push the ship to lighten the situation and to her intense relief, at that moment the frigate slid into the water. 'It was a moment of despair,' she said in a speech later, 'The agonizing situation seemed a lifetime.' It was a story she would often tell when launching ships in the future, always saying how she could breathe easily when all had gone according to plan. It was a personal touch that people enjoyed, and she had certainly gained from the experience.

Once complimenting a woman on 'your wonderful baby', she looked up and saw that what she had supposed was a young mother turned out to be a woman of over seventy. 'It taught me a lesson,' she revealed. 'You should always look at the woman first, and then at the child. In that way you have a better idea of guessing the relationship.'

Alexandra's legendary clumsiness did not always help in the early days when she still felt awkward. On 17 May 1953, she accompanied her mother to the Empire Youth Sunday Service in St Paul's Cathedral and having not yet studied under Mademoiselle Anita she was inexperienced at walking in high heels and tripped as she walked in procession up the aisle. Even thirty years later she had a mishap in Hollywood of a similar nature when dancing with Fred Astaire. Although she had enjoyed country dancing at Heathfield, as she grew older she always worried about dancing in public in case she tripped. While dancing with eighty-three-year-old Fred Astaire in November 1982, the Princess did indeed trip as she feared, partly out of nerves. 'Astaire did something fiddly,' said Angus, 'and they both fell over.'

Princess Alexandra can take consolation in the fact that she is not the only member of her family to embarrass themselves in public, and there have been times when her brothers' clumsiness has proved more serious. The Duke of Kent celebrated his seventeenth birthday at Government House in Singapore while on a tour of the Far East with their mother in 1952. A cake was made in honour of the occasion and Eddie was given a *kris*, a long-bladed dagger, to ceremoniously cut it. Flourishing the dagger in the air he accidentally caught Princess Marina in the eye. All in the room gasped as blood gushed down her face on to her dress. As Marina was taken out, the Prince thought he must have blinded her, but the Princess reappeared later with a plaster over her eye, a doctor confirming that only the soft tissue of her eyelid had been scratched and the quantity of blood more alarming that the wound.

On occasions Princess Alexandra has found herself at the centre of a political storm, having been unwittingly embroiled. In October 1980 Alexandra and Angus flew to Australia to undertake engagements in Melbourne (the centenary of the Melbourne Exhibition Building),

Canberra, Adelaide, Victoria, Portland and Alice Springs. Even before they arrived there was unease about the visit because it was to take place in the run-up to a General Election and political fervour was high. The Royal Family always disassociate themselves from politics and for this very reason Alexandra's visit had been quite deliberately planned so as not to coincide with the election itself. In retrospect she would have been better advised to postpone her visit until after voting. As the tour came at the end of a long and sometimes bitter campaign, each Party leader feared the other might use the Princess's visit to his own advantage. It was therefore initially agreed that if she was to meet the Prime Minister then she should also be seen with the Leader of the Opposition.

In 1965 her cousin, the Queen, had found herself in exactly the same unusual situation, arriving in West Germany amid a pre-election battle between Chancellor Erhard and Willy Brandt, leader of the Social Democrats. In Berlin the two men had a heated argument as to who should sit beside the Queen in the car, which resulted in both travelling with Her Majesty, but refusing to speak to each other. Fully aware of this, it is surprising that Princess Alexandra was allowed to be placed in the same embarrassing position. As it was, she was met at Canberra airport by the then Conservative Prime Minister, Malcolm Fraser (who was to retain his premiership until the General Election of March 1983), the Leader of the Opposition boycotted the event, perhaps hoping to gain more republican votes. He also refused an invitation to a reception with the Ogilvys.

On a planned visit to the Festival Centre in Adelaide, the Princess decided to watch part of a play rehearsal, unaware that the production was Martin Sherman's *Bent* about the treatment of homosexuals in Nazi Germany, which includes scenes in a Dachau concentration camp. She watched a scene from early on in the play involving a Berlin nightclub in 1934 and afterwards chatted with an actor playing the role of a transvestite. As photographers suddenly saw the potential in a picture of a Princess and a 'queen' and reached for their cameras, Alexandra made a hasty and embarrassed exit, fearing the connotations that could be made of such a photograph.

This was Princess Alexandra's fourth visit to Australia and at the outset political disharmony seemed to blight the tour. Several of the engagements on the itinerary were cancelled at the last minute; a strike amongst refuse collectors in Melbourne meant the streets were piled high with decaying rubbish in sweltering heat and when she arrived in Portland she found workers had gone on a four-day week and her visit was mistimed to coincide with a day off. Embarrassed officials diverted Alexandra to a nearby hospital for an unscheduled tour, but it was not what she had planned. Enthusiastic crowds turned out in force to see her, as always, she and Angus enjoyed the successful engagements, such as inaugurating a new railway in Alice Springs and opening the National Federation of Fitness and Physical Achievement in Victoria but the Princess was disappointed that arrangements had not gone according to plan.

Politics had also angered the Princess back in Britain. Alexandra was invited down to Sussex to undertake duties in Bognor Regis and she happily accepted. It was a seaside town she had visited in childhood and Princess Marina had spent holidays there with her sisters prior to the First World War, so there were family associations. Bognor had also been fashionable with royalty since one of Alexandra's ancestors, Princess Charlotte (granddaughter of George III), stayed there in the late eighteenth century. Alexandra's own grandfather, George V, had convalesced at Bognor after a serious illness in 1929 and granted the town the suffix 'Regis'.

On her itinerary was the unveiling of a plaque on a new entertainment complex. When she arrived nothing had been built other than one single wall on which had been placed the said plaque, which she duly unveiled. A short time after her visit Princess Alexandra was furious to learn that the wall had been demolished by the council within forty-eight hours and that she had to all intents and purposes been used as a publicity gimmick. Her visit had been intended to encourage investors in the project. She did not consider this to be one of her roles and her staff were instructed to undertake more intensive research into her engagements in the future.

The year in which the Lonrho affair caused Angus to resign from his directorships was one of the most distressing for Princess Alexandra. His income was reduced, the future of their home was in the balance and the inevitable aroma of scandal surrounded them. At the end of that year, with Angus recovering from pneumonia, she looked forward to a visit to Italy and a trip to the Vatican. She had always had a deep faith, always taking Holy Communion in her own church, and it would be another spiritual experience for her to attend Mass at the Vatican. No doubt in her mind were the traumas of the year. At the service she received Communion, blissfully unaware that as a confirmed member of the Church of England she was not to be given it in a Roman Catholic church. She had scarcely left the Vatican before a furore broke out. Princess Alexandra is in line of succession to the throne and in 1701 an Act of Settlement was issued to prevent descendants of the Catholic James II inheriting the crown. When Prince Charles, closer obviously to the throne than Alexandra, wanted to attend a private Mass with the Pope at the Vatican, politicians, the Church and the Queen intervened to prevent him. The Coronation service, it was pointed out, has the Sovereign promise to uphold the Protestant religion and the Queen is officially Head of the Church and Defender of the Faith. Princess Alexandra had put the Queen in an embarrassing position, said Church authorities. It was a minor public embarrassment for Alexandra; privately of course the Queen had no words of admonishment. A few months later Alexandra surprisingly hit the headlines again at a rock concert.

Princess Alexandra's taste in music is varied. From her father she seems to have inherited a love of jazz. She likes Schubert, Chopin, and once packed the works of Vivaldi and Fauré in her suitcase for a tour of Australia, hoping to find time to practise. When opening the Young Men's Christian Association in Grimsby she was to be given a gift in honour of the occasion and requested the harpsichord works of Scarlatti. In the knowledge of this classical interest, and personal friendships with Sir Malcolm Sargent, Sir William Walton and Malcolm Williamson (Master of the Queen's Music since 1975), it surprises many to learn that she also likes contemporary pop music, possibly as a result of her own children's tastes, and particularly enjoys the songs of Elton John. When she met the singer after the performance, he was momentarily speechless when the Princess asked him if he took cocaine. The Press could not believe their ears and when Princess Alexandra read her words quoted in the next day's newspapers, doubtless she could not believe her words.

What the Princess had initially intended was to express her surprise at the singer's boundless energy, and meant jokingly to say that he must take something to keep him going. However, out of context her question appeared extraordinary. Later Alexandra wrote to Elton John to apologize for the embarrassment caused, which had been unintentional. Elton John has remained popular, not only with the Ogilvys but has since performed for the Royal Family at Windsor Castle, dined with the Queen Mother and Princess Margaret privately, and is very friendly with the Duke and Duchess of York. The 'cocaine' episode was one of the rare occasions when Princess Alexandra could have avoided a sensation through a better choice of words.

If asked what advice they can give to new members of the family undertaking public duties for the first time, royalty always insist that you can only learn through experience and Princess Alexandra would not refute this. In the Nineties she now has forty years of working experience to draw on, and rarely does she ever now make a mistake. If launching a ship she is prepared for any eventuality, she avoids engagements where politics or religion might place her in a potentially embarrassing position and knows how to choose her words with care. But it is only through experience that she can avoid the gaffes that some members of the Royal Family make today. In comparison to the less experienced she does merit the title of the Princess who never puts a foot wrong.

The Lonrho episode drew Alexandra and Angus noticeably closer together and although financially worse off, Angus found more time to involve himself in his wife's working life. Soon after they were married Angus was quoted as saying, 'I don't bore Alexandra with my daily routine, and she doesn't bore me with hers.' Although he had nearly always accompanied her on overseas tours, he suddenly became more visible at functions in Britain, not on the day-to-day visits that the Princess undertakes (Appendix II) but he suddenly became more apparent at evening functions, charity concerts, film premières, fund-raising receptions, giving the Princess support in the background. Angus even represented Alexandra at memorial services, when she was otherwise unable to attend, and, for example, flew with her to Monaco in November 1982 for a service to the memory of Princess Grace, and in April 1983 for a memorial service for ex-King Umberto of Italy.

When Angus tendered his resignation to his various companies, two of them – the Rank Organization and the Metropolitan Estate and Property Corporation – refused to let him go, and he was later offered the job as a financial adviser and directorship of Sotheby's, positions he still holds today. In 1983 his position at Sotheby's hung in the balance when two American journalists set out to take over the company, but he remained on the board. Unlike the early years of their marriage, Angus has never again taken on too many commitments at once. Especially as his health seemed to deteriorate and Alexandra was particularly concerned about the fact that her husband smoked sixty cigarettes a day. Her father's brother, George VI, had died prematurely from lung cancer, exacerbated by smoking, and her cousin Princess Margaret had a cancer scare in 1985, necessitating an exploratory lung operation.

To ease the situation for Alexandra and Angus the Queen offered them a grace-and-favour property in Hyde Park. It stretched from Kensington Gardens in the west, where Alexandra had lived with Princess Marina at Kensington Palace, to Hyde Park Corner in the south-east within sight of Buckingham Palace. It was the perfect location. One of the Royal Parks owned by the Crown, Hyde Park has several properties within its boundaries that belong to the Queen. Thinking she could help her cousin, the Queen offered her cousin Ranger's Lodge, which had been empty for some time and was immediately available. The idea being that Alexandra and Angus could perhaps sell Thatched House Lodge, now worth considerably more than the estimated £150,000 they had paid for it, which would give them some capital. Being grace-and-favour, the Ogilvys would have nothing more than the cost of upkeep, money would be saved on travel if Alexandra was centrally based, and no doubt the Queen saw the advantages of having the Princess within easy reach of Buckingham Palace and Kensington Palace where she could be given extra official duties.

As soon as the offer became public knowledge there was an outcry. Members of Parliament complained that there was no reason for a Princess, whom they naturally considered to be wealthy through no other reason than being royal, to be given a free house. The plight of the homeless in London was raised, unemployment, the Civil List, and critics called the whole idea obscene. Princess Alexandra knew that it would be impossible for them to live there without a constant barrage of criticism, and at heart she must have felt affection for Thatched House Lodge and appreciated the healthy environment at Richmond out of the London smog. The Queen's offer was declined and the Ogilvys have remained in their marital home. As a concession they accepted a small apartment in St James's Palace, one of twenty, where the Princess can change and freshen up between engagements and stay overnight if necessary. It is used chiefly if Alexandra has duties during the daytime and evening, when the trek back to Thatched House Lodge to change into evening wear would take too long. Especially with the ever increasing traffic problems in London. The apartment also became a temporary home for their daughter, Marina, when she needed to be in central London, and because St James's Palace holds many royal offices, including the Prince of Wales' and the Lord Chamberlain's, plus Princess Alexandra's own, there has never been any hint of complaint. The only problem Alexandra has encountered with St James's Palace was when damp caused plaster to fall off the walls on top of her, landing her with a £15,000 bill for a new damp course.

St James's Palace was originally built by Henry VIII. Work began in 1532 and a range of buildings were constructed around four courtyards – Colour Court, Ambassadors Court and Friary Court, a fourth being destroyed by fire in the nineteenth century. Many rooms still retain their original Tudor fireplaces, and there is a passage from St James's Palace into Clarence House which enables the Queen Mother to attend functions in the Throne Room or Tapestry Room without having to go outside. It is in Friary Court that Princess Alexandra has her small three-roomed office suite. Visitors to the office are surprised at how un-royal it appears. Two outer offices are typically functional with filing cabinets, two large desks strewn with paperwork, where the administrative side of Princess Alexandra's working life is carried out.

The office at Friary Court is headed by Princess Alexandra's Private Secretary. A post held until April 1991 by Miss Mona Mitchell, who had been appointed in 1968. Highly regarded, Miss Mitchell was made a Commander of the Royal Victorian Order by the Queen for her work. It was in keeping with Princess Alexandra's style that when Mona Mitchell wrote on her employer's behalf her letters were always friendly in tone, so unlike the laconic, curt letters so often sent out by

Buckingham Palace. 'If you have any specific queries please do not hesitate to contact me again,' she would write when I enquired about one of Princess Alexandra's engagements that I wished to discuss on the radio. The goodwill it seemed to offer in turn coloured one's opinion of the Princess, providing an impression of approachability. Sir John Garnier, who has long associations with royalty since first serving on the royal yacht *Britannia* in 1956 and eventual appointment as Naval Equerry to the Queen in 1962, is now Princess Alexandra's Private Secretary, and has two administrative assistants.

Behind the two offices is a minuscule sitting room that barely accommodates the desk and two armchairs it contains. Unlike Prince Charles, who might grant an interview in his St James's Palace office, or the Princess Royal, who you may meet in her room at Buckingham Palace, Princess Alexandra has not to date granted an interview with any writer or journalist so has little need of a larger, more comfortable sitting room. To her it is simply a place to meet up with her lady-in-waiting, Lady Mary Mumford, or equerry, Major Peter Clarke. Most of Princess Alexandra's staff are long-serving. Lady Mary Mumford became a lady-in-waiting in 1986, replacing Lady Mary Fitzalan Howard who had been with the Princess for twenty-two years. Major Clarke has even longer associations with the Kent family. In 1961 he was seconded from the 14th/20th King's Hussars as Assistant Private Secretary to Princess Marina, before eventually becoming Comptroller to Marina and later to Princess Alexandra. There are also two extra ladies-in-waiting who work for the Princess on a rota basis. Mrs Peter Afia and Lady Nicholas Gordon Lennox. Ladies-in-waiting are always personal friends and receive little more for their duties than their expenses and a small clothing allowance.

Princess Alexandra seldom undertakes less than 130 engagements a year in Britain, plus one or two overseas tours. One visit to Australia, for example, may involve fifty separate functions and it is as an overseas ambassador that the Princess is possibly at her best. She is associated with some seventy organizations (see Appendix II), and has deliberately kept her patronages to a convenient number so that she can attend engagements for each as often as possible. Although a working member of the Royal Family, Princess Alexandra does not actually receive any money from the Civil List towards her expenses, under the Civil List

Act. The Queen, her husband and children receive an allowance, except the Prince and Princess of Wales whose income derives from the revenue of the Duchy of Cornwall. The Queen Mother, Princess Margaret and Princess Alice are also included in the Civil List, but not the Duke of Kent, the Duke of Gloucester or Princess Alexandra.

The revenue for the Duchy of Lancaster goes directly to the Queen and with this she finances the Privy Purse, which offsets expenditure not covered by the Civil List. From this money she herself gives an allowance to the Kents, Gloucesters and Princess Alexandra for the work they do. In the year 1990 Princess Alexandra's allocation was £154,000, which will remain unaltered until a review in the year 2000. It is not an income for Alexandra to spend as she wishes, but is purely to cover her expenses for carrying out duties.

A large percentage of this money goes on staff wages and national insurance contributions and administration, amounting to roughly 70%. The remainder barely covers the cost of official entertaining, heating, lighting, resident staff's community charges and travel. Usually when overseas it is the host country that covers the expenses, but in Britain the Princess has to pay for her official cars. She has to reimburse British Rail if travelling by train and the Queen's Flight if using a helicopter or aircraft. Although Princess Alexandra does not pay income tax on this allowance as it is not personal income, she is not exempt from Customs and Excise duties and pays VAT on her purchases. Scarcely is there any money over in the budget for official clothes – a necessary part of the job – which Angus, therefore, pays for. He does, of course, pay income tax on his earnings. Whilst many mistakenly believe that the Civil List allowance is taxpayers' money, it comes from the revenue of the Crown Estates. In the year ending 31 March 1990, the gross income from Crown lands totalled £101 million of which less than £6.5 million was returned to the Royal Family to cover the cost of duties. In addition, from the Privy Purse the Queen paid £435,000 to her cousins for their expenses. It only takes basic arithmetic to see that more goes to the Treasury than the Royal Family take out, even when the expenses of Buckingham Palace, Windsor Castle and *Britannia* are taken into consideration. It must be galling to Princess Alexandra to hear criticism of the 'cost' of the Royal Family, when her own family have had few resources, and so frequently the vast number of engagements she carries out seldom receive news coverage other than in local newspapers for the areas she visits.

How Princess Alexandra looks is one of the fundamental requirements of her job. She has never been a leader of fashion like the Princess of Wales, or indeed her own mother, yet occasionally when she was younger a coat or hat she wore would catch on with girls of her generation. Because money for clothes was tight when young she frequently wore off-the-peg outfits at considerably less cost than designer creations, and it was telling that a Marks and Spencer sales assistant was among the guests invited to her wedding. Throughout the late Eighties and early Nineties Princess Alexandra's wardrobe became noticeably more elegant. Although always chic, maturity suited her and her classic well-cut coats, suits and dresses fell in line with fashion. She has, unlike the Princess of Wales, always patronized only three or four designers at any one time. John Cavanagh was an early favourite and the Princess learned a great deal from him, although he experienced difficulties in making her more adventurous once she had been to Mademoiselle Anita's, and, of course, Norman Hartnell created formal gowns for State occasions. Once she began public duties she branched out to designers of her own choice, going first to Maureen Baker of Susan Small (it was Alexandra who introduced her to Princess Anne, which led to a commission to make the latter's wedding dress in 1973), and the Princess has remained with her for twenty-five years. Sometimes for a tour Alexandra will allow one designer to make the whole collection, such as on her first visit to Australia when the designer Leslie Kaye made eighteen separate outfits.

The celebrated couturier Victor Stiebel made many of Alexandra's evening gowns; a great favourite with society ladies, Stiebel also made many of Joyce Grenfell's stage costumes. Today Princess Alexandra still favours Maureen Baker, Jean Muir, and is now a long time client of David Sassoon of Belville Sassoon. She buys at least one outfit from Sassoon every season, the blue and white outfit that she wore for her son's wedding in 1988, for example, a silver and white evening gown for a Buckingham Palace State banquet for the President of Nigeria in 1989 and a yellow outfit for the Ascot races that same year. Gina Fratini is another favoured designer, but Princess Alexandra still gets pleasure from shopping for ready-made clothes in the West End of London.

Although a policeman will frequently be in tow for the sake of security, the Princess can usually shop and not be recognized. 'Nobody expects to see a member of the Royal Family in a shop,' said one assistant, 'so customers seldom look twice. At the most they think, doesn't that woman look a bit like Princess Alexandra?' Alexandra would hate to lose such liberty.

Although designers can, and do, visit Princess Alexandra at Thatched House Lodge or St James's Palace for fittings, she enjoys visiting their own showrooms and will often go armed with samples of material and a definite idea of the style she requires. She knows the restrictions imposed on all female members of the Royal Family – nothing too flimsy that can be seen through or blown up by the wind, nothing too restricting as the Princess has to bend to get in and out of cars, stoop to talk with children and people in wheelchairs. Garments must not crease and must look as good from the back as from the front because it is an angle people so frequently see, and colours are usually fairly bold so that the Princess will not only stand out in a crowd, but photograph well. Although Alexandra wears fewer hats these days, some are necessary to coordinate with her outfits for church services, Ascot or Trooping the Colour. Popular royal milliners are John Boyd and Frederick Fox.

As royalty wear hats far less than they used to, Princess Alexandra pays great attention to the cut and condition of her hair. For many years her hairdresser has been Michael Rasser of Michaeljohn, who also styles the Princess Royal's hair and occasionally Lady Sarah Armstrong-Jones's, and Princess Alexandra will often ring his salon herself to make an appointment. She has deliberately kept her hair long not only to provide a variety of styles, but it helps accommodate a tiara – a necessary part of the royal uniform.

Princess Alexandra does not possess vast quantities of jewellery and for daytime engagements will wear very little. Around her neck is a permanent gold chain, a gift from Angus, which remains almost hidden, enabling her to wear another decorative necklace or choker at the same time, again often gifts from her husband and simple in design. One necklace, for example, is a plain polished gold circlet set with a single diamond. On her right hand she wears two eternity rings, one set with emeralds and diamonds, the other with rubies and diamonds, and on the same hand a ring once belonging to her mother. On her left hand she wears her own wedding ring and platinum engagement ring with its sapphire and diamond setting.

Surprisingly, Alexandra inherited very little jewellery from Princess Marina. Most of it was left to Edward and Michael rather than Alexandra, believed to be a Greek tradition based on the idea that sons have to give jewellery to their wives, whereas daughters will be provided for by their own husbands. In the Sixties Princess Alexandra used to wear a diamond tiara with high festoons set with single pearls, on a pearl band, but this now belongs to Princess Michael of Kent. Another diamond tiara with circlets of diamonds containing pearl drops was again worn by Alexandra but has not been seen since Princess Marina's death. Rumour has it that the tiara was sold to pay death duties. Many of Marina's pieces of jewellery have been worn in recent years by the present Duchess of Kent, Alexandra's sister-in-law.

A small amount of Princess Marina's jewellery now belongs to Alexandra. An impressive cabochon emerald choker with a detachable emerald drop (which can be worn separately as a brooch) was Marina's, once belonging to Princess Nicholas of Greece, Alexandra's grandmother. A pair of pearl button earrings that she frequently wears again once belonged to her Greek grandmother. Other treasured pieces include three diamond brooches in the shape of stars which Alexandra has also worn as hair decorations; two ruby and diamond brooches in the shape of flowers, and a diamond and ruby bracelet that Alexandra's father gave to Princess Marina in 1936 when their daughter was born. At the time of Prince Michael's christening in 1942, Princess Alexandra was photographed wearing a small brooch containing two square rubies surmounted by diamonds. She still wears it today, but it has now become the clasp of a bracelet. At the time of her wedding Alexandra had another brooch, set with pearls and diamonds, turned into the centrepiece of a pearl choker, which again she still wears.

Although tiaras are a necessary symbol of royal position, the Royal Family seem to own very few. The Queen has come off best with no less than seven tiaras and one diadem, her most familiar tiara of interlaced diamond circles with pearl drops, once belonging to Princess Marina's grandmother, the Grand-Duchess Vladimir of Russia. The Queen Mother has four, but favours a modern tiara made for her by Cartier in 1953. Princess Margaret had to buy her own, and the Poltimore tiara for which she paid £5,500 just before her wedding is one of the most impressive of all the family. Princess Marina's seem to be worn by the present Duchess of Kent and Princess Michael, and Princess Alexandra was forced to have her own made up. For her wedding she borrowed her mother's, but for the pre-wedding ball at Windsor Castle she was seen for the first time wearing one of her own design which she has now used for thirty years. Originally she owned a circlet of seven flowers made of diamonds and pearls. In 1962 Collingwood (who have had royal customers since the reign of George IV and were first given a Royal Warrant by Queen Victoria) took the circlet to pieces and created a tiara around five of the flowers, and matching earrings from the remaining two. To complete the suite, Angus gave her a matching necklace as a wedding present. With typical ingenuity and thrift, the pearls can be removed from the necklace and be replaced with turquoises. Later some sapphires were purchased for the tiara so that this too can be altered at whim to look like different pieces.

In her collection may be diamonds, rubies, emeralds, sapphires and pearls, but one of Princess Alexandra's favourite items is a gold charm bracelet, to which charms have been added periodically on special anniversaries, and although probably worth far less than her more spectacular pieces, it is of greater sentimental value and frequently adorns her wrist. In the summer of 1976, Lady Monckton of Brenchley, the widow of Walter Monckton, Edward VIII's Attorney-General, and a general royal confidante, made a plea on behalf of Princess Alexandra to the Duchess of Windsor for the return of some of the Royal Family's jewels, especially those she was believed to possess that once belonged to Queen Alexandra. However, the appeal fell on stony ground. Had she been successful Princess Alexandra might have had the pleasure of wearing the jewels of her great-grandmother and namesake.

When Princess Alexandra attends an evening function in tiara and evening dress, one particular item becomes significant. A miniature portrait of the Queen set in diamonds, worn on a riband of chartreuse yellow silk. The Royal Family Order of Queen Elizabeth II, bestowed as a personal symbol of royal favour at the Queen's discretion. It is not given to members of the Royal Family as a matter of course and there are only eight holders at the present time. The Princess of Wales, for example, was honoured with this symbol of Her Majesty's gratitude in 1982. It has not yet been given to the Duchess of York or Princess Michael of Kent. A further honour Princess Alexandra has received is that of Grand Cross of the Royal Victorian Order, again restricted in its bestowal and not yet granted to the Princess of Wales or the Duchess of York. These royal symbols mark the esteem in which Alexandra is held. Now even less common, she is also a holder of King George VI's personal order. When dignitaries or visiting Heads of State see Princess Alexandra in tiara and honours, it is rarely their first meeting. Frequently she is the member of the Royal Family sent to greet them at the airport on their arrival in Britain. In May 1989, for example, she and Angus travelled to Gatwick Airport to meet President Babangida of Nigeria. From Gatwick the couple escorted the President on a train that took them to Victoria Station, where the Queen, Prince Philip, the Prince and Princess of Wales and Princess Margaret were waiting on Platform Two to meet the train before the final carriage procession to Buckingham Palace. It is Princess Alexandra, therefore, who has provided their first taste of royalty, put them at their ease and offered help and advice. It is no coincidence that she has been designated this task so often.

Alexandra has played a key role in the arrival of a visiting Head of State, and royal protocol once again comes into force when Princess Alexandra is made aware of her position. As the Queen introduces female members of her family, one by one they curtsey if the visitor is a monarch, and (as with the State Visit of King Juan Carlos of Spain in 1986) will kiss on each cheek if also a family friend; male members of the family bow and shake hands. In the line-up Princess Alexandra and Angus are always last in the line, and even though Alexandra is in line of succession and her brother Prince Michael is not, having relinquished his rights to marry a divorcee, she still has to stand behind her two brothers and their wives. Male members of the British Royal Family take precedence over females. Obviously if anyone present was lower in order of succession than Alexandra they would stand after her, but there seldom is anyone. At State Banquets, again Angus and Alexandra enter last. For a State Banquet given in honour of King Juan Carlos at Windsor Castle, while 177 non-royal guests were already in place at the table the Royal Family entered to the National Anthem, the Queen leading the procession escorted by the King of Spain, followed by Prince Philip with the Queen of Spain, and all members of the Royal Family, and Princess Alexandra at the rear with William Whitelaw and Angus last of all with Lady Whitelaw. Possibly this is why the Ogilvys blend so much into the background when other leading members of the Royal Family are present. When President Kaunda of Zambia paid a State Visit to Britain in 1983 at a banquet on 22 March, after the President had been introduced to Alexandra and Angus (the Princess with a broad grin simply said, 'We have met before, I think') it was noticeable that while other guests chatted quietly in the Music Room before the procession into the Ballroom, Angus and Alexandra stepped back and spoke only to each other. Revealing also, perhaps, on another occasion in a similar line-up, after the visiting dignitary, the Prince and Princess of Wales walked along the line and greeted each member of their family formally. When the Princess of Wales reached the Duchess of Kent they hugged and kissed, and giggled with each other. 'You look so cold!' said the Duchess sympathetically. Diana then moved on to the Ogilvys, kissed Alexandra on the left cheek before moving on to Angus. Not a word was spoken between them. Was there, some speculated, resentment that in a life so wrapped up in protocol Alexandra had to curtsey to a commoner who now ranked above her? Certainly the Ogilvys had remained in the shadows at the Prince and Princess of Wales' wedding in 1981, and in the official photographs, taken by Patrick Lichfield at Buckingham Palace, Angus and Alexandra amongst the sixty people in the group look on severely from the *back* row.

Schooled by an earlier generation of royalty, it would seem that Princess Alexandra laments the loss of dignity that some young members of the Royal Family have introduced. She has herself worked hard to draw a fine line between approachability while still maintaining some of the necessary mystique. Although she married a commoner, having opted to marry only someone she loved, she can make it known very firmly that he ranks *below* her. Often when overseas with her husband, her hosts have expected Angus to enter a room first as the man, but she has pointed out that he must walk behind her for reasons of protocol. If anyone, because of her friendliness, becomes overfamiliar they can be quickly frosted out and are left in no doubt of her displeasure. Only very close personal friends are allowed to call her by her Christian name, and even close members of her team, like Mona Mitchell, who have met with her on an almost daily basis for over twenty years, are still expected to curtsey when they meet for the first time that day. It is because of these standards, not in spite of them, instilled into her by Princess Marina that Alexandra is so successful as a working royal and others could follow her example. When she attends a function there is a royal aura of dignity about her and nobody ever feels short-changed.

When with other members of the Royal Family, whether publicly or privately, Princess Alexandra always stands back and lets them take the lead. For this reason, it is when attending engagements alone or with Angus that she is at her regal best. In Britain Angus will accompany his wife on engagements that he finds most interesting, such as when she opened the redesigned golf course, aviary, maze and grotto at Leeds Castle in Kent in 1988, or as in the spring of 1990 when they went to the annual exhibition staged by the Royal Photographic Society at Hamilton's Gallery in London. Both are keen photographers. Overseas he is more to the forefront and the couple have especially enjoyed trips to America together. In June 1984 they went to New Orleans for the World Exposition and amongst the many engagements was a Gala Performance given by the English National Opera at the Metropolitan Opera House, Alexandra being Patron of the English National Opera. Throughout the tour Angus was by the Princess's side. In 1990 they returned again, this time to Los Angeles, where part of the itinerary included a BAFTA Gala at which the actor Michael Caine was being honoured for his 'creative contribution to the international entertainment industry'. The Princess also opened the Festival of Britain in Orange County – the largest British arts and consumer goods promotion staged in North America that year. Angus's presence, although not strictly official, eases Alexandra's job and means that they can talk to twice as many people. He becomes both an escort and an ally.

Each year some 400 invitations arrive at Friary Court requesting an official visit from Princess Alexandra, more than would ever be practical to undertake. Priority must always be given to those from which she is Patron, President, or in some way connected, who naturally feel that they have a right to some of her time. She has deliberately kept the number to a manageable level so that her involvement can be total. One advantage of a long royal career such as Alexandra has had is that time and again she can see the fruits of her labour. In 1975, for example, she opened a new hospital in Basingstoke, and at the end of 1990 opened their new Body Scanner Suite. The fifteen-year association had enabled her to keep in touch with the progress of the hospital. In November 1990 she opened a Scanner Suite at the Royal Lancaster Infirmary and in April had opened the Screening and Assessment Centre of Breast Test in Cardiff. From each she had built up a knowledge of the subject, her own medical training enabling her to talk on a practical level to doctors, nurses and patients, rather than talking in mere platitudes. As a result of her medical knowledge it is not surprising that much of Princess Alexandra's work is concerned with health. Her first official role was as Patron of the British Junior Red Cross and she went on to become Vice-President of the British Red Cross Society, Patron of Princess Mary's Royal Air Force Nursing Service, and Queen Alexandra's Royal Naval Nursing Service. She is also Patron of the Guide Dogs for the Blind Association and President of the Royal Commonwealth Society for the Blind. In 1990, for example, she attended engagements involved with training disabled people for employment, cancer research, mental health, child blindness, drug addiction, and Age Concern. Forever conscious of her own good health and faculties, she works particularly hard for those who have lost their sight and when she first took on the patronage of Guide Dogs for the Blind she took her own blindfold and covered her own eyes in an attempt to discover for herself what it would be like walking with a guide dog when unable to see. Again in 1990 she opened the World Health Organization Meeting on the Prevention of Childhood Blindness at the International Centre for Eye Health in London, attended a gala concert in Greenwich to raise money for Guide Dogs and a play in Scarborough in aid of Sight Savers (Royal Commonwealth Society for the Blind), went to a garden party at Buckingham Palace to celebrate the seventy-fifth anniversary of St Dunstan's, an organization that cares for men and women blinded in the Services and their families, and went to an exhibition of paintings by Graham Rust in London, again to raise money for the blind.

In 1968 Princess Alexandra became interested in the work of the

Cystic Fibrosis Research Trust, which had been founded by Mr Joseph Levy, a close business friend of Angus Ogilvy's. Cystic Fibrosis is a life threatening children's disease which affects one child in every two thousand and when the Trust was set up in 1964 was a major cause of infant mortality. One child is born with Cystic Fibrosis every day in the United Kingdom.

The disease is hereditary and is caused by a single abnormal gene present in each parent, but which does not affect the parents in any way. One person in twenty carries this gene and when two carriers have children there is a one in four chance of a baby being born with Cystic Fibrosis. A congenital disease, the child has a high susceptibility to bacterial infection in the lungs and a malfunctioning of the pancreas interfering with digestion and therefore growth. Before the Research Trust was set up children with Cystic Fibrosis rarely reached adulthood. Through research, although the cause could not be removed, the ill effects could be controlled. In 1968 Princess Alexandra agreed to become Patron of the Trust and has taken a very active involvement. In the wake of her patronage, by 1974 some £500,000 had been raised to find a cure and improve methods of treatment. 'The genetic science and biochemistry research which is involved in seeking a cure for Cystic Fibrosis is complex,' said the Trust's Director, Barbara Bentley, 'and the understanding of such complexities by the Princess has impressed many of our scientific colleagues.'

Local branch groups were set up in the first decade and played a major role in helping parents of children with Cystic Fibrosis to cope with the problems – of emotion, understanding and communication. Through being able to share the ordeal, the feeling of isolation which affects the parents of any handicapped child is overcome. 'Our Branch Membership set great store by their Royal Patron,' Barbara Bentley told me, 'and are eager to have her join them on as many occasions as possible, far more, in fact, than it would be humanly possible to attend. Most of these valiant people are parents or past parents, and to meet the Princess puts good heart into them for their lifetime struggles with Cystic Fibrosis.' Once again, through her long association, Princess Alexandra has been able to share in dramatic events. In August 1989 intensive genetic research finally discovered the Cystic Fibrosis gene. The discovery has paved the way to perfect and expand the means for carrier detection and early diagnosis of Cystic Fibrosis, as well as new methods for improved management and treatment. Over the years Princess Alexandra has already met with an increasing number of adults with Cystic Fibrosis who before research would not have lived beyond childhood, some of whom have undergone heart-lung transplants.

One of the highlights of Princess Alexandra's patronage, the Trust feel, must have been when in 1989 she joined 2,000 members – parents, past parents, patients, doctors, scientists, nurses, executives and staff – in Westminster Abbey at a Service of Thanksgiving and rededication conducted by the Archbishop of Canterbury on 23 February. The service was to mark the Trust's Silver Jubilee, and by coincidence that same year the faulty gene was finally discovered after twenty-five years of research. Princess Alexandra joined the congregation in remembering those who had died and those who were rededicating themselves to the fight ahead. One of the trumpeters whose voluntary rang out to herald her arrival was a CF child; a pair of identical CF twins carried a Book of Remembrance the length of the Abbey, and a heart-lung transplant girl read one of the lessons. The Princess spoke with them afterwards and to as many of the congregation as she could. Many felt afterwards that she had been there, not as a member of the Royal Family, but as one of them.

While the discovery of the elusive gene received national media coverage being a turning point in the Trust's work, Princess Alexandra has been keen to point out that it offers only light at the end of the tunnel and did not mean the end of the road. It did not by any means signal that the Trust's work was over, it was merely the frontier of discovery and there is still much to do. 'Our main objective,' says the Director, 'is to find a cure; to care for those alive today with Cystic Fibrosis; and to educate both government and the public in the complex problems which burden those with Cystic Fibrosis.' Princess Alexandra will continue to play her part.

The Cystic Fibrosis Research Trust is but one of the seventy organizations with which Alexandra works. Each is as worthy, complex and demanding on her time. In 1964 she became Chancellor of the then new University of Lancaster and each year has spent at least two days with the students, bestowing degrees in July and December, meeting and talking with as many students as possible. When she once received a letter from the Students' Union before a University ball, hoping to establish who and how many the Princess would dance with, they were told that Alexandra would not decide in advance and dance with as many students as she could. At the University are 5,200 full-time and 780 part-time students plus 490 academic staff, and whenever she visits she really does attempt to meet as many as she can and in 1990 this involved four full days in Lancaster.

Once Princess Alexandra had accepted the Chancellorship of Lancaster University in 1964, Princess Marina had followed suit to become the first Chancellor of the University of Kent in 1966. Both feared initially that their own lack of academic qualifications would be a disadvantage. Both found favour with the students through their lack of them. Princess Marina actually gave a party for seventy students at Kensington Palace in the liberal Sixties when students were frequently long-haired and 'hippies'. When it was suggested to her that the students should be told to have haircuts and dress smartly, Princess Marina disagreed. 'No certainly not,' she said. 'They must come as they wish and behave as they wish.' Princess Alexandra has followed her mother's dictum.

The demand for Princess Alexandra will continue and there is no apparent lessening of the number of engagements she accepts. Indeed since her children, James and Marina, have left home she has the opportunity to undertake even more with less personal demands on her time. No longer does she have to keep school holidays free, for example. The esteem in which she is held is shown in the way that all of her charities and organizations are happy to pay tribute to her; many, such as the Guide Dogs for the Blind Association and the Cystic Fibrosis Research Trust, have even named their premises 'Alexandra House' so that her name will be permanently associated with them even after her death.

In the same way, she has been able to follow in her great-grandmother's footsteps because of a link with the name – Queen Alexandra's House Association, Queen Alexandra's Royal Naval Nursing Service, the Royal Alexandra Hospital for Sick Children in Brighton, and the annual Alexandra Rose Day appeal (formed to help organizations caring for 'the aged, the young, the sick and the disabled') – have all gladly accepted her patronage, initially on the strength of her name and now as a result of her abilities.

Alexandra Rose Day typifies both royal continuity and Princess Alexandra's style. Inspired by her great-grandmother, Alexandra Rose Day was established in 1912 to raise funds for hospitals. Queen Alexandra's father, King Christian IX of Denmark, instituted a 'Children's Help Day' in his own country and raised money by walking through the streets of Copenhagen collecting donations himself. After visiting a priest in Denmark who raised money for the poor by selling the roses in his garden, Queen Alexandra formulated the idea of a Rose Day and, under the supervision of Miss Christine May Beeman, 15,000 ladies, dressed in white muslin, collected money on the streets of London by selling white artificial roses. On that day, 26 June 1912, Queen Alexandra drove from Marlborough House to the Mansion House and back again and collected money *en route*. She had introduced the British public to the idea of selling emblems in support of charity, and on that first Alexandra Rose Day almost £20,000 was collected.

'It was a beautiful idea,' said the London *Evening News* that night, 'that all London should wear her favourite flower, and by so doing help her favourite charities, was an inspiration.' By 1920 London hospitals had benefited by over £750,000. Today the tradition continues under the patronage of Princess Alexandra, and collections are made all over the country in June. Each May the Princess attends a Rose Ball at the Grosvenor House, which in 1990 raised £43,000, and on Sunday 3 June 1990 for the first time an Alexandra Rose Day Polo Match was played at Smith's Lawn, Windsor, to raise further funds through sponsorship.

Each year Princess Alexandra tours the depots during the collections, just as her great-grandmother did, but what appeals to her about this charity is that Alexandra Rose Day involves so many people and is a year-long event. Handicapped people make linen roses by hand to be sold; a Campaign Director organizes events nationwide from sponsored swims to a sponsored wheelchair push, supported by many groups from the Fire Service to the Police Force. At the end of the day, over thirty-five different charities benefit, from Age Concern to the Multiple Sclerosis Society. Like the Princess herself, Alexandra Rose Day works quietly behind the scenes and has a far lower profile than many similar causes, but thousands of people benefit in the end. Under the one umbrella title of a day now bearing her name, the lives of many have been enhanced.

On one of her early visits to Australia Alexandra was dubbed 'Princess Understanding' for her sympathy and compassion. If ever faced with noisy demonstrations she has not ignored them but has broken away from her entourage and walked over to hear the reasons for the protest. On each occasion her understanding has turned jeers into cheers. Faced with demonstrators outside Liverpool University complaining about poor quality housing she soothed tempers by discussing the conditions, offering sympathy and promising to do all she could. On overseas tours she has frequently helped minority causes through personal intervention. When she discovered in Hong Kong that blind women were bottom of the social scale, simply by inviting a blind woman to a society function she raised their social standing. An artless act, but it took a Princess to do it.

Although on the working front Princess Alexandra's royal career, that has spanned the Fifties, Sixties, Seventies, Eighties, and is now into the Nineties, has been an unqualified success, the question has arisen as to whether her own personal life has suffered as a result. When she reaches the milestone of her thirtieth wedding anniversary in 1993 her marriage will have been deemed a success, especially in the light of the failed marriages of Princess Margaret and Princess Anne. Of a trio of non-royal husbands only Angus Ogilvy has stayed the course. To the outside world Sir Angus and Lady Ogilvy presented a picture of the ideal husband and wife, the perfect mother and father. Yet behind closed doors at Thatched House Lodge many a drama had been enacted, which on 9 October 1989, was to become common knowledge. The Ogilvy dirty linen was to be laundered in public and Princess Alexandra's 'understanding' image was in danger of becoming permanently soiled. By an ingrate of a daughter!

10

In the Shadow of Marina

[ii]

In November 1990 Princess Alexandra's daughter Marina was photo-graphed for the *Daily Mail* wearing black leather thigh boots and a very short Lycra mini dress, admitting that it was her favourite outfit. In her right hand she carried a gun, and when interviewed by journalist Jenny Nisbet, Marina confessed that she enjoyed wearing rubber corsets. Although the Queen saw the article we shall never know her reaction, or that of Princess Alexandra. Tagged a 'royal rebel', Marina has been photographed for a tabloid newspaper sitting on a throne wearing a crown, was reduced to tears by Robert Kilroy Silk in a BBC television interview, and in February 1991 was voted 'Rear of the Year' by a jeans manufacturer.

'I'm not on the Civil List so it doesn't matter what I do. I'm a very distant cousin of the Queen and I don't have a title. I have my own life, my own family and my own surname,' Marina told reporters defiantly, never being afraid of controversy. Currently twenty-sixth in line to the throne and destined to be pushed even further down the line of succession by any subsequent children of the Prince of Wales, Duke of York, Prince Edward and even her brother James, Marina revels in her independence and unconventional lifestyle. Even if it does raise a few royal eyebrows. On a Channel 4 chat show with Jonathan Ross, when asked if she saw her parents, Marina paused momentarily, gave an embarrassed smile and replied, 'Sometimes.' Her silence spoke volumes.

On the surface Marina would seem the antithesis of her mother. While Alexandra is dressed by Jean Muir and Belville Sassoon, is never seen with a hair out of place and if called upon at the last minute to launch a ship would be there on the dockside completely unruffled, Marina favours Vivienne Westwood, Gaultier and Pamela Hogg, a specialist in leather and rubber, has her hair hennaed by her husband, keeps her make-up in a shoebox and never carries a handbag. Yet, in her own life there were occasions when Princess Alexandra rebelled, felt oppressed by royal life and admitted that she found 'luxury faintly stifling'. She did not always match up to her mother's expectations and there were clashes over clothes. Where Alexandra and her daughter differed fundamentally is that one was born a Princess, the other wasn't. While there would seem advantages in not having a title, the royal prefix gave Alexandra a golden key. It opened doors and gave her a path in life to follow. She had a function, a duty, and a secure future because of it. It was the key to opportunity, a passport to travel the world, and she dedicated herself to a life of service. Miss Marina Ogilvy, however, grew up in a different world. She was kept in the background, sheltered from the royal way of life and told that she would never need to undertake any royal duties. It must have been confusing. It may even have led to a feeling of inferiority. The reversal of Alexandra's mother who told her 'you are not a girl, you are a Princess', young Marina must have felt that she was not a Princess, just an ordinary girl.

Although she has almost turned her back on royal functions, had she been nurtured in the correct way, Marina has the outgoing personality that would actually have made her good at royal engagements. She enjoys meeting people, she appreciates travel, and is obviously not frightened of media attention. A title might actually have made the world of difference to her life. Children might not have any conception of what a title means, but as she played with her cousins Prince Edward, Viscount Linley, Lady Sarah Armstrong-Jones, Lady Helen Windsor, Lord Nicholas Windsor and the Earl of St Andrews, she must have been aware that there was something lacking in her name. It's all too easy later in life to say 'I don't want a title anyway,' but as children there is a fear of being different, of feeling left out. It must have been puzzling to Marina. Not only that, she was brought up in the belief that she could be herself and live an 'ordinary' life, yet she still had to conform to royal standards. At the age of five while travelling in a car in a State procession she allegedly jumped up and down shouting

'Knickers!' at the crowds. It gained her the attention she desired and angered her father.

Marina also appears to have suffered as a second-born child through always being measured against her brother, James. He has certainly been able to cope with a non-royal life, has enjoyed staying out of the limelight and has never caused his parents any embarrassment. He married the beautiful Julia Rawlinson, whose father Charles is senior adviser to the Norman Grenfell Group of merchant bankers, and James now has a successful career with a banking and investment company. It is a conventional path that can have caused Alexandra and Angus few concerns.

It is impossible to know now whether Princess Alexandra's attitude differed towards her two children, or if Marina sometimes felt excluded. When James was born, for example, his christening took place at Buckingham Palace, yet Marina had a smaller ceremony at St James's Palace. It may be fanciful, but it could show that the first-born son held greater significance in his parents' eyes. Marina later confessed to school friends that whenever she had problems that she wanted to discuss with her parents 'they weren't at home often enough' to discuss them. In her teenage years she suffered from various illnesses including glandular fever and anorexia. Left to her own devices, Marina always veered towards unconventional friends. They were people who could offer a stimulus and excitement.

Although not as academically brilliant as her brother, Marina, like Princess Alexandra, excels at music and was offered a place at the Guildhall School of Music in London. By this time she had met and fallen in love with photographer, Paul Mowatt. Eventually she moved in with him.

Marina took her photographer boyfriend to Thatched House Lodge to meet her parents and supposedly met with an unfriendly reception. As Princess Alexandra is so used to meeting strangers of all classes, colours and creeds, it seems hard to believe that she would at this time be deliberately cool towards a friend of her daughter's, although most certainly reserved. The problems began in August 1989 when Marina and Paul Mowatt visited Thatched House Lodge to tell Princess Alexandra that she was pregnant and did not intend to marry until the following summer. It was naive of Marina to believe such an announcement would be accepted lightly. Few mothers would be happy at this news, let alone a member of the Royal Family whose reputation was as yet unblemished.

To Princess Alexandra's horror, what began as a personal worry turned into a public nightmare when in September 1989 Marina Ogilvy took the unprecedented step of contacting *Today* newspaper, selling them her side of the story, which was eventually published on Monday 9 October in six full pages. There was nothing Princess Alexandra could do to put her side of the story. It seemed unforgivable to her that her daughter had betrayed the family who relish their privacy. Perhaps Marina knew that it was the one weapon that would hurt her parents most. Whilst news that Princess Alexandra's daughter becoming an unmarried mother would certainly have hit the newspapers eventually, it could not have carried the same weight had Marina not taken the action she did.

To Jonathan Ross in a television interview Marina gave her reasons for the story as 'wanting to tell the truth'. In the article she claimed that when she went to the doctor's for the results of her pregnancy test she was told that an appointment had been booked for her to see a gynaecologist. She believed that it was a trick and what would appear to be a routine test would actually turn into an abortion. When they went to Thatched House Lodge to tell Alexandra that she was to be a grandmother, Marina says her mother appeared to be aware of the situation already and asked 'Have you done it?' which was inferred as meaning 'Have you had the abortion?'

Marina Ogilvy branded Princess Alexandra a hypocrite, accused her father of drinking too much, and said that they insisted she either have an abortion or get married instantly by special licence. Neither of these courses of action was Marina prepared to take. She wrote to the Queen seeking advice, but quite naturally did not receive a reply. Instead the Queen entered into lengthy telephone conversations with Alexandra from Balmoral where she was staying at the time. Just as Her Majesty could not have gone against Princess Marina's wishes when the Duke of Kent first wanted to marry Katharine Worsley, so Marina Ogilvy's letter placed the monarch in an embarrassing situation.

Whatever the original intentions of Marina's outpourings to *Today*, once the initial sensation had died down, the sympathies of the public

and the Press lay with Princess Alexandra. It was known that because
of the nature of her position she could not respond to any allegations,
and the general feeling was that Marina had quite literally got herself
into trouble. At the end of the day Alexandra came through the episode
with dignity, while Marina will forever remain synonymous with her
newspaper outburst. For a time Princess Alexandra was completely
overshadowed by her daughter's situation, but quietly carried on with
her full engagement diary receiving nothing but support from those
with whom she came into contact. What had upset Alexandra and
Angus most was not so much the fact that Marina was pregnant, and
certainly not that the father was not royal, but that she had sold her
story to the Press, and worded it in such a way that it would reflect
badly on them. In the *Daily Mail* Lynda Lee Potter wrote: 'Marina has
tried to project herself as a timid, hurt young girl who craved affection,
but it seems to me that it is her parents alone who have shown the
loving.' Ultimately it was *because* Alexandra and Angus could do
nothing other than retain a dignified silence that they gained the most
public sympathy. It seemed impossible to visualize the sneering, callous
portrait that Marina had painted of her mother, but Alexandra's deep
concern for her family's reputation can be accepted.

Whether through Alexandra and Angus's intervention or a change of
heart on the part of their daughter, Marina and Paul Mowatt eventually
decided to marry *before* the baby was born. In some small way it
brought an air of respectability to the situation and Alexandra and
Angus quashed rumours of a family rift by giving their daughter the
fullest support, in public at least. Marina, who had once cooperated so
fully with the media, equally went out of her way to keep the wedding
a secret, perhaps not wanting to be seen going back on her decision not
to marry until later that year. At first they were going to marry at
Kingston-upon-Thames Registry Office, but plans were changed when
this became common knowledge. Another date was set, but friends
revealed 'This will probably be changed now you all know about it,'
to put the Press off the scent. Eventually the wedding took place on
Friday 3 February 1990, at St Andrew's Church on the outskirts of
Richmond Park. The best man had a pony-tail; the six-months pregnant
bride wore black.

Nobody seemed to notice at the time, but for Marina's wedding

Princess Alexandra wore a burgundy velvet suit with a matching hat trimmed with Persian lamb, first seen publicly twelve months earlier when she opened the Florence Nightingale Museum in London on 4 February, 1989. Marina opted for a black crushed velvet dress with a short red bolero jacket and a wide black hat. Nobody had anticipated a white wedding. Was Princess Alexandra's choice of outfit deliberate, in contrast to the new blue Belville Sassoon suit made for James's wedding, or was the whole affair so uncertain that she did not have time for something new to be made? Cynics noted that the suit looked purple – the colour of royal mourning.

It was an informal wedding for someone who was then twenty-fifth in line to the throne, who might easily have married with all due pomp and ceremony in Westminster Abbey or St Paul's Cathedral had circumstances been different, the personalities of the bride and groom more conventional. Princess Alexandra was the only member of the Royal Family to be present, even though the Prince of Wales is Marina's godfather. The guests numbered a mere thirty-one. At the wedding reception afterwards, held at the Duke of York's Barracks, off the King's Road in Chelsea, Princess Alexandra and Angus Ogilvy were conspicuous by their absence, having returned to Thatched House Lodge in their Rolls Royce looking as if they had just attended a funeral rather than a wedding. They had witnessed the ceremony with smiles firmly in place, determined to support Marina, but it was with some sadness that it was not the full white wedding they had wished for their only daughter. In Princess Alexandra's mind must have been the wedding of James to Julia Rawlinson, at St Mary the Virgin Church, Saffron Walden in Essex, attended by the Queen, the Princess of Wales, Prince and Princess Michael of Kent and many members of the Windsor Family. It was a ceremony that went without a hitch. The bride was late, Prince Edward was two minutes later than the bride, but it was the happiest of days for Princess Alexandra.

Although they do see Marina and Paul occasionally, Alexandra and Angus see far more of James and Julia. They spend Christmas at Sandringham, while the Mowatts stay away. In June 1990 they accompanied Princess Alexandra to King Constantine of Greece's lavish fiftieth birthday party at Spencer House in London with royalty from all over Europe, but Marina and Paul Mowatt remain deliberately out of the royal circle. *good*

On 26 May 1990, Princess Alexandra's first grandchild was born at Queen Mary's Hospital in Roehampton, south-west London, by caesarean section. At first Marina called her baby daughter 'Moog'. She herself had been known by her family as 'Mo' after her initials, and James is known as 'Jo' for the same reason, and no doubt 'Moog' came from '*Mo Ogilvy*'. Eventually the baby was christened Zenouska Mowatt, a name created by her parents. It included Zen, after the cult book *Zen and the Art of Motorcycle Maintenance*, and Eno, after Marina's favourite musician, Brian Eno. Princess Alexandra said she was 'delighted by the unusual choice'. There was little else she could say. *The author is correct.*

In this Ogilvy family battle there were no winners, only survivors. Each still bears the scars. The apparently gentle Alexandra had shown an iron streak when it came to defending the Royal Family's honour. There had not been a *known* illegitimate child in the family for ninety years and Princess Alexandra was prepared to do all in her power to prevent her granddaughter being the first. Ironically she had allowed her son James to live with his future bride before marriage, some say she gave it her blessing, for the situation received no publicity, <u>not now being unusual for any young couple, and</u> maybe she believed that a trial period of living together would prevent a divorce later on. One wonders what the Ogilvy family reaction would have been had James fathered a child before he was married. Almost certainly there would have been no question of an abortion. The key statement that Marina made to the Press was that when she asked her father which came first 'Queen and country or your own daughter', Angus replied 'Queen and country.' Through no fault of her own, it was what Princess Alexandra had been taught – that her duty to the Crown came first.

Although Princess Alexandra was a successful mother, she had experience only of how royal children are brought up and as her children matured it became difficult for her to accept their independent lifestyle. She cannot even go shopping without an armed detective in tow, yet Marina and James have been free to travel the world unhampered by security or crowds of onlookers. Theirs will always be an alien world. To many the saga that will haunt Princess Alexandra has changed their opinion of her, their view now coloured by Marina's revelations. Had

Alexandra accepted her daughter's lifestyle without a fight she could have seemed too good to be true. As it was, the tough stance she took was a display of human emotion. Many a mother could identify with the Princess and would have taken the same course of action in her position. Although Alexandra feared that her own reputation was on the line, ultimately forty years of public affection did count for something in the end. The compromise reached has satisfied all. If Marina had decided to have an abortion she would have blamed her mother for the loss of the child for the rest of her life and Alexandra would have suffered from guilt. One can appreciate also Marina's stance of wanting to marry Paul after the baby was born, knowing that otherwise it may well have been said that she was marrying him not for love, but simply because she was pregnant. As it is, their love has shone through and is unquestionable, and in the years to come Zenouska will thank them for making her birth legitimate.

It was the Queen who managed to have the final, subtle word. By the tradition of the Royal Marriages Act 1772, it was she who had to give her consent to the union of Marina Ogilvy and Paul Mowatt, and for the sake of history this is recorded with a hand-written vellum document. For more than 200 years the wording has remained unchanged and has always begun, depending upon the monarch's relationship to the recipient, 'My trusty and well-beloved cousin ...' From the Queen's Private Secretary came a message to the Crown Office in the Lord Chamberlain's department that these words were to be deleted from Marina's document. It was no less than a public declaration that the Queen strongly disapproved of her cousin's behaviour. She had seen the *Today* article as a bitter attack on Princess Alexandra that she could not forgive. An attack that had been unnecessary and had achieved nothing other than a certain notoriety for Marina. Whilst the deletion of a few simple words from the marriage consent may seem superficial, it was the only way the Queen could make a public statement without actually speaking out and causing even more of a scandal. Taken in its historical context the Queen's change of wording on the document has even greater significance, almost as if her feelings are written on vellum for posterity. Within a short time of Zenouska's birth Princess Alexandra met her daughter and granddaughter and the reconciliation began. Princess Alexandra cradled Zenouska in her arms at Thatched House Lodge, and from that moment any past animosity began to melt. The lifestyles of the Mowatts and the Ogilvys will always be divergent, their styles of communication at odds, but ultimately it could well be Zenouska who will cause a strengthening of family bonds.

There is an irony in the fact that Princess Alexandra, who has led such a successful public life, should have encountered so many family problems behind the scenes. Unlike Princess Margaret who has had the spotlight focused on her personal life, eclipsing completely the good works she has undertaken. Some of the tragedy in the Kent background seems to haunt the family to this day. Just when Alexandra's life seems to be running smoothly, fate gives the Kents another blow. The situation with her daughter Marina had followed hot on the heels of distressing allegations that her mother, Princess Marina, had once had an affair with the entertainer Danny Kaye. An accusation Alexandra repudiates. Since the death of Danny Kaye in March 1987, such implications became easy with neither party alive to defend themselves. Indeed in the 1940's when 'The Margaret Set' was making headlines, it was Princess Margaret who was supposed to be cavorting with Mr Kaye. They had met backstage at the London Palladium and Margaret later invited him to lunch, and when the Princess danced the can-can at the American Ambassador's residence in Prince's Gate, at a private party, it was revealed that Danny Kaye had coached her. When the Queen's sister went to see the show *Call Me Madam*, she learned that the Lord Chamberlain had censored the line 'Even Princess Margaret goes out with Danny Kaye,' to her great amusement. Perhaps after Danny Kaye's death one Princess M became confused with another ... Either way Princess Alexandra's family was once again at the centre of controversy.

Particularly close to her brothers, Edward and Michael, Princess Alexandra's public smile has belied the emotional turmoil she has suffered with them in the last two decades. Since the death of Princess Marina, Alexandra has almost taken over a maternal role towards them and both feel that they can share their worries with their only sister. For Edward, Duke of Kent, the late Seventies presented particular personal concerns. Firstly came the question of finance, with the ever-increasing cost of maintaining Coppins on his Army pay. Like Alexandra he received a Civil List allowance (due to the Queen's refund) but this was insufficient to cover the expenses for the royal duties he undertook. Unable to fulfil such a packed schedule as his sister he felt unable to request an increase, and he did not have the advantage that Alexandra had of a husband to supplement her allowance. Eventually, after much agonizing, the problem was solved through the sale of Coppins, the family home, and the acceptance of a grace-and-favour apartment at York House – part of St James's Palace where Alexandra has her office and *pied-à-terre*. They also bought the lease of Anmer Hall, a late-Georgian house on the Sandringham estate in Norfolk. After a lengthy discussion with the Queen, Edward also resigned from the Army and took up the post of Vice-Chairman to the British Overseas Trade Board. His experience of official overseas tours being a distinct advantage, as was his mastery of languages.

During this period of upheaval, in July 1977, Katharine, the Duchess of Kent, discovered that she was pregnant. They already had three children, Alexandra's nieces and nephews, George, Earl of St Andrews (named after Edward and Alexandra's father, the late Duke of Kent); Lady Helen Windsor (named after Princess Marina's mother) and Lord Nicholas Windsor (after Princess Marina's father). The youngest at this time was seven, and at the age of forty-four there were concerns about Katharine's health at an age when childbearing is considered unwise. The baby was due in February 1978, the month of her forty-fifth birthday.

At first the Royal Family were elated by the unexpected news, and any fears Princess Alexandra may have had she kept to herself. Unlike her own pregnancies when she had withdrawn from public life almost as soon as her condition was known (Alexandra withdrew from engagements in July 1963 and her son was not born until 29 February 1964), by the late Seventies many women continued to work throughout. In 1977 Princess Anne was also expecting a baby, her first child born that November, and appeared throughout Jubilee Year even when very heavily pregnant. The Duchess of Kent compromised by easing her workload, resting more than usual, but felt healthy enough until the fifth month when she suddenly suffered severe pain. The Duke cancelled a planned trip to Iran and drove Katharine to the King Edward VII Hospital for Officers, Marylebone, in London, just a short distance from York House. After an agonizing thirty-six hours, the Queen's gynaecologist, George Pinker, delivered a stillborn baby on 5 October. Katharine knew that it signified her last chance of having any more children. It was to have a profound effect on her.

Having come to terms with the initial shock of an unplanned pregnancy at her age, Katharine and Edward had been excited about the forthcoming baby. Its loss devastated them both, but for a time the Duchess managed to maintain the royal mask that betrayed no emotion. She resumed engagements eighteen days after leaving hospital and to the outside world seemed to have recovered. Princess Alexandra was one of the few people who knew of the private depression that her sister-in-law was suffering and it became a time for Kent family unity.

The first public sign that all was not well came on a visit to the Royal Northern College of Music in Manchester, which the Duchess of Kent abruptly cut short in February 1978. It was the day her baby had been due. With the support of her family she had tried to carry on as normal, but a deep depression was slowly taking hold. One by one she would cancel her engagements at the last minute, unable to face crowds, fearful of seeing mothers with young babies, frightened of making a fool of herself in public. A planned tour of New Zealand was indefinitely postponed. Although the Duke could have gone on alone, he was anxious about leaving his wife. With York House so close to her office and part of the same building as their St James's Palace flat, Princess Alexandra would visit Katharine to offer words of comfort and support. As important, she was there for her brother to unload his fears.

Part of Katharine's problem was still a nagging pain inside her and she feared that it might be something serious, possibly something doctors had kept from her which might even have terminated her pregnancy. After tests in March the Duchess was found to have a gall bladder problem and found herself back in hospital for an operation. This did nothing to raise her spirits and only deepened her depression. After a period of convalescence over Easter, as the summer came there was hope that she might resume her public role and engagements were pencilled tentatively in the diary, but again were cancelled at the eleventh hour, the Duchess having lost her confidence. In the winter of 1978, Edward and Alexandra, both sharing a love of music and opera with Katharine, thought that some involvement in music might be therapeutic and they persuaded her to join a choir. Possessing a clear soprano voice, she joined the Bach Choir under the guidance of its musical director, Sir David Willcocks. The Duchess knew that Sir David would only accept her if her voice was good enough. It was, and this boosted her morale. It had been a mutual love of music that had initially drawn the Duke and Duchess together and she became involved in the Leeds International Pianoforte Competition and Patron of the Northern College of Music. By December 1978, when the Duke and Duchess of Kent joined the Royal Family at Windsor Castle for Christmas, Katharine seemed brighter. They stayed in the Edward III Tower with their eldest son, Prince and Princess Michael of Kent, and James and Marina Ogilvy. Just along the corridor in the Lancaster Tower were Princess Alexandra and Angus Ogilvy, Princess Margaret, Viscount Linley, Lord Frederick and Lord Nicholas Windsor, Princess Anne and Captain Mark Phillips, like the most exclusive hotel guest list in the world. All aware that 'Katie' had been suffering from depression each in their own way tried to show her love and support. Of the assembled gathering Princess Alexandra had been the first member of the Royal Family there that she had ever met when Edward had brought her to Coppins thirty years earlier to meet Princess Marina, and the two had a rapport. Alexandra tried hard to show her sister-in-law that the family did care and were there to back her up, and was perhaps conscious of her own royal training that had given her strength in any crisis. A training that Katharine had lacked.

When the whole entourage moved on to Sandringham for New Year, the Duke and Duchess of Kent went to Anmer Hall, and the Ogilvys stayed with them rather than in the main house with the Queen. Just when Katharine seemed so much better, that January her mother Joyce, Lady Worsley, died. As an only daughter, Katharine had been particularly close to her mother and the loss proved devastating. Within weeks of the funeral she was so depressed that she suffered a complete nervous breakdown. For more than a month only her immediate family, including Princess Alexandra, were allowed to visit. Although there was little Princess Alexandra could do for Katharine, her brother Edward now needed her more than ever and it was her strength that pulled him through. The road to recovery was to be long and arduous. Just when the Duchess appeared to be fully recovered she would suffer a relapse. In 1983 she again suffered stomach pains that made her relive the loss of her baby five years before. Once more she was admitted to hospital and this time an ovarian cyst was removed. It seemed to be an unending catalogue of medical problems, and it was not until 1985 that the Duchess of Kent emerged from a dark tunnel of depression. Today she is back undertaking a full programme of engagements and devotes her spare time to the Samaritans, who understand perhaps more than any organization the problems of depression. When the Duchess speaks, anonymously, to a distraught caller, her gentle voice can offer hope based on personal experience.

Having conquered the tragedy, the Kent family have been drawn closer, and with many interests in common Alexandra and Angus will frequently socialize with Edward and Katharine either at York House or Thatched House Lodge, and when the Royal Family began spending Christmases at Sandringham again in 1988 after a twenty-five-year gap due to extensive restoration work on Windsor Castle, the Ogilvys joined the Kents at Anmer Hall. Their son James and his wife Julia are always there; their daughter Marina and husband Paul choose to stay away. Not invited, to her embarrassment, is Princess Alexandra's younger brother Prince Michael and his wife Marie-Christine. Neither are they invited to Balmoral in the summer. 'The Queen only has room for her immediate family,' say Buckingham Palace, but Prince Michael is just as much a cousin to the Queen as Princess Alexandra.

During the drama of the Duchess of Kent's nervous breakdown, Princess Alexandra also had to cope with the problems of Prince Michael. At a dinner party with their Gloucester cousins at the family home 'Barnwell' in Northamptonshire in 1971, Michael had met for the first time the statuesque Marie-Christine von Reibnitz. At that time married to Thomas Troubridge, a merchant banker friend of Prince William of Gloucester's. Five months later Prince William was tragically killed while taking part in an air race at the age of thirty-one. In 1977 while the Kent family were suffering anxiety about the Duchess of Kent's baby, Prince Michael met Marie-Christine again. First at a luncheon for the Red Cross, of which Princess Alexandra is Patron, and then by coincidence near Thatched House Lodge when both were riding in Richmond Park. By this time Marie-Christine was separated from Thomas Troubridge and was attempting to get the marriage annulled. As a Roman Catholic if she divorced she could not marry again in Church, but an annulment would be like wiping the slate clean as if the marriage had never occurred.

Prince Michael was then thirty-five and although there had been dalliances, some questioned whether he would ever marry. In Marie-Christine he found many attractive qualities. She was certainly striking in appearance and in teenage years had been nicknamed the Amazon because of her height. She had the wit and intelligence, like that of Wallis Simpson, to captivate a Prince's heart. Prince Michael was also drawn to her voice, low with just the trace of a foreign accent like Princess Marina's.

Three years younger than Prince Michael, Marie-Christine was born in Czechoslovakia, and at a few weeks old moved with her parents, Baron Günther von Reibnitz and Countess Mary Szapary, to Austria. Within a few years her parents divorced and in 1950 Marie-Christine went to Australia to live with her mother, who married for a second time to Count Thadeus Rogala-Koczorowaska. Marie-Christine was educated at a convent in Rose Bay, Sydney, and on completion moved to Vienna before finally settling in London, where she launched her own interior design company, Szapar Designs.

When Prince Michael told his sister that he wanted to marry, Princess Alexandra knew there would be difficulties and once again the Queen was to be placed in an awkward position. As Marie-Christine was separated, the question of whether she received an annulment or a divorce was paramount. If she, as a divorcee, wanted to marry Prince Michael history would be repeating itself. For the sake of marrying a divorcee, Wallis Simpson, Edward VIII had been forced to abdicate. At the risk of her own personal happiness, the Queen's own sister Princess Margaret had faced fierce opposition when she wanted to marry Group Captain Peter Townsend because he had been divorced. The Queen could not allow Prince Michael to then go ahead and marry a divorcee without provisos. The supreme irony is that Princess Margaret is now herself divorced, Princess Anne is separated and on the verge of divorce. Should either wish to remarry, the Queen will be faced with a dilemma by her own sister or daughter. With Marie-Christine, however, there was an added complication. As a Roman Catholic she could not marry anyone in the line of succession under the 1701 Act of Settlement which had been passed to keep the British Royal Family Protestant. Prince Michael was then sixteenth in line to the throne, just ahead of Princess Alexandra.

In April 1978 Marie-Christine succeeded in having her marriage to Thomas Troubridge annulled by the Vatican, her grounds had been that her former husband had denied her children. In order to marry, the Queen and Prince Michael solved the problem through his renunciation of any rights to accession, which instantly moved Alexandra up a place in the line, and compromised with the agreement that as long as any subsequent children were raised in the Anglican faith they would not be excluded from their rights. Although this placated the Queen and complied with the Act of Succession and the Royal Marriages Act of 1772, the very fact that the Catholic Marie-Christine would have Anglican children did not satisfy the Pope who refused them a Church wedding.

The couple were eventually married in a civil ceremony on 30 June, 1978, at the *Rathaus* in Vienna, members of the Royal Family being exempted from registry office weddings in England. The reason being that it was assumed royalty would never want a civil ceremony. Princess Alexandra and Angus Ogilvy were amongst the small family contingent to attend the wedding, which included Princess Anne, Lord Mountbatten and the Duke of Kent. Some five years were to pass before Pope John Paul II agreed that their union could be recognized by the Roman Catholic Church and on 29 July 1983 Princess Alexandra and Angus witnessed a final small ceremony in London at which her brother's marriage was finally blessed. By this time Marie-Christine had the title 'Princess Michael of Kent', and the couple had taken up residence at Kensington Palace. In their ten-roomed apartment are many reminders of the Kent background, Princess Marina's books, a portrait of Prince Nicholas of Greece, and many of the late Duke of Kent's *objets d'art*.

Princess Alexandra has been a symbol of stability and reassurance throughout her brother's marital difficulties, always there in the background for guidance and support. Those who know the Ogilvy family well feel that Alexandra is the strongest of the family, head of the household, almost taking the place of Princess Marina. Princess Michael of Kent has gone on to become one of the most controversial members of the Royal Family in recent years, especially following her own revelations that she did not wish to spend her life 'kissing babies and cutting ribbons' (the Prince and Princess receive nothing from the Civil List and carry out engagements at their own expense); and the much publicized episodes concerning her father's involvement with Hitler's ss, and the plagiarism in her first book *Crowned in a Far Country*. The Queen has said Marie-Christine is 'more royal than the rest of us' when discussing Princess Michael's manner; Lady Colin Campbell revealed that 'Princess Margaret would rather drink a cup of poison than have a drink with Princess Michael,' and Viscount Linley when interviewed by *Ritz* magazine when asked what he would give his worst enemy for Christmas replied 'Dinner with Princess Michael of Kent'. Her critics loved him for it. Princess Michael has never helped her own cause with well-publicized comments such as, 'The English love failure. I only really feel content when I'm in America,' and, 'The English distrust foreigners – the wogs begin at Calais.' Had she really thought about it, her late mother-in-law Princess Marina was as 'foreign' as could be yet was accepted with open arms by the English.

Only in recent years has Marie-Christine learned from Princess Alexandra's discretion and conscientiously steered clear of controversy. Alexandra has learned only too well that controversy comes unbidden without any help from mistimed comments. Despite the problems Princess Alexandra has experienced within her own family, the deliberate decision to remain in the shadows only serves to enhance her reputation as the years go by. The collapse of Princess Margaret's and Princess Anne's marriages has made her own thirty years with Angus Ogilvy seem stronger in comparison and now on a par with the Queen's. Within the family itself the problems encountered by Alexandra's brothers, through no fault of their own, made her choice of partner uncomplicated. In the Nineties when the state of the Prince and Princess of Wales' marriage is discussed or the Duchess of York is admonished for her lack of dignity, Princess Alexandra is shown to be a paragon of virtue.

Unnoticed, Princess Alexandra will frequently slip into Clarence House for a quiet tea with her aunt, the Queen Mother. Throughout Alexandra's childhood, as Queen Elizabeth, she had brought unity to Britain, became a focus for attention during the war, and gained nothing but admiration for her unfailing comfort to those who had lost their homes and loved ones during the blitz, and the news that she had learned to use a revolver 'so that I shall not go down like all the others'. It is this calm dignity and strong inner fighting spirit that Princess Alexandra most exemplifies. While the world debated the love affair of Princess Margaret and Peter Townsend, the Queen Mother retained a low public profile, made no comment, and emerged from her daughter's situation with no blot on her own character. If Princess Margaret seemed wayward and unconventional no blame was ever laid at the Queen Mother's door. Like a mirror reflection, Princess Alexandra equally made no public comment when her own daughter, Marina, caused controversy. Even though mud was thrown at Alexandra's character, so clean was her image that none of it was able to stick. With the passing of the Queen Mother, Princess Alexandra will stand out as one of the last of a former generation of royals, taught never to show emotion, to place duty before personal desire and above all uphold the dignity of the monarchy. When respected author Douglas Keay watched Princess Alexandra in Australia sitting through forty minutes of speeches in sweltering heat, her back ramrod straight and never once touching the chair, he later asked her how she did it. 'Upbringing,' she replied with the wistful smile, so like Princess Marina's. 'Don't forget, Queen Mary was my grandmother.' When the Queen Mother rode in an open landau for a ninetieth birthday tribute on Horse Guards Parade on 27 June 1990, whether sitting in the carriage or on the dais for the hour-long parade, her back too remained equally straight, never once leaning back for support, displaying no signs of fatigue. As Queen Mary had said to a young member of her family, 'We are Royal. We are *never* tired.' Time and again Princess Alexandra displays evidence of her grandmother's training. Queen Mary would not be disappointed.

Shortly after his engagement to Princess Alexandra, Angus Ogilvy received a telephone call from Kensington Palace. It was Princess Marina, his mother-in-law to be. 'I have been informed that at your dinner parties you are introducing my daughter as Alexandra,' she said. 'This really will not do. If the mystique of the monarchy is to be maintained my daughter must be introduced as *Princess* Alexandra and afterwards referred to as Ma'am.' It was an early lesson for the 'commoner' husband. Of the many personal problems that have arisen within Alexandra's family the fundamental differences of upbringing appear to have been the underlying cause. In her own case her mother had wished for a union with a European Prince, and had Alexandra followed her desired path a royal husband would not have faced the long period of adjustment that Angus needed. Their children would have been titled and as such might not have developed the complex that Marina Ogilvy so obviously had. Katharine Worsley faced opposition at first from Princess Marina, and the depression she eventually suffered can only have been made worse by the glare of media attention. As plain Mrs Katharine Kent she could have received treatment and regained her health without the added pressures of public duty. Even though Marie-Christine von Reibnitz said of her family '900 years of breeding must be worth something' and has been angered by any writer who has dared to call her a 'commoner' she has, nevertheless, found integration into the Royal Family difficult and even after more than fourteen years of marriage is still made to feel an outsider. When Angus Ogilvy was admitted to King Edward VII Hospital suffering from exhaustion after the Lonrho affair, both he and Alexandra knew that the pressures upon him would never have been as great had it not been for the simple fact that he had been married to a member of the Royal Family. Just as *Today* newspaper would have had no interest in Marina Ogilvy's everyday story of a family rift had her mother not been Princess Alexandra. Even as a schoolgirl Marina knew why she, as Mrs Ogilvy's daughter, received so many invitations for tea from the other girls' mothers.

Within the Windsor family itself both the non-royal Lady Diana Spencer and Miss Sarah Ferguson encountered long periods of adjustment after entering the world that Princess Margaret once likened to being 'trapped in a gilded cage'. True acceptance within the family takes decades. Few today would consider Queen Elizabeth the Queen Mother to be anything other than royal, but she encountered blatant hostility in the early years of her marriage as Lady Elizabeth Bowes-Lyon – not from the general public, but from the Family who felt that she was 'not like one of us'. By the time of her ninetieth birthday she had become like a piece of England itself, beyond criticism, it was sacrilegious to say a word against her.

That Princess Alexandra is also held in such high regard did not really become truly apparent until the end of 1989. By the time she celebrated her fifty-third birthday on Christmas Day, surrounded by her immediate family at Sandringham, having received more than the usual number of birthday cards and letters of support and nothing but praise from the media, there was a general feeling that Princess Alexandra like her Aunt Elizabeth was beyond attack. Her daughter Marina had within her power the ability to blacken her mother's character, destroy her reputation. Although no day will ever again seem as black as the one Princess Alexandra experienced on reading her own daughter's view of her in the newspaper, it proved the ultimate test. That she survived did not surprise her family. As a teenager Alexandra once expressed a fear that the Queen might believe fabricated stories that were being written about her. 'You might just as well think that Her Majesty doesn't know the difference between real diamonds and paste,' she was told. To the general public Alexandra will always be voted one of the jewels in the Royal Family's crown, and throughout 1990 she discovered how discerning the public really are. Within days of Marina's revelations Princess Alexandra carried out engagements in London, Hampshire, Leicestershire, Devon, Somerset and Norfolk. From launching a new Harbour and Coastal tug for the Alexandra Towing Company in Great Yarmouth to opening a new Housing-with-Care scheme in Plymouth, from visiting a Red Cross Training Centre in Taunton to hosting a Diplomatic Reception at Buckingham Palace, Princess Alexandra was cheered *en route* and received nothing but warmth and support. Not censured for failing as a mother but reappraised through her handling of the situation, in a strange way it was as if Marina Ogilvy had actually done her mother a favour.

In December 1990 Princess Alexandra spent her first Christmas and birthday away from the leading players of the Royal Family. For over fifty years she had gone to Sandringham or Windsor, but decided instead to have a quiet Christmas at Thatched House Lodge, spending part of the time with the Duke and Duchess of Kent at their new home in the village of Nettlebed, near Henley-on-Thames. An eight-bedroomed Queen Anne house with its own apple orchard and wood-land views, Princess Alexandra said when she first saw it that the interior reminded her of Coppins. George, Earl of St Andrews, Alexandra's eldest nephew was also there. In January 1988 George had married Canadian divorcee Sylvana Palma, the daughter of Mr Max Tomaselli and Mrs Josiane Demers, and for the Kents there must have been a feeling of *déjà vu*, for not only was Sylvana divorced but she was also a Roman Catholic, albeit a lapsed one. Like Prince Michael of Kent, George St Andrews renounced his rights of succession to the throne in order to marry, but made history by becoming the first member of the House of Windsor to be married in a registry office. By renouncing all rights, including those of his children, George was able to have a civil ceremony and although he will eventually inherit his father's title, he will not be allowed the prefix 'His Royal Highness'. Through him the Dukes of Kent will cease to be royal. Their first son, christened Edward after his grandfather, is known as Lord Downpatrick. Born on 2 December 1988, he really will be able to lead an 'ordinary' life, and unlike the other Kent children has not had a nanny or a chauffeur and has never needed security protection. Alexandra, Edward and Michael are now the last of the Kents who will ever bear the titles of Prince and Princess. Their eventual demise will close a chapter in royal history.

The Eighties had proved an emotionally difficult time for all branches of the Kent family for varying reasons, but in times of trial they had remained united. Throughout 1990, after Alexandra and Angus's trauma with Marina, it seemed as if the Kents became even closer, both publicly and in private. When the Duke and Duchess of Kent made their annual pilgrimage to the Wimbledon Lawn Tennis Championships, as Princess Marina and the late Duke of Kent had done in the years before them, on finals day that July Princess Alexandra was there in the royal box beside them. While the rest of the Royal Family were at Sandringham that Christmas attending the christening ceremony of nine-month-old Princess Eugenie of York in the Church of St Mary Magdalene, it was one of the rare occasions when Princess Alexandra was missing. Instead the family was represented by Alexandra's son, James, who had been chosen as one of Eugenie's five godparents. Away from the cameras and the protocol, Princess Alexandra toasted the latest addition to the Royal Family from afar and slipped quietly into the background.

Watching a film of the York christening, which had taken place just two days before Christmas, Princess Alexandra might have reflected on her own baptism over half-a-century before. In common, babies Alexandra and Eugenie had worn the same Honiton lace christening

[Handwritten marginal note:] Thought that the children of George would be in line of succession to the throne. If the son is raised as a protestant, he should still be in line of succession, after his grandfather, the Duke of Kent.

robe, but there were significant differences which mirrored the changing face of royalty. Princess Alexandra's godparents had been a reigning monarch and his Queen Consort, the Queen of Norway, two Princesses, an Earl and a Count. Princess Eugenie's are the untitled James Ogilvy, Susan Ferguson, Alistair Ross, Julia Dodd Noble and Lulu Blacker – the Duke of York's cousin, the Duchess's stepmother and three close friends. Princess Alexandra's had taken place in the privacy of Buckingham Palace; Princess Eugenie's christening took place at a public church service. Like Alexandra, Eugenie (even if she undertakes royal duty) will always be overshadowed by her more important Wales cousins, and will be superseded by any brothers she may have. From a new generation, however, Eugenie faces a future that can never be like Princess Alexandra's past.

By a quirk of fate, soon after Princess Alexandra's christening there were rumours of war. A war which drew the monarchy and its people closer. The Gulf War of 1991 occurred within weeks of Princess Eugenie's christening, a war that was to call the Royal Family's role and relevance into question as we approach the twenty-first century.

The Secret of Success

There was a general hush among the small gathering of onlookers as the actress, Noele Gordon, fell in a dead faint at Princess Alexandra's feet. Shown that evening on a Midlands television bulletin, without soundtrack, viewers later admonished the popular actress for being drunk in front of royalty. Others assumed she had passed out at the sight of the Princess, but in reality it was Alexandra who had caused the 'soap' star's lack of decorum.

On an official visit to new television studios in Birmingham Princess Alexandra watched a rehearsal. 'Something awful has just happened to my son and I have to faint,' Noele Gordon explained.

'Go on then, show me,' the Princess dared.

Noele Gordon collapsed at Alexandra's feet to a polite round of applause. Later the Princess roared with laughter when she discovered that the actor playing Noele Gordon's son was returning to the series after a long absence and thought the crowds lining the streets outside the studio were to welcome him back, not realizing that Princess Alexandra was officially opening the new television centre. It was the kind of story that appealed to her. Once when visiting the BBC studios she became separated from the official party and bumped into comedian, Bob Monkhouse, who assumed she was a member of the public.

'Hello darling, you shouldn't be in here, you know,' he told her.

'I must be getting back,' said the Princess, 'the people I've come with will be missing me.'

The comedian then offered her tickets to see his show which she enthusiastically accepted. When someone rushed forward to tell him who Princess Alexandra was, Bob Monkhouse replied, 'I'm the one who makes the jokes around here.'

Once voted the least arrogant member of the Royal Family in an opinion poll, it is Princess Alexandra's ease of manner and obvious enjoyment of her work that has maintained her popularity. Unpretentious in her approach, when she visited Alice Springs in 1980 she shocked officials by choosing to explore the area by bicycle. She wanted to see the region for herself, at her own pace. It would be difficult to visualize the Queen making such a decision, yet Alexandra managed it with dignity. 'Don't forget that nowadays we have to compete with the Beatles and Elizabeth Taylor,' she had said in the Sixties and she has always managed to walk the fine tightrope, maintaining that balance between being human yet seeming royal.

Princess Alexandra has tried to adhere to Walter Bagehot's dictum of not allowing too much daylight in upon the magic for fear of destroying the mystique. For this reason she has consciously steered clear of revealing trivia about herself. We do not know what she has for breakfast, what her favourite television programme is or whether she uses an ozone-friendly hairspray, and she is not sure that we should know. Yes, it makes the Royal Family more human, less remote some would say, but whilst she would not wish royalty to take on divine status, Alexandra does see advantages in the mystique. Her human qualities that shine through, such as delight at not being recognized and being offered free tickets to a television recording, are all the more apparent without trivial revelations. Many journalists felt as Alexandra reached her fiftieth birthday in 1986 (the year in which so much was made of the Queen's sixtieth birthday) that she should break her rule and give an interview about herself. Yet the two members of the family who have never given an interview, Alexandra and the Queen, are the two who have actually done most to retain the mystique. When the Queen Mother gave not so much an interview as a tour of her garden at Royal Lodge to be shown on television at the time of her ninetieth birthday, viewers were left feeling none the wiser.

'And are you against the use of pesticides, Ma'am?' Sir Alastair Burnet probed with great reverence, repeating the question twice as if the answer was going to be a great revelation.

'I don't know anything about them,' replied the Queen Mother with a smile, wandering towards the azaleas as if she were about to accept a bouquet from a small child. Although 'at home' in her own garden, she was still wearing her familiar upturned-brim hat with matching coat and dress, a style that once caused author Alan Hamilton to roguishly refer to her as 'the royal lampshade'.

Far more revealing than a formal interview are Princess Alexandra's natural actions that say far more about her character. I have seen her at a film première on the bitterest of days walk over to the Press party and say, 'Thank you for waiting, you must be frozen,' showing a genuine concern, certainly in comparison to the stars of the film who had previously swept into the cinema concerned only that the wind did not ruin their hairstyle and that the Press managed to get a shot of their best side. At theatrical galas she has made sure that her guests in the royal box are seated comfortably before she sits down herself, displaying an inherent courtesy. It is the simplest of actions that people remember.

When she enters a room on an engagement it is usually so quietly that few realize she is there, until suddenly she is upon you, stretching out an ungloved hand, asking a searching question with a gleam in her eye as if she genuinely wants to know the answer. Her technique is to often include several people in the conversation at the same time so that it does not turn into a royal interrogation. Always there is laughter. Even when faced with the unexpected, experience has taught her how to handle any situation.

For the woman Henry 'Chips' Channon once described as 'a whirlwind of a girl', public life offers a constant stimulus on which she thrives. No longer an ebullient teenager, her outgoing personality has nevertheless been an advantage. Her Aunt Mary, the late Princess Royal, and Aunt Alice, the Dowager Duchess of Gloucester, were never comfortable about public life, always suffered from nerves and appeared over formal. Princess Alexandra enjoys the fact that by its very nature her public life is varied. One day visiting a home for the blind who have to be able to hear and touch her, the next conferring degrees on students for whom the sight of her at this climactic moment in their education they will carry with them through life. Once saying of herself, 'God, I must be so boring,' before anyone comes into contact with Princess Alexandra the inevitable question arises, 'Is she really as nice as she seems?' In my 'royal' career I have always found Alexandra to be a favourite, and having spoken with people from all walks of life who have come into contact with royalty for whatever reason, I find people are always happy to share their experiences, their moment of glory, be they good or bad. Not once have I been told of any disappointment with Princess Alexandra's performance.

'I met Princess Margaret once,' said a Sky TV presenter, just seconds before we went on air, 'and quite frankly she was bloody rude.'

'I was at a dinner party once with Princess Margaret,' said another broadcaster as we recorded a programme for the British Forces Overseas. 'She took one mouthful of the soup, put down her spoon and lit a cigarette. That effectively ended the first course. We all had to stop.'

The Queen, the Princess Royal, even the Princess of Wales, have occasionally offended members of the public by their approach, be it deliberate or unconscious on their part, but ask anyone about their meeting with Princess Alexandra and their response is enthusiastic. One could recount details of the 5,000 plus engagements she has carried out since 1954 and it would be a catalogue of success. Before the Queen abolished the debutante system, a tiaraed Princess Alexandra would sit regally on the dais beside Her Majesty at presentation parties in the Throne Room at Buckingham Palace; she has been a Counsellor of State in her time acting as 'deputy' monarch in the Queen's absence, opened turbine factories, switched on the Christmas lights in London's Regent Street (1983), even attended rugby and football matches in the course of duty. When other members of the Royal Family are present, be it the Festival of Remembrance each November or Trooping the Colour every June, Princess Alexandra is always there in the background showing parity and support. Her life is full, varied, and often to the media so boringly successful that it is seldom considered newsworthy. It must be galling that in four decades of public life, in recent years she has gained notoriety with the younger generation only as the mother of Marina Ogilvy.

So, is the 'niceness' natural or merely a public image? Those who have worked closely with the Princess are adamant that Alexandra has no pretensions. As with Princess Marina there is an underlying toughness below the surface, a resilient inner core of steel that makes her less vulnerable than she appears, which manifests itself more in determination and strength of will than anger or negative energy. Those I know who only ever met Princess Marina on an official level remember her as quiet, gentle and reserved. Those I also know who worked for the Kents and saw Marina behind closed doors paint a slightly different picture. She could be tough, always a stickler for protocol, and very capable of showing any displeasure. Yet, like Alexandra, the firmness was tempered with humour and grace, and she detested gossip. Whereas the Queen knows all that is going on within her various households, Princess Marina only ever wanted to hear good news about anyone. If her friends or even her lady's maid had anything salacious to impart, Marina would refuse to listen and admonish them for tittle-tattle. Her humour was never malicious and she had a gift for mimicry. If, for example, she heard her butler, Bysouth, complaining or arguing with a member of her staff she would frequently stand giggling behind the door like a schoolgirl giving her family a running commentary of all she could hear. As a result, Princess Alexandra's childhood was strict but tempered with love and laughter.

In a biography of Princess Marina, the author J. Wentworth Day* summed up the Duchess of Kent as a mother, writing of Marina: 'She brought up the two Princes and Princess Alexandra in a thoroughly down-to-earth democratic way, but with a proper sense of their own inherited responsibilities.'

This was then the foundation upon which Princess Alexandra's life was built; never molly-coddled by her mother, and forever conscious of her obligations. Because they were inherent, Alexandra has never longed for the freedom of an ordinary life as Princess Margaret and Princess Anne did in their youth; if she rebelled it was as an immature method of gaining attention, it was never an attack on her status. Neither, in adult life, has she ever seriously broken the unwritten rules of royal conduct. She has never sworn in public, like Princess Anne; she has not shown ill-temper as her cousin Prince Philip has; criticism has never been levelled at her for a lack of decorum, nor have there ever been complaints that she has shirked her duties or not pulled her weight. The early training instilled by Queen Mary has never been forgotten or ignored.

*J. Wentworth Day, HRH Princess Marina (Robert Hale, 1962).

Princess Alexandra benefited from two intelligent parents who were appreciative of the arts, music and literature, and their own interests have rubbed off on their daughter. At Thatched House Lodge she has collected many beautiful antiques, creating an elegant setting for private life and public duty. In her own home she has been able to entertain such distinguished guests as Prince Naruhito of Japan, just as Princess Marina did with the dignitaries of her day at Kensington Palace. She shares her parents' love of the cinema, favourite films in recent years being *Yentl*, *Heat and Dust*, and *My Left Foot*, the story of Christy Brown who suffered from Cerebral Palsy. Were she not interested in these areas, the whole royal way of life and work would be anathema to her, being a world where patronage of the arts is part and parcel of royal duty. A royal career is like any other job; if you do not enjoy it or lack a flair for the work, it can never be well carried out.

In her private life Princess Alexandra has suffered more than her fair share of unsettled weather. In adult life there has been the inevitable emergence of further details about her father's sexual proclivities before he was married. Details that she could not be shielded from, although how much Princess Marina was aware will never be known. Bisexual, Prince George had affairs with both sexes, having a liking for black women and blond men, many procured at the Embassy Club in London's Bond Street which he frequented with his brother David (the late Duke of Windsor). At one time he expressed a desire to marry one of his mistresses, Poppy Baring, until a little royal detective work found her past unsuitable for a royal future as a Duchess of Kent. His alleged affair with 'The Master', Noël Coward, became London society gossip only through the latter's boasting, although the appearance of some love letters written by George to a man in Paris almost created a scandal, diverted only because the Prince purchased his letters back.

When he became involved with the American Kiki Whitney Preston of the 'Happy Valley Set', he became addicted for a time to cocaine and morphine, and only his discretion, and the fact that he was mysteriously spirited away to a private clinic, avoided yet another potential scandal. Although some felt that George was pushed into marriage with Princess Marina, theirs appears ultimately to have been a love match and the Greek Princess had a calming influence on the wayward English Prince. Fatherhood became the making of him and he found great pleasure and pride in his three children. Princess Alexandra is able to console herself in the fact that the father she knew was a completely different character to the foolish teenager who sought constant stimulation and excitement.

In her own married life Princess Alexandra has been strengthened by the support of Angus Ogilvy. It was not a union that either rushed into lightly and they were certain of solid foundations before they took the final step. Although not royal, Angus felt that his family background was such that he had what he described as 'one foot on the steps of the throne' at least and was fully aware of the lifestyle ahead. For the Princess, Angus has been a source of encouragement and advice. He has supported her in her duties both financially and practically as an escort, prepared to stand in his wife's shadow, content to walk three paces behind. If they hold a reception at Thatched House Lodge for one of Alexandra's organizations, he will be the first to greet the guests so that the Princess can 'make an entrance'. She arrives last, even in her own home, because of protocol. Having now known each other for forty years, Alexandra and Angus are a strong, loyal team. They have not drifted apart now that the children have left home, and proved early critics wrong who suggested that a marriage between a Princess and a commoner could never last.

Princess Alexandra has conquered a potentially difficult lifestyle by consciously drawing a clear division between that which she considers to be her private life as a wife and mother, and that which is public as a member of the Royal Family. Modest about her achievements, her success lies in the fact that she can walk with Kings but has never lost the common touch. Self-sacrificing, she has a dedication to duty and a strong desire to uphold the traditions of the monarchy. Although she jokes that the Royal Family now has 'lots of new stars to fill the centre of the stage. I'm now in the back row of the chorus,' there is no sign of her workload slackening, her popularity is undiminished. In the Nineties Princess Alexandra may have a lower public profile than the Princess of Wales or the Duchess of York, but it is those who work tirelessly behind the scenes, often uncredited, that keep the royal show on the road.

Princess Alexandra's arrival into the world on Christmas Day was considered to be a good omen. As a symbol of hope, she has never broken that early promise.

Princess Alexandra Factfile

Full Title	Her Royal Highness Princess Alexandra, The Honourable Lady Ogilvy, GCVO.
Born	Friday 25 December, 1936, at 3 Belgrave Square, London.
Christened	9 February, 1937, at Buckingham Palace by the Archbishop of Canterbury, Dr Cosmo Lang.
Names	Alexandra Helen Elizabeth Olga Christabel
Godparents	King George VI Queen Elizabeth Alexander, Earl of Athlone Princess Beatrice *(youngest child of Queen Victoria and Prince Albert)* Princess Nicholas of Greece Queen Maud of Norway Count of Toerring-Jettenbach
Ailments	Appendicitis, February 1948 Adenoids removed, April 1951 German Measles, Summer 1951 Mumps, Winter 1953 Glandular fever, March 1958 Tonsils removed, May 1962 Wisdom teeth removed
Education	1943–6 Mrs Parnell, York Cottage, Iver. 1946–7 Private tutor at Coppins. 1947–52 Heathfield Boarding School (left December 1952). 1953–4 Mademoiselle Anita's Finishing School, Paris.

1956–8	Trained as a nurse, taking a course in child welfare, at Great Ormond Street Hospital, London.
Engagement	Announced on 29 November, 1962.
Marriage	Wednesday 24 April, 1963, at Westminster Abbey. Husband is the Honourable Angus James Bruce Ogilvy (born 14 September, 1928), the second son of 12th Earl of Airlie. Knighted in the New Year's Honours List 1989.
Children	1 James Robert Bruce Ogilvy, born 29 February, 1964. Married Julia Rawlinson on 30 July, 1988, at Saffron Walden Church, Essex. 2 Marina Victoria Alexandra Ogilvy, born 31 July, 1966. Married Paul Mowatt on 3 February, 1990, at St Andrew's Church, Richmond. Daughter Zenouska Mowatt born 26 May, 1990, at Queen Mary's Hospital, Roehampton, London.
Residences	Thatched House Lodge, Richmond, Surrey. Friary Court, St James's Palace, London.
Interests	Music (from Jazz to Classical) Playing the piano Riding Walking Salmon fishing Tennis (taught by Dan Maskell) Skiing Photography Swimming

APPENDIX II

HRH Princess Alexandra, The Hon. Lady Ogilvy Patronages and Official Appointments

Patron and President

Action for Blind People	Patron
Alexandra House (Royal United Service Short Stay Residence for Service Children)	Patron
Alexandra Rose Day	President
Alzheimer's Disease Society	Patron
Anchor Housing Trust	Patron
Bethlem Royal and Maudsley Hospitals	Patron
British Association of Cancer United Patients (BACUP)	Patron
British Red Cross Society	Vice President
British School at Rome	President
Calcutta Tercentenary Trust	Patron
Care for Mentally Handicapped People	Patron
Central School of Speech and Drama	Patron
Children's Country Holidays Fund	President
Compass Theatre Limited	Patron
Crisis	Patron
Cystic Fibrosis Research Trust	Patron
Drug and Alcohol Foundation	Patron
Durham Light Infantry Association	Patron
Elizabeth Fitzroy Homes	Patron

English National Opera	Patron
Ernest Read Music Association	Patron
Fairbridge Drake Society	Patron
Florence Nightingale Museum Trust	Patron
Friends of the Osborne and Lillian H. Smith Collections	Patron
Girls Venture Corps Air Cadets	Patron
Guide Dogs for the Blind Association	Patron
Hellenic College of London	Patron
Jacob Sheep Society	Patron
Kew Guild, The	Patron
King Edward's Hospital Fund for London	Honorary Member – General Council
Leeds Castle Foundation	Patron
Light Infantry Club	Patron
London Academy of Music and Dramatic Art	Patron
Mental Health Foundation	Patron
Motor Allied Trades Benevolent Fund	Patron
National Association for Mental Health (MIND)	Patron
National Birthday Trust	Patron
National Florence Nightingale Memorial Committee of Great Britain and Northern Ireland	Patron
National Kidney Research Fund	Patron
New Bridge, The	Patron
People's Dispensary for Sick Animals	Patron
Queen Alexandra's House Association	President
Richmond Fellowship, The	Patron
Royal Alexandra Hospital for Sick Children	Patron
Royal Brompton National Heart and Lung Hospital	Patron
Royal Brompton National Heart and Lung Hospital Development Trust Fund	Patron
Royal Commonwealth Society for the Blind	President
Royal Humane Society	President
Royal Overseas League	Vice Patron
Royal School Hampstead	Patron
Royal Star and Garter Home for Disabled Sailors, Soldiers and Airmen, The	President
St Christopher's Hospice	Patron
Scottish Artists Benevolent Association	Patron
17th/21st Lancers Regimental Association	Patron
Tavistock Clinic	Patron

World Wide Fund for Nature – UK	President
Young Women's Christian Association of Great Britain	Vice Patron

Regiments and Service Organizations

Canadian Scottish Regiment (Princess Mary's), The	Colonel in Chief
King's Own Royal Border Regiment, The	Colonel in Chief
Light Infantry, The	Deputy Colonel in Chief
Princess Mary's Royal Air Force Nursing Service	Patron and Air Chief Commandant
Queen Alexandra's Royal Naval Nursing Service	Patron
Queen's Own Rifles of Canada, The	Colonel in Chief
Royal Hong Kong Police Force and Royal Hong Kong Auxiliary Police Force	Honorary Commandant General
Royal Yeomanry, The	Deputy Honorary Colonel
17th/21st Lancers	Colonel in Chief

University

University of Lancaster	Chancellor

Honorary Fellowships

College of Anaesthetists	Honorary Fellow
Royal College of Obstetricians and Gynaecologists	Honorary Fellow
Royal College of Physicians and Surgeons of Glasgow	Honorary Fellow

Freedoms

City of Lancaster	Freeman
City of London	Freeman
Worshipful Company of Clothworkers, The	Honorary Freewoman

Overseas Visits Made by HRH Princess Alexandra

1953–4	**France**	Lived in Paris where she stayed with the family of the Comte de Paris, attending a finishing school and studying French and music.
1954	**Canada and United States**	Accompanied her mother, the Duchess of Kent, on her tour of Canada and the United States in August and September.
1956	**Mediterranean**	Accompanied the Queen and the Duke of Edinburgh on a Mediterranean cruise in March.
1959	**South America**	Accompanied the Duchess of Kent on her tour of Latin America, visiting Mexico, Peru, Chile and Brazil in February and March.
	Australia, Thailand, Cambodia, India and Turkey	Visited Queensland for its centenary celebrations, which began in August. The Princess visited twenty-two cities and towns in Queensland and afterwards visited other parts of Australia. On the return journey paid short visits to Thailand and Cambodia and made brief stops at Delhi and Istanbul, arriving back in London in October. (This was the Princess's first Commonwealth tour alone.)
1960	**Federal Republic of Germany**	As Colonel-in-Chief The Queen's Own Rifles of Canada, visited the 2nd Battalion in Germany for the regiment's centenary celebrations in July.

	Nigeria	Three-week visit as the Queen's special representative at the Independence celebrations of the Federation of Nigeria from 1 October.
1961	**Far East**	Six-week tour of the Far East in November and December. After a private visit to Vancouver, official visits to Honolulu, Wake Island, Hong Kong, where the University was celebrating its 50th anniversary, Japan and Burma. Also visited Thailand privately, returning via Aden and Tripoli in December.
1962	**Netherlands**	Visited the Netherlands, with Princess Marina, for the silver wedding celebrations of Queen Juliana and Prince Bernhard.
	Sweden	Visited Sweden in May to open the British Trade Fair in Stockholm.
	Greece	Visited Greece to be a bridesmaid at the marriage of Princess Sophia and Don Juan Carlos of Spain on 14 May.
1963	**Spain**	Visited Spain, with Mr Ogilvy, in May after her marriage.
1965	**France**	Visited Paris in May.
	Japan, Hong Kong, Iran and Jordan	Accompanied by Mr Ogilvy, visited Tokyo to attend the British Exhibition; they spent ten days in Japan sightseeing and were entertained by the Emperor Hirohito and other members of the Japanese Imperial Family as well as the Prime Minister. They also visited Hong Kong for a weekend, Tehran for five days as guests of the Shah of Iran, and Amman for three days as guests of King Hussein of Jordan. They also visited Jerusalem and Malta.
1966	**Netherlands**	Visited Amsterdam with Mr Ogilvy and her mother, Princess Marina, Duchess of Kent, to attend the wedding on 10 March of Princess Beatrix to Jonkheer Claus van Amsberg; Princess Alexandra was one of the witnesses to the marriage.
1967	**Burma, Hong Kong and Australia**	Visit to Burma in February with Mr Ogilvy, at invitation of Burmese Head of State, General Ne Win, followed by visit to Hong Kong and private visit to

		Australia as guests of the Prime Minister.
	Canada	Official visit with Mr Ogilvy to Canada May–June, during which the Princess opened the British Columbia International Trade Fair and made an extensive tour including Yukon and Northwest Territories.
	Sweden	Visit to Sweden in September to open British Petroleum's new refinery at Gothenburg on 12 September.
	United States and Canada	Visit to North America in October, beginning with stay in United States – her first official visit. During her stay she opened the British Fortnight at the Neiman-Marcus store in Dallas. She and Mr Ogilvy then went to Canada to carry out engagements in connection with British Week in Toronto.
1968	**Sweden**	Opened British Week in Stockholm in September.
1969	**Singapore**	Represented the Queen in August during 150th anniversary celebrations of founding of modern Singapore.
	Kenya, Swaziland, Malagasy and Mauritius	After a brief stay in Nairobi, visited Swaziland in September with Mr Ogilvy for the first anniversary of the country's independence. Visited the Malagasy Republic and paid a three-day visit to Mauritius.
	Austria	Visited Vienna and opened British Week on 10 October.
1970	**Sweden**	Visited Gothenburg in June to name a tanker built for the World Wide Shipping Group at the shipyard of Gotaverken A/B.
	United States	Visited United States to open the new British Overseas Airways Corporation passenger terminal at Kennedy Airport, New York, in September.
	Argentina	In November opened British Industrial Exhibition, of which she was patron, in Buenos Aires.
1971	**New Zealand**	Visit to New Zealand in April with Mr Ogilvy, for centenary celebrations of Auckland, also visiting Napier for three

		days and Wellington briefly.
	United States	To inaugurate British Trade Week in San Francisco in September, afterwards visiting Los Angeles for two days.
1972	**United States**	Visit to New York in April for the inaugural banquet of the Variety International Convention, and for the dedication of the Mental Retardation Institute of New York Medical College.
	Afghanistan, Hong Kong and Cyprus	Visit to Afghanistan in October at the invitation of HRH Princess Bilqis, *en route* for Hong Kong to visit the Royal Hong Kong Police Force and the Royal Hong Kong Auxiliary Police Force, of which the Princess is Honorary Commandant General. On the return journey the Princess visited Princess Mary's Royal Air Force Hospital at Akrotiri, Cyprus.
1973	**Federal Republic of Germany**	After a brief stay in Bonn, visited Stuttgart for the opening of an Exhibition of British Design mounted by the Design Council and the Central Office of Information in February.
	Canada	Visited Nova Scotia in July for the bicentenary celebrations of the arrival of the Scottish settlers.
1974	**Austria**	In February, visited Vienna for the re-opening of Vienna's English Theatre.
	France	In May, at Epinay-sur-Orge, near Paris, inaugurated the External Medico-Professionnel (a unit for the treatment of handicapped children) at the Colonie Franco-Britannique de Sillery.
	Brazil	In August, following short visits to Brasilia and Rio de Janeiro, opened the British Industrial Exhibition at São Paulo.
	Poland	In October visited Poland at the invitation of the Council of State of the Polish People's Republic, carrying out engagements in and around Cracow and Warsaw.
	West Berlin	*En route* for London visited West Berlin for two days.

	Mauritius	In October travelled to Mauritius for installation ceremony as Chancellor of the University.
1975	**Mauritius**	As Chancellor of the University, visited Mauritius in October to preside at degree congregations.
1976	**Monaco**	Visited Monaco in May for the Grand Prix, accompanied by Prince Michael of Kent and Mr Ogilvy, at the invitation of Prince Rainier and Princess Grace.
	Italy	Visited the British School at Rome (of which she is President) in October, accompanied by Mr Ogilvy.
	France	Visited Paris in November, accompanied by Mr Ogilvy, for a presentation at the British Embassy by the National Wool Textile Export Corporation and a Gala Performance on the occasion of the re-opening of the Comédie Française in aid of the European Organization for Research on the Treatment of Cancer.
1977	**Hong Kong**	Visited Hong Kong with Mr Ogilvy in February for the opening of the 1977 Festival of the Arts and a programme of other engagements including a visit to the Royal Hong Kong Police Force.
	Oman	Visited the Sultanate of Oman, *en route* for London from Hong Kong.
	Malta	As Patron of Queen Alexandra's Royal Naval Nursing Service, visited Royal Naval Hospital, Mtarfa, in July, accompanied by Mr Ogilvy.
	Iran	Visited Tehran in October as Patron of the British Cultural Festival.
	Mauritius	As Chancellor of the University, visited Mauritius to preside at a graduation ceremony, accompanied by Mr Ogilvy.
	France	Accompanied by Mr Ogilvy, visited Paris in November for the opening of a Marks and Spencer store and a dinner party held at the British Embassy to mark the Queen's Silver Jubilee.
1978	**Australia**	At the invitation of the Government of the Commonwealth of Australia, a visit with Mr Ogilvy in September for the

		opening of the Annual Show of the Royal Agricultural Society of Victoria in Melbourne and also for a programme of other engagements in Canberra, Victoria, New South Wales, Queensland and the Northern Territory.
	Egypt	Visited Egypt with Mr Ogilvy in November at the invitation of President Sadat.
1979	**Saint Lucia**	Accompanied by Mr Ogilvy, represented the Queen at the Independence celebrations in February.
	Italy	Visited Venice in May with Mr Ogilvy for the unveiling of the Porta della Carta after restoration by the Venice in Peril Fund.
	Gibraltar	As Patron of Queen Alexandra's Royal Naval Nursing Service, visited the Royal Naval Hospital in June and, with Mr Ogilvy, carried out a programme of engagements.
	Fiji	Visited Fiji in August to open the South Pacific Games at Suva.
1980	**Hong Kong**	Visited Hong Kong in February, accompanied by Mr Ogilvy, for the opening of the Mass Transit Railway.
	Canada	As Colonel-in-Chief of both regiments, visited in April The Queen's Own Rifles of Canada in Toronto, Ontario, and the Canadian Scottish Regiment (Princess Mary's) at Victoria, British Columbia.
	Burma, Thailand, Hong Kong and Australia	In September and October with Mr Ogilvy, visited Burma, Thailand and Hong Kong before arriving in Australia to carry out engagements in Canberra, Victoria, South Australia, the Northern Territory and Western Australia.
1981	**France**	Accompanied by Mr Ogilvy, visited Paris in February to open the Gainsborough Exhibition at the Grand Palais, and to undertake engagements at the Hertford British Hospital and the British Cultural Centre.
1982	**United States**	Accompanied by Mr Ogilvy, visited Washington in May for the opening of

		'Lutyens 1982: A British Embassy Showcase'.
	Thailand	Accompanied by Mr Ogilvy, visited Bangkok in October for the Rattanakosin Bicentennial celebrations at the invitation of the King and Queen of Thailand.
1983	United States	Accompanied by Mr Ogilvy, visited Washington in April for the Dedication of the Ditchley Bells.
	Austria	Visited Vienna in November for the 20th anniversary celebration of Vienna's English Theatre.
1984	United States	In June, accompanied by Mr Ogilvy, visited Houston, New Orleans (attended Louisiana World Exposition), Denver and New York for engagements, as Patron, connected with the tour of English National Opera.
	France	With Mr Ogilvy, visited Cannes in October on the occasion of the celebrations to mark the 150th anniversary of the 'discovery' of the town by Lord Brougham.
	Mexico	Visited Mexico in November, accompanied by Mr Ogilvy, on the occasion of the 40th anniversaries of the British Council in Mexico City and of the foundation of the Anglo-Mexican Cultural Institute,
1985	Switzerland	Accompanied by Mr Ogilvy, visited St Moritz in February for the celebrations to mark the centenary of the Cresta Run.
	Belgium	In April visited Belgium on the occasion of the 70th Anniversary of the foundation of Talbot House (Toc H) in Poperinghe, West Flanders.
	United States	Visited Minnesota with Mr Ogilvy in September for the opening events of the British Festival of Minnesota at Minneapolis/St Paul.
	Canada	In November, accompanied by Mr Ogilvy, visited Canada for the 125th Anniversary celebrations of The Queen's Own Rifles of Canada and the opening

		of the Royal Agricultural Winter Fair in Toronto.
1986	**Thailand and Hong Kong**	Accompanied by Mr Ogilvy, visited Thailand in April at the invitation of the King and Queen and subsequently, as Honorary Commandant General of the Royal Hong Kong Police Force, visited Hong Kong.
	United States	Visited New York in June with Mr Ogilvy for the re-opening of the British Airways Terminal at John F. Kennedy Airport.
	United States	In October, accompanied by Mr Ogilvy, carried out engagements in Kentucky, Washington D.C., Maryland and New York.
1987	**United States**	With Mr Ogilvy, in April/May, visited Philadelphia for the opening of the Magna Carta Exhibition on the occasion of the Bicentennial of the United States Constitution, and Washington D.C. for the opening of an exhibition of Italian drawings from the Royal Collection.
	Italy	In May, as President, visited the British School at Rome.
	Cyprus	As Patron and Air Chief Commandant of Princess Mary's Royal Air Force Nursing Service, visited Princess Mary's Royal Air Force Hospital, Akrotiri, in May.
	Belgium	Attended a reception in June held by the British community at Supreme Headquarters Allied Powers Europe to celebrate the official birthday of the Queen.
1987	**Federal Republic of Germany**	In September visited the Federal Republic of Germany for the opening of the British Promotion at Karstadt Department Store in Nuremberg.
	Pakistan	Accompanied by Mr Ogilvy, visited Pakistan in October as guest of the Government of Pakistan.
	India	Visited the Henry Moore Exhibition at the National Gallery of Modern Art, New Delhi, with Mr Ogilvy in October.

1988	**Cayman Islands, Montserrat, Anguilla, British Virgin Islands, Turks and Caicos Islands**	A visit with Mr Ogilvy (except for Cayman Islands) in November.
	Bermuda	Accompanied by Mr Ogilvy, visited Bermuda in November.
1989	**Canada**	As Colonel-in-Chief visited the Canadian Scottish Regiment (Princess Mary's) at Victoria, British Columbia, in September for the celebrations to mark the 75th anniversary of the regiment.
	Caribbean Dependent Territories	In October visited Montserrat and the British Virgin Islands in the wake of the destruction caused by Hurricane Hugo.
	India and Nepal	With Sir Angus Ogilvy visited India (including the Tercentenary Celebrations of Calcutta) at the end of October and Nepal at the beginning of November.
1990	**Germany**	Took the Salute at The Queen's Birthday Parade of the British Forces in Berlin in May.
	Portugal	Visited Portugal in June, accompanied by Sir Angus Ogilvy, on the occasion of the Bicentenary of the Factory House, Oporto.
	France	In September visited Paris with Sir Angus Ogilvy for a gala performance at the Théâtre du Châtelet in aid of European Organization for Research and Treatment of Cancer.
	United States	Visited Southern California, accompanied by Sir Angus Ogilvy, for the opening of the Festival of Britain in Orange County in October.
	Hong Kong	As Honorary Commandant General visited the Royal Hong Kong Police Force in October accompanied by Sir Angus Ogilvy.
	Spain	Visited Madrid in November with Sir Angus Ogilvy for the opening of the British Council School at Pozuelo.

Princess Alexandra's Engagement Diary for May 1991

1st   Attended a dinner arranged by the Royal Star and Garter Home for Disabled Sailors, Soldiers and Airmen, at Hampton Court Palace.

2nd   Attended the Floral Luncheon of the Forces Help Society and Lord Roberts Workshops at the Savoy Hotel, London WC2.

As Patron of the Calcutta Tercentenary Trust was present in the evening, with Sir Angus Ogilvy, at a Reception held by the Trust at the Royal Geographical Society, Kensington Gore, London SW7.

Afterwards attended a performance of Gluck's *Orfeo and Euridice* by the Monteverdi Choir and English Baroque Soloists at the Queen Elizabeth Hall, South Bank Centre, London SE1.

7th   Attended, with Sir Angus Ogilvy, a Memorial Service for Mr Nicholas Phillips at St George's Church, Hanover Square, London W1.

In the afternoon attended a reception at St James's Palace for members of Queen Alexandra's Royal Naval Nursing Service and Princess Mary's RAF Nursing Service who served in the Gulf.

9th   Opened the Manor Cheshire Home at Brampton, Cambridgeshire.

12th   Attended a Gala Performance at the Theatre Royal, Haymarket, in aid of the Richmond Theatre Restoration Appeal.

14th   Attended a Garden Party held by the Richmond Fellowship at 8 Addison Road, London W14.

15th   Visited the Lochend YWCA in Edinburgh, Scotland.

Attended a concert in the evening as part of the Perth Festival of the Arts, Perth City Hall.

16th Attended a rehearsal of *Peace Child* by the Perth Youth Theatre at the Coaching Hall, Bell's Sports Centre, Perth, and was received by Her Majesty's Lord Lieutenant for Perth and Kinross (Major David Butter) and the Lord Provost of Perth (Councillor Alex Murray).

20th Visited the Chelsea Flower Show, London.

21st As Colonel in Chief, attended a Reception at St James's Palace for personnel of the 17th/21st Lancers who served in the Gulf.

Attended the re-opening of the Metropolitan Benefit Societies' Almshouses at Balls Pond Road, Islington, London N1.

22nd Attended a Gala Evening at the British Interior Design Exhibition, in aid of the National Kidney Research Fund, at The Design and Decoration Building, 107a Pimlico Road, London SW1.

23rd Opened 'Town Thorns', the fourth residential centre of BEN–Motor and Allied Trades Benevolent Fund, at Easenhall, near Rugby, Warwickshire.

Launched the Coventry Befriending Scheme at the Drop In Centre at Wellington Gardens, Coventry.

Opened Deerwood Grange, the home for elderly infirm people run in partnership by the North Birmingham Health Authority for Mental Health (MIND), Four Oaks Estate, Sutton Coldfield.

Princess Alexandra was represented by Sir Angus Ogilvy at the Memorial Service for the Viscount De L'Isle, VC, KG, in the Guards' Chapel, Wellington Barracks.

28th Opened Augusta Court, the new Housing-with-Care Scheme of Anchor, at Winterbourne Road, Chichester, West Sussex.

29th In the morning named the new Shoreham Harbour lifeboat for the Royal National Lifeboat Institution at Shoreham, West Sussex.

In the afternoon opened the new Day Centre for the Worthing and District Association for Mental Health at Durrington, West Sussex.

Undertook a weekend of engagements in North Yorkshire, including a Thanksgiving Service to mark the 60th Anniversary of Guide Dogs for the Blind.

Princess Alexandra and the Royal House of Windsor

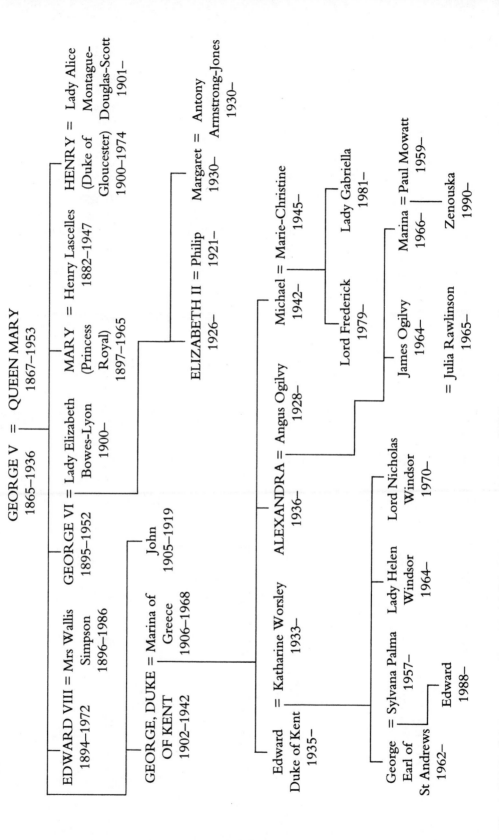

GEORGE V = QUEEN MARY
1865–1936   1867–1953

EDWARD VIII = Mrs Wallis   GEORGE VI = Lady Elizabeth   MARY = Henry Lascelles   HENRY = Lady Alice
1894–1972   Simpson   1895–1952   Bowes-Lyon   (Princess   1882–1947   (Duke of   Montague-
              1896–1986   1900–   Royal)   Gloucester) Douglas-Scott
                                                              1897–1965   1900–1974   1901–

GEORGE, DUKE = Marina of   John
OF KENT   Greece   1905–1919
1902–1942   1906–1968

                                             ELIZABETH II = Philip   Margaret = Antony
                                             1926–   1921–   1930–   Armstrong-Jones
                                                                                       1930–

Edward = Katharine Worsley   ALEXANDRA = Angus Ogilvy   Michael = Marie-Christine
Duke of Kent   1933–   1936–   1928–   1942–   1945–

                                                                      Lord Frederick   Lady Gabriella
                                                                      1979–   1981–

George = Sylvana Palma   Lady Helen   Lord Nicholas   James Ogilvy   Marina = Paul Mowatt
Earl of   1957–   Windsor   Windsor   1964–   1966–   1959–
St Andrews   1964–   1970–
1962–   = Julia Rawlinson
                                                             1965–   Zenouska
Edward   1990–
1988–

Genealogy of Princess Marina of Greece (1906–1968)

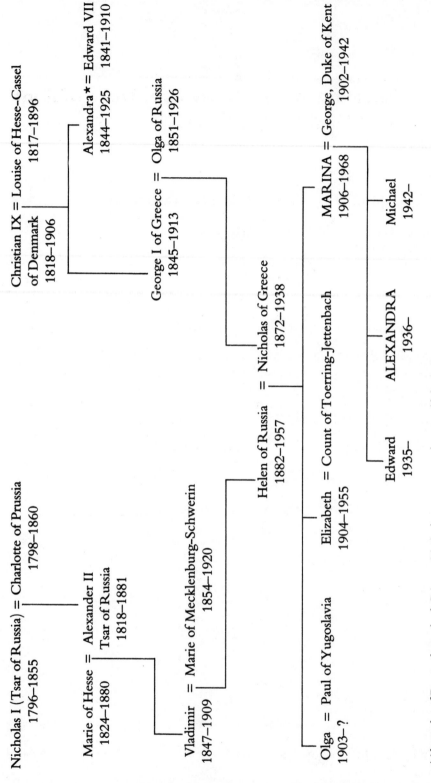

Nicholas I (Tsar of Russia) = Charlotte of Prussia
1796–1855   1798–1860

Christian IX = Louise of Hesse-Cassel
of Denmark   1817–1896
1818–1906

Alexandra ★ = Edward VII
1844–1925   1841–1910

Marie of Hesse = Alexander II
1824–1880   Tsar of Russia
1818–1881

George I of Greece = Olga of Russia
1845–1913   1851–1926

Vladimir = Marie of Mecklenburg-Schwerin
1847–1909   1854–1920

Helen of Russia = Nicholas of Greece
1882–1957   1872–1938

MARINA = George, Duke of Kent
1906–1968   1902–1942

Olga = Paul of Yugoslavia
1903–?

Elizabeth = Count of Toerring-Jettenbach
1904–1955

Edward
1935–

ALEXANDRA
1936–

Michael
1942–

*Alexandra of Denmark was both Princess Marina's great-aunt, as her grandfather's sister, and the Duke of Kent's grandmother.

Genealogy of Prince George, Duke of Kent
(1902–1942)

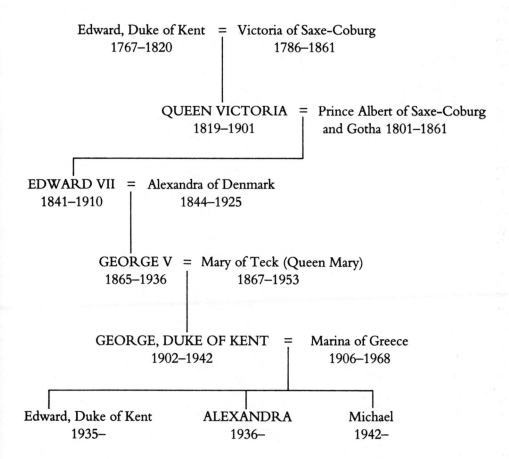

Edward, Duke of Kent = Victoria of Saxe-Coburg
1767–1820   1786–1861

QUEEN VICTORIA = Prince Albert of Saxe-Coburg
1819–1901   and Gotha 1801–1861

EDWARD VII = Alexandra of Denmark
1841–1910   1844–1925

GEORGE V = Mary of Teck (Queen Mary)
1865–1936   1867–1953

GEORGE, DUKE OF KENT = Marina of Greece
1902–1942   1906–1968

Edward, Duke of Kent   ALEXANDRA   Michael
1935–   1936–   1942–

Bibliography

Airlie, Mabell, Countess of, *Thatched With Gold* (Hutchinson, 1962)

Aronson, Theo, *Royal Family – Years of Transition* (John Murray, 1983)

Bloom, Ursula, *Princesses in Love* (Robert Hale, 1973)

Bloom, Ursula, *The House of Kent* (Robert Hale, 1969)

Bolitho, Hector, *Their Majesties* (Max Parrish, 1952)

Brown, Craig, and Cunliffe, Lesley, *The Book of Royal Lists* (Sphere, 1983)

Brown, Ivor, *Royal Homes* (Batsford, 1958)

Cathcart, Helen, *Princess Alexandra* (W. H. Allen, 1967)

Colville, John, *Footprints in Time* (Collins, 1976)

Cowles, Virginia, *The Last Tsar and Tsarina* (Weidenfeld & Nicolson, 1977)

Crawford, Marion, *The Little Princesses* (Cassell, 1950)

Duff, David, *Alexandra, Princess and Queen* (Collins, 1980)

Duncan, Andrew, *The Reality of Monarchy* (Heinemann, 1970)

Edgar, Donald, *Palace* (W. H. Allen, 1983)

Ellis, Jennifer, *The Duchess of Kent* (Odhams, 1952)

Ellison, Grace, *The Life Story of Princess Marina* (Heinemann, 1934)

Fincher, Jayne, and Garner, Valerie, *My Young Friends* (Weidenfeld & Nicolson, 1989)

Furness, Audrey, *Princess Alexandra's Wedding Book* (Purnell, 1963)

Gordon, Noele, *My Life at Crossroads* (W. H. Allen, 1975)

Graham, Tim, *On the Royal Road* (Weidenfeld & Nicolson, 1984)

Hall, Trevor, *The Royal Family Today* (Colour Library, 1983)

Hamilton, Alan, *The Royal Handbook* (Mitchell Beazley, 1985)

Hedley, Olwen, *Kensington Palace: The State Apartments* (Pitkin, 1976)

Hoey, Brian, *Monarchy* (BBC Books, 1987)

Hudson, Derek, *Kensington Palace* (Peter Davies, 1968)

James, Paul, *Anne: The Working Princess* (Piatkus, 1987)

James, Paul, *Diana: One of the Family?* (Sidgwick & Jackson, 1988)

James, Paul, *Margaret: A Woman of Conflict* (Sidgwick & Jackson, 1990)

James, Paul, *The Royal Almanac* (Ravette, 1986)

James, Paul, and Russell, Peter, *At Her Majesty's Service* (Collins, 1986)

Keay, Douglas, *Royal Pursuit* (Severn House, 1983)

King, Stella, *Princess Marina: Her Life and Times* (Cassell, 1969)

Lacey, Robert, *Majesty: Elizabeth II and The House of Windsor* (Hutchinson, 1977)

Laird, Dorothy, *How The Queen Reigns* (Hodder & Stoughton, 1959)

Longford, Elizabeth, *Elizabeth R* (Weidenfeld & Nicolson, 1985)

Louda, Jiří, and Maclagan, Michael, *Lines of Succession* (Orbis, 1981)

Masters, Brian, *Great Hostesses* (Constable, 1982)

194

Menkes, Suzy, *The Royal Jewels* (Grafton, 1985)

Nicholas, Prince, of Greece *My Fifty Years* (Hutchinson, 1926)

Nicolson, Harold, *Kind George The Fifth* (Constable, 1952)

Pope-Hennessy, James, *Queen Mary* (Allen & Unwin, 1959)

Robinson, John Martin, *Royal Residences* (Macdonald, 1982)

Rose, Kenneth, *Kings, Queens and Courtiers* (Weidenfeld & Nicolson, 1985)

Russell, Peter, *Butler Royal* (Hutchinson, 1982)

Saville, Margaret, *Royal Sisters* (Pitkin, 1953)

Strong, Sir Roy, *Cecil Beaton: The Royal Portraits* (Thames & Hudson, 1988)

Weir, Alison, *Britain's Royal Families – The Complete Genealogy* (The Bodley Head, 1989)

Wentworth Day, J., *HRH Princess Marina, Duchess of Kent* (Robert Hale, 1962)

Whiting, Audrey, *The Kents: A Royal Family* (Hutchinson, 1985)

Wheeler-Bennet, John, *King George VI* (Macmillan, 1958)

Ziegler, Philip, *Crown and People* (Collins, 1978)

Index